WHAT THE HELL DO YOU HAVE TO LOSE?

JUAN WILLIAMS

WHAT THE HELL DO YOU HAVE TO LOSE?

Trump's War *on* Civil Rights

PUBLICAFFAIRS

New York

5158

PublicAffairs
Hachette Book Group
1290 Avenue of the Americas, New York, NY 10104
www.publicaffairsbooks.com
@Public_Affairs

Printed in the United States of America

First Edition: September 2018

Published by PublicAffairs, an imprint of Perseus Books, LLC,
a subsidiary of Hachette Book Group, Inc. The PublicAffairs
name and logo is a trademark of the Hachette Book Group.

The publisher is not responsible for websites (or their content)
that are not owned by the publisher.

Print book interior design by Six Red Marbles Inc.

Library of Congress Cataloging-in-Publication Data

Names: Williams, Juan, author.
Title: What the hell do you have to lose? : Trump's war on
civil rights / Juan Williams.
Description: New York : PublicAffairs, [2018] | Includes bibliographical
references and index.
Identifiers: LCCN 2018015518 (print) | LCCN 2018033869 (ebook) |
ISBN 9781541788275 (ebook) | ISBN 9781541788268 (hardcover)
Subjects: LCSH: African Americans—Civil rights. |
African Americans—Social conditions. | African Americans—History. |
Civil rights—United States—History. | Civil rights
movements—United States—History. | Trump, Donald, 1946- |
Racism—United States. | United States—Race relations. |
United States—Politics and government—2017-
Classification: LCC E185.615 (ebook) | LCC E185.615 .W49157 2018 (print) |
DDC 323.1196/073—dc23
LC record available at https://lccn.loc.gov/2018015518

ISBNs: 978-1-5417-8826-8 (hardcover), 978-1-5417-8827-5 (e-book)

LSC-C

10 9 8 7 6 5 4 3 2 1

*This book is dedicated to **Herbert H. Denton Jr.** [1943–1989] and **Henry Hampton** [1940–1998]—mentors. 'Call all to the light; praise the good and the right.'*

Contents

Introduction

D URING HIS SUCCESSFUL CAMPAIGN for the presidency, Donald Trump's message to black voters was that supporting Democrats left them with bad schools, high crime, and higher unemployment. In asking them to join his campaign, Trump famously threw an explosive and simple question at black people: "What the hell do you have to lose?"

The president should know the answer.

When Trump was seven years old in 1954, the Supreme Court in the famous *Brown v. Board of Education* case outlawed racially separate public schools.

Then, when he was eighteen, Congress passed the 1964 Civil Rights Act, opening the way to an era of rapid progress in race relations.

Now seventy-two years old, Trump has lived through the astonishing growth in the black middle class. He just has to pick up the paper to see incredible advances in black political power that have taken place in his lifetime, including the election of the first black president.

As a casino owner, beauty competition sponsor, and television personality, he had a front row seat from which to watch the rush of black talent to the front line of the nation's culture from music (Michael Jackson), to beauty contests (Vanessa Williams as the first black Miss America), to television (Oprah) and sports (Michael Jordan).

Having attended a military academy for high school, Trump might have noticed that in 1980 Vincent Brooks became the first black student to lead the cadets at West Point. How about the front-page headlines that greeted Colin Powell when he became the first black chairman of the Joint Chiefs of Staff in 1989? Did he miss that too? These days, trailblazing black people hardly get any attention. In 2017, when Simone Askew became the first black woman to lead the cadets at West Point, it was buried inside the papers. I can understand if Trump missed that one.

As a businessman, however, he could hardly have ignored the rise of black people into the ranks of top executives. In his time, a black woman broke through racial and gender ceilings to become the head of Xerox. In his lifetime, black men have taken the top jobs at American Express, Merrill Lynch, Merck, and Time Warner. He saw entertainment moguls Bob Johnson and Oprah Winfrey become the world's first two black billionaires, reaching a threshold he himself often claims to have achieved, though the record is far from clear. And at Carnegie Hall, just a few blocks from his Fifth Avenue apartment, Trump might have noticed that another black billionaire, Robert F. Smith, made the front pages when he was elected as chairman of the board.

I'm just seven years younger than Trump. But I'm black. The changes he sniffed at make up the prime story of my lifetime.

Let me boil this down for Trump. Take a look at two men—my father and me—and do a generational comparison.

The difference between the life my father led as a black man—he was born in 1902—and the life I lead today as a black man—I was born in 1954—are so different I might as well live on another planet.

As a first stop, go to restaurants in downtown Washington, DC. They were closed to my dad and other black people as late as the 1960s. Today I've been welcomed in fancy restaurants in DC and even farther south, from Richmond to Birmingham to New Orleans. The same is true for hotels that kept out my dad. How about housing? I bought my first house in a neighborhood once governed by "restrictive covenants" that legally banned a black man like my dad from buying a house. My father's heart would have swelled with pride and wonder to see my daughter's Georgetown law degree. Georgetown University did not accept its first black student until the 1950s. And what might Daddy have said about me having lunch with another black man at the White House, when he realized the other guy was Barack Obama, the first black president of the United States?

He'd say that's a different planet. I agree. And we'd both give thanks for all the progress toward racial equality in a nation whose founding ideals of liberty and justice have always sat uncomfortably beside the reality of slavery.

The country still has a long way to go before approaching racial equality. But the revolution in race relations during the last fifty years—the majority of Donald Trump's life—has been absolutely mind-boggling.

Instead of asking black people what they have to lose by voting for him, Trump needs to ask himself, "How the hell did I miss all of this?"

But let's be honest. Trump did not just happen to overlook it. He intentionally put on blinders because he finds comfort and political advantage in seeing a distinctly different reality. He wants to see black failure and misery. That view justifies his distaste for black people—some might say his racism. He locks his eyes on the worst of black American life because it makes him and other white people into victims of the trouble in black neighborhoods; he is the hero defending whites against the approaching barbarians.

On the campaign trail he used his awful depiction of black life as a regular feature of speeches to whip up his heavily white campaign crowds.

Trump has "opened the door to assertions of white identity and resentment in a way not seen so broadly in American culture in over half a century, according to those who track patterns of racial tension and antagonism in American life," the *New York Times* reported near the end of the 2016 presidential campaign.

Specifically, Trump has "electrified the world of white nationalists," the newspaper noted. A company that tracks social media revealed that "almost 30 percent of the accounts Mr. Trump retweeted...followed one or more of 50 popular self-identified white nationalist accounts."

His colorful speeches to raucous white crowds conjured scary pictures of black neighborhoods full of gunfire and desperation that threatened white people, risked infecting white neighborhoods, and required support for police, even bad police, who had to cope with these out-of-control black folks. "I mean, honestly, places like Afghanistan are safer than some of our inner cities," he said.

He described these impoverished areas as representative of all black life. As a public avatar of white contempt, Trump encouraged Americans to damn poor black people for living with poverty and violence. By his logic, the black people in those neighborhoods made the choice to be there, to stay there. They blame racism for their problems and ask for welfare, he said. But in Trump's world, black people don't see that they are failing themselves because "you take a look at the inner cities, you get no education, you get no jobs, you get shot walking down the street."

President Obama responded to one of Trump's negative speeches about black America this way: "You may have heard [Trump] say that there's never been a worse time to be a black person. I mean, he missed that whole civics lesson about slavery or Jim Crow."

"Does Trump have the faintest clue what black America is really like?" asked Eugene Robinson, a columnist in the *Washington Post*. Another black columnist, Leonard Greene of the *New York Daily News*, decided to respond directly to Trump's question about what black voters have "to lose" by supporting him. "No. 1: My dignity. No. 2 My self-respect. No. 3: My standing among family and friends, black or white, and anyone who has ever held me in high regard. No. 4: My future...."

Thirty years ago I wrote *Eyes on the Prize—America's Civil Rights Years 1954–1965*, a best-selling book about the modern civil rights movement. The project included a six-part PBS television series. Twenty years ago I wrote a celebrated biography of the first black Supreme Court justice, Thurgood Marshall. And since then I have authored books on African American religion, black colleges and universities, as well as my disappointment with so many current black leaders.

Trump's name never came up in any of my books.

Keep in mind that prominent white people did speak out against racism. To name a few, they include the famous conservative actor Charlton Heston, who marched with Dr. King; Earl Warren, the conservative, former Republican governor of California who became chief justice of the Supreme Court and used his power to lead a unanimous vote to end school segregation; and Frank Sinatra, a singer whose work for civil rights led the NAACP to give him its Lifetime Achievement Award.

Trump will never get any award from the NAACP.

A rich, politically connected white man with a big voice in newspapers and his own show on television, Trump had ample platforms and every opportunity to speak out about racism. He never did.

Keep in mind that changes in race relations could not have taken place without several leading white Americans speaking to other white people about racial wrongs. The model of this might be Atticus Finch, the fictional white Alabama lawyer in the best-selling novel, *To Kill a Mockingbird*. He bucked the racist culture of a small Southern town to represent a black man wrongly charged with rape and to speak out about corrupt racial attitudes.

Enough real-life white men in an all-white US Senate took the risk to cast votes to pass the 1964 Civil Rights Act. To say that was a risky political move is an understatement. White Democrats knew it would antagonize the many white Southern segregationists in their party, known as Dixiecrats. To this day that vote stands as a historic inflection point in the nation's racially divided politics, the biggest since the Civil War. It is the moment when the solidly Democratic Southern states began shifting to the current reality of the predominately Republican South.

Then there are mortal risks taken by all the people, black and also white, who, despite the threat of segregationist violence, got on the buses to go to the March on Washington. There are the legal risks taken by people who stoked political pressure and raised money to pass the 1965 Voting Rights Act and 1968 Fair Housing Act. The threats these activists faced down, and the changes that resulted, stand as monumental achievements for a generation of Americans, black and white, who grew up in a legally segregated, white-majority country.

During these same years, Trump played no role in bringing about racial progress in America. If anything, he attempted to stall it. As a businessman, he was distressed by the changes, specifically when blacks tried to rent apartments in his previously all-white properties. The federal government sued him, and he was forced to settle one of the biggest housing discrimination cases in history.

Trump's silence on race throughout his long life is a bit like the dog who did not bark in the Sherlock Holmes story "The Adventure of Silver Blaze." In that case, the dog never barked because it recognized his owner as the man stealing a horse. In Trump's case, he didn't even bother to look.

The spark of idealism—the optimism that drives young people to question and protest and change the world—never ignited in Trump. This young white man's attention flew by the fight for equal rights for blacks, the calls for women's rights, and the Great Society drive to lend a hand to the poor.

Perhaps Donald Trump never spoke on equality because he didn't see oppression as a crime. His millionaire dad's resentment of immigrants and minorities led him to attend a KKK rally in 1920s New York. Then young Donald was sent to a private high school and universities with few black people. Coming of age among hippies, antiwar protests, and music asking, "What's Going On?," Trump remained unconnected to his times. He kept his distance from the romanticism of the 1960s peace-and-love culture of rebellion against war and the civil rights movement with its rejection of racism.

His inner drive was all about moving up in New York's high society and making money in New York's real estate business. He showed no natural desire to reach out to the poor folks below, be they black, white, Latino, immigrants, or women.

His distaste for black people is tied to his lack of empathy for the poor. Black people have the highest rates of poverty, welfare, and crime of any racial group. In absolute numbers, most poverty in the United States is among white people. That is no surprise since whites, at 70 percent of the population, are the largest racial group in the country. Similarly, white people commit most crimes. But the white poverty rate, like the white crime rate, is at a lower overall percentage than poverty and crime rates among blacks and Latinos.

Also, much of white poverty and street-level crime is hidden. Poor white people are generally outside cities, in small towns and rural areas like Appalachia that are far from Trump's life in midtown Manhattan. Black poverty can also be found in rural areas, like the Mississippi Delta. But unlike its white counterpart, black urban dysfunction is a staple of the eleven o'clock nightly news in big cities—major media markets—including New York.

There is a lot of history here.

Black people who moved up north to escape the worst of Southern segregation in the mid-twentieth century found themselves isolated by housing and school segregation and kept out of good paying jobs in the North. Trump was less concerned with that sad human situation and racism than he was with his own anxiety about crime and the impact it had on the value of his buildings.

Trump belongs to a long tradition of white Americans who were happy to ignore our national history of racism and pretend it didn't exist. Trump's experience, specifically his anxiety over black crime, fits with the complaints of older political conservatives and neoconservatives, a type often described as "a white liberal who has been mugged." This is how Trump and his cohort view black people: as a population of potential muggers.

Then there is the matter of social status. As Trump grew up it was hard to find any blacks, Latinos, or Jews in top-tier positions among America's social elite. There were few if any black titans of Wall Street. The same held true for Madison Avenue advertising magnates, real estate developers, and the owners and top executives of major television and newspaper companies. This is the world Trump aspired to join, and black people had no place in it.

But even when older white conservatives speak honestly of their fear of the chaos of black crime and poverty, they reassure me that they are not racists. They profess to be speaking out against the damage done to people of all colors by the wrongheaded acceptance of crime and welfare dependency. They regard being called a racist as the worst, the lowest possible insult.

At first, I took them at their word and received their attitude as good news. But over time, an incredible impulse revealed itself in people who professed to be good.

In my experience, whenever I pointed to obvious racism on the part of other white people—in hiring statistics, police brutality, and more—these same white, conservative truth-tellers suddenly became defensive. The reflex puzzled me. Why should one white person resist believing a different white person is racist? But slowly I realized it was a fear that the same charge might be leveled at them. They didn't want to hear about anyone being called a racist.

This exercise in racial denial took center stage when Hillary Clinton, the Democratic candidate for president, said half of Trump's backers were "deplorables," and defined the group as "racist, sexist, homophobic, xenophobic, and Islamophobic." That was not a rash generalization—it was based on polling data.

Earlier that summer, a Reuters poll found "nearly half of Trump's supporters described African-Americans as more 'violent' than whites... more 'criminal' than whites, while 40 percent described [blacks] as more 'lazy' than whites." These results fit well with a later Reuters poll from 2017, which found that 39 percent of Americans believe "whites are currently under attack in this country." That included 63 percent of Republicans, despite what Jennifer Rubin, a *Washington Post* columnist, described as "the absence of any evidence that whites as a group are disadvantaged in schooling, employment, income, public accommodations, political power or any other area." But Trump's supporters reacted to Clinton's "deplorables" comment by accusing her of "playing the race card" and defaming good people who did not agree with her policies and politics. They trashed her campaign with charges of using "identity politics" to stir up people of color, a key constituency of the Democratic Party, even as Trump supporters had nothing to say about to the almost all-white makeup of the GOP. Their passionate defense was notable because it required looking away from Trump's willingness to use white racial resentments to fire up white voters.

It also required ignoring Trump's public behavior. When a black ESPN television host called Trump a "white supremacist" during his first year in office, the president's press secretary demanded the television anchor be fired. Trump's political supporters rallied to his side by saying the charge lacked factual basis; it was just another example of oblivious liberal hatred of Trump.

Wait a second. Let's go back and look at the record of what American voters were thinking when they elected Trump.

In August 2016, just a few months before he was elected president, 51 percent of Americans polled by YouGov said that they would describe Trump as a racist. A Pew poll in October found that 54 percent of Americans agreed that Trump does not "respect black people very much." And a Quinnipiac poll a month earlier found most voters agreed, "The way Donald Trump talks appeals to bigotry." Overall, polling research showed that as Trump took control of the presidential race in 2016, whites felt "bias against white people is more of a problem than bias against black people." Two professors who surveyed negative attitudes toward black people from 1950 through the 2016 election concluded that a large percentage of white Americans agreed "improvements for black Americans...are likely to come at a direct cost to whites." These anxious white attitudes about race predated Trump's campaign.

Since President Nixon campaigned by appealing to the "Silent Majority," who were disgusted with hippies, feminists, and black militants, Republicans have appealed to white resentment. But as far back as President Eisenhower, Republicans have been careful to separate themselves from openly racist groups like the KKK and the John Birch Society.

Trump exercised no such restraint. He took advantage of white anxieties, fears, and outright racism. AP polls found 51 percent of Americans now express explicitly anti-black attitudes compared to 48 percent in a similar 2008 survey. That timeframe is important because Barack Obama, the first black president, took office in 2009. Republicans showed higher levels of racial grievance against blacks in the polls—79 percent, as compared to 32 percent of Democrats.

Before he ran for president Trump's biggest calling card was his leadership of the racist birther movement. He questioned whether the first black president was really an American. He demanded a birth certificate to prove that Obama was born in the United States. His deceitful tactic had impact. Fifty-nine percent of Trump's supporters told pollsters in May 2016, as the GOP primary was being decided, that Obama was not born in the United States.

The suggestion that Obama was not an American also led Trump to publicly scoff at the idea that Obama earned admission to an Ivy League school. He dismissed the idea that the black president was bright enough to have once won the esteemed title of editor of the *Harvard Law Review*. Trump also demanded Obama's college transcripts and derided him as an "affirmative action" president.

Before he launched the birther attack, Trump's bitter racial attitude was evident on social media. The *Washington Post* reported that in eight years of using Twitter, Trump was three times as likely to accuse black people of racism as he was to point out white racism. "Trump's use of words like 'racist' and 'racism' is perhaps best understood in the context of a modern conservative movement that has come to believe, against all evidence, that whites face more discrimination than blacks," the *Post* reported in an analysis. "...Trump has given validation to that belief."

And then the KKK endorsed Trump's candidacy for president. They told their followers that voting against Trump is "treason to your heritage," in the words of former Klan leader David Duke. Trump went on CNN and said he knew nothing about Duke. This was suspect, considering that Trump understood Duke well enough to have called him a "bigot, a racist" in 2000. Yet following his CNN interview he offered the lame excuse that he didn't denounced Duke this time because he hadn't heard the question.

Trump's evasions later prompted Tim Scott of South Carolina, the only black Republican in the Senate, to condemn Trump: "Any candidate who cannot immediately condemn a hate group like the KKK does not represent the Republican Party. If Donald Trump can't take a stand against the KKK, we cannot trust him to stand up for America against Putin, Iran or ISIS."

Trump offered no apology. His failure to condemn the Klan became his biggest dog whistle: words intended to give him space to escape charges of racism while still appealing to racists. This became obvious in the summer of 2017, several months into his presidency, when white supremacists, including members of the KKK, marched in Virginia with torch-bearing neo-Nazis. President Trump said the appalling group, openly carrying guns, included many "fine people" who only marched in opposition to taking down Confederate statues. So in his mind, "fine people" stand side by side with Nazis.

Trump never condemned the Nazi group for its threatening march against blacks, Jews, and immigrants. He never said a word about their responsibility for the violence, including one racist who used a car to kill a woman marching in opposition. At best, Trump blamed "both sides." The Daily Stormer, a white supremacist website, thanked the president: "No condemnation at all.... When asked to condemn, [Trump] just walked out of the room.... God bless him."

Trump's behavior led 56 percent of Americans to tell Fox News pollsters weeks after Charlottesville that he is "tearing the country apart." Sixty-one percent disapproved of his words and actions in handling race relations. A Pew poll after the violence found 58 percent of Americans declaring racism is now a "big problem" for the country, the most Americans to say that since polling firms started regularly asking the question twenty years earlier, in 1995.

Trump acted as if nothing happened. After the Charlottesville attack he went on to take several provocative steps on race. He made a political display of pardoning a white sheriff found guilty of racial profiling of immigrants, Arizona's Joe Arpaio. Then he made a show of giving local police departments surplus, high-powered military weapons at a time of national concern over police shootings of black men. He also ended a program to protect undocumented immigrants, mostly Latinos, who came to the United States as children, from deportation.

"By playing into white fears of crime and concerns that minorities are taking their jobs, he's signaling to his white supporters that he's a politician who is finally taking their problems seriously," wrote German Lopez for *Vox*. Lopez quoted a researcher who described Trump's use of racially coded language as particularly pernicious in its design, allowing "people who are racially anxious and who are easily fired up with racial narratives to deny to themselves that it's race that's agitating them." Many of Trump's appeals to white racial anger, Lopez concluded, "are masked under broad concerns—over the waste of taxpayer money and crime—but they're really appealing to underlying racial resentment."

Trump masterfully put a twenty-first-century twist on the politics of segregation going back to the 1940s, 1950s, and 1960s. When Alabama governor George Wallace blocked the schoolhouse door to stop black people from attending the state university, he said he acted in the name of Southern tradition and heritage. He never said he was a white supremacist. Trump is playing a similar game. Without ever talking about racism, he goes off on big government waste of tax dollars on social programs and crime by immigrants and black people. It was an appeal to racial resentment that allowed Trump and his supporters to deny their racist feelings as long as they didn't call names and only expressed disagreement with government programs and policies they identified as designed to help poor black people. This was true even if the programs, from Obamacare to student loan programs, helped more whites than blacks and Latinos.

His tactics gave cover to his base voters even as the press reported that Trump's campaign for president had excited extremist, racist hate groups. After all, Trump's run for the White House literally started with a speech full of attacks on Mexican immigrants as rapists and thieves. On the campaign trail he hammered every violent crime by an undocumented immigrant as if such crimes were the country's major source of danger. He brought crying mothers and fathers of the victims of these crimes on stage, to applause from mostly white followers.

During Trump's first year in office the FBI saw a spike in activity among racist groups. The bureau confirmed that it had one thousand investigations underway into racist organizations that had turned to violence. But Trump's backers continued to downplay the significance of the news that the leaders of the KKK endorsed Trump's campaign. Even more incredible, they managed to look away as he thrilled the "alt-right," a loose affiliation of racist, sexist, and Anti-Semitic hate groups that often openly advertise themselves as white supremacists. In fact, he hired Steve Bannon as his campaign manager. Bannon once said the Civil War was a "war of Southern independence." He said the South wanted to secede not to keep black people as slaves so much as to fight for "economic development." Bannon is also a man who said his website, Breitbart, was "the platform for the alt-right" and allowed leaders of racist groups control over stories that appeared on the website.

During a European speaking tour in early 2018, after he was forced to step down from the Trump administration, Bannon told a right-wing French group to "let them call you racist. Let them call you xenophobes. Let them call you nativist. Wear it as a badge of honor." Telling an audience to relish accusations of racism is a startling break from most conservative American politicians of the last half century. Even when playing racial politics, conservatives have gone out of their way to condemn outright racism and argue they are making the case for color-blind policies.

Despite stirring up racist groups and embracing Bannon, Trump denied charges of racism. Instead, he blamed the media for smearing him.

There is a tradition here. It is a tradition of denial.

From the start most white Americans did little to challenge the reality of their nation exploiting black people as legally held slave labor. Few people joined the abolitionist movement against slavery. Slave owners, including some of the Founding Fathers, said they did not create slavery but accepted it as a reality. President Lincoln spoke of the importance of keeping the country together even as the abolitionists pointed to the inhuman reality of slavery. It was abolitionists who identified slavery as the real issue behind the Civil War and called out the shocking hypocrisy on display between the harsh reality of slavery and the Founding Fathers' inspiring pledge to equality—"all men are created equal." This was a time when white slave owners regularly tore black families apart and used black women as whores. The whole country was forced to submit to the rules of white supremacy through organized white violence, including public lynching.

And history records the incredible contributions of brave white and black Americans who stood up in the face of tradition and business profits to condemn legal segregation, including federal laws enforcing the denial of personal rights and voting rights that resulted in the treatment of blacks as second-class citizens.

The most stunning reality I discovered while writing the history of the modern civil rights movement was the sacrifice made by so many people no one ever heard of.

A hundred years after the abolitionists, another group of American heroes took to the streets as protest marchers, boycotted buses and businesses, and sometimes went to jail to stand up for equal rights. They pushed open the doors of the voting booth as well as the lunch counter to end legal racial segregation in modern America.

Yes, everyone knows about Dr. Martin Luther King Jr. He is a genuine hero and deserved that honor long before he was assassinated. He became a martyr for the greatest social movement in American history. Today a monument to his epic contributions to the nation is prominent in the nation's capital, on federal land between the memorials to presidents Thomas Jefferson and Abraham Lincoln. But the idea of one man, even King, doing all the work is a cartoonish illusion. The inspiring reality is that so many people, most of them anonymous in the public mind to this day, risked everything—some going to jail and some dying—to make the gains that made the movement go.

The modern civil rights story is truly astonishing because so many people with neither King's high profile nor his leadership ability took big personal risks. Some lost their jobs. Others had their mortgages withdrawn from the bank. Many suffered jail time, beatings, and death—to stand up against racist laws, challenge racist traditions, and defy white segregationist political power. Keep in mind, these ordinary heroes faced not only burning crosses on their lawns but an even larger number of whites who just accepted second-class treatment of blacks as a reality of politics and traditions they didn't want to deal with.

The insight that stays with me from the experience of writing *Eyes on the Prize* is that the long, painful history of American racism was upended by so many anonymous people who stood up to make a difference. I am talking about young and old, black and white, in addition to leaders like King. They may be unknown, but the power of their ideas and commitment is beyond dispute.

Even if you buy into the idea that history is made by great leaders (and I do—that's why I write biographical pieces), most Americans still do not know how many titans led the civil rights movement— people such as Ella Baker, Fannie Lou Hamer, C. T. Vivian, Fred

Shuttlesworth, and Dave Dennis. All of them had leadership roles in civil rights organizations. They all made incredible sacrifices for the greater good. Yet only a few people know their names. Trump is certainly not among them.

How about this name? Mose Wright.

He was a sixty-four-year-old man when he saw his fourteen-year-old great-nephew, Emmett Till, snatched out of bed and taken away to be sadistically beaten, shot, and then tossed into a river. Wright became the first black man to dare to testify against whites charged with murdering a black person in Mississippi. He stood in the witness box and pointed directly at the men who kidnapped the boy. Wright had to leave his home, say good-bye to family and friends, and flee the state after he testified. The all-white jury found the men not guilty, although they later admitted to the murder.

Now that is a sacrifice. But who remembers Mr. Mose Wright?

How about the black schoolteachers in Alabama?

They usually avoided civil rights activism for fear of being fired by the all-white school board. But when Amelia Boynton, a middle-age black woman, was beaten by Selma police in 1965 for trying to register to vote, more than a hundred of those black teachers got together, put on their Sunday go-to-church clothes, and went to the registration office to show support for Boynton and try to register. They, too, were beaten.

Those teachers risked everything for the greater good.

How about the black college student Diane Nash? She was a student at Fisk University in Nashville in 1961 when segregationists bombed a Greyhound bus traveling from Washington, DC, to New Orleans. The segregationists' aim was to stop a group of black and white students from engaging in an interracial Freedom Ride. The bombers saw it as a violation of Southern Jim Crow laws.

Nash's response was to organize students to travel to Alabama despite the threat of more violence and warnings that they might be killed. While Nash coordinated the rides, a second group of students boarded a new bus to travel from Nashville to Birmingham. They rode the buses, pressuring the federal government to send agents to enforce the law and attracting hundreds more young people, black and white, to join the fight.

Here is another name: Viola Liuzzo. In the popular telling of American history few know of her heroism. Who, you ask?

Liuzzo was a white Detroit housewife who took it on herself to get in her car and drive all the way to Alabama to support the Selma march for voting rights in 1965. As she was driving back home, the KKK chased her car, and she was shot to death.

Have you ever heard of the Reverend Jim Reeb? This Unitarian minister also went to Selma to support the movement to give voting rights to black Americans. Segregationists asked the Northerner what he was doing down there supporting blacks. They called him a "nig-ger' and hit him in the head with a club, killing him.

Do you know about Jimmie Lee Jackson? A twenty-six-year-old black man, he was with his grandfather and mother at a voting rights march, also in Selma, and saw his grandfather beaten. When he de-fended his mother from being hit by an Alabama state trooper, he was shot by another trooper and later died.

I've met James Meredith. I've met John Lewis. I've met Diane Nash. I've met Rosa Parks. I know the scars they carry, some of them on their face or on their skull. (That's the case with Lewis, who had his head bashed in by Alabama state police.) Somehow Trump, who was alive as these people were risking their lives with incredible acts of self-sacrifice, is unfamiliar with these heroes. They were worlds away from the wealthy Manhattan in-crowd of developers, hedge fund managers, and fashion models he admires.

Just compare John Lewis, Diane Nash, and Rosa Parks to the pres-ident. Trump was in his late teens and early twenties when so many people in his generation paid a high price to lead, organize, and push Americans to open their eyes to the wrong of treating blacks as infe-rior, second-class citizens.

Their success opened the door to cultural shifts beyond race. Suddenly, equal rights for women began to come to fruition, the movement for LGBT rights gained momentum, and so did changes in immigration law to allow more people of color from around the globe to come to the United States in greater numbers than ever.

Trump made no effort to help anyone but himself.

This indifference reflects a self-absorbed idea that life for white people would be easier without activists pushing for racial justice and if there was less attention to difficult racial issues rooted in the long history of bias against black people.

His attitude is epitomized in his campaign slogan, "Make America Great Again," a not-so-subtle call to go back in time. Those words hit a resonant chord with twenty-first-century white supremacists as well as neo-Nazi groups and people still holding to the distant, discredited cause of the slaveholding Confederate states. It was this revanchism that brought out the KKK to support him.

Since the Confederate states lost the Civil War and the right to hold blacks as slaves, there is a long record of racists working to turn back the clock on gains made by black Americans. Whites-only schools, whites-only churches, whites-only labor unions, and segregationist politicians resisted the rise of proud black people defying threats of segregationist violence to call for the nation to live up to the Declaration of Independence's promise that "all men are created equal." Even racially moderate whites regularly dismissed civil rights activists as troublemakers and counseled patience and silence instead of action.

Here is Dr. King, in his 1963 "Letter from a Birmingham Jail," writing to moderate white clergymen who criticized his protests against segregated stores as "unwise and untimely."

> I must confess that over the past few years I have been gravely disappointed with the white moderate. I have almost reached the regrettable conclusion that the Negro's great stumbling block in his stride toward freedom is not the White Citizen's Councilor or the Ku Klux Klanner, but the white moderate, who is more devoted to "order" than to justice; who prefers a negative peace, which is the absence of tension, to a positive peace, which is the presence of justice...who

paternalistically believes he can set the timetable for another man's freedom.

In the modern context, for example, when African Americans protest repeated cases of young black men killed by police, President Trump sees only valiant police protecting white America against a race of people with high rates of criminal activity. He is oblivious to black people as fellow Americans suffering injustice.

He sees white people who care about these issues as weak, politically correct saps, unwilling or unable to speak honestly about the crime rate in black neighborhoods. He sees Black Lives Matter, a movement protesting harsh treatment of blacks by police, as a group of people who hate the police.

These protests started in 2012 after Trayvon Martin, an unarmed black seventeen-year-old, was shot to death as he walked home from the local Florida market because he looked suspicious to a neighborhood watch volunteer. The group gained even more press attention when it led protests after a white policeman shot and killed an unruly but unarmed eighteen-year-old, Michael Brown in Ferguson, Missouri. As a candidate, Trump regularly derided Black Lives Matter as a threat to law and order.

All of this prompted Patrisse Cullors, one of the group's founding members, to tell the *Los Angeles Times* that she sees no benefit in talking to the president. "We wouldn't as a movement take a seat at the table with Trump, because we wouldn't have done that with Hitler," Cullors said. She called him the "epitome of evil, all the evils of this country," including racism, sexism, homophobia, and capitalism. Cullors said Trump is "killing our communities," and concluded, "The answer is not to sit with him but to resist him and to resist every single policy."

Kareem Abdul-Jabbar, the famous basketball player and now a writer, put his feelings about Trump this way:

"Trump represents the last wisp of the rich white plantation owner holding on to the glories of the past," Abdul-Jabbar wrote, pointing to statistics on the rising share of people of color in the United States. "For African Americans, America just got a little more threatening, a little more claustrophobic, a lot less hopeful.... People of color cannot merely play defense anymore. They must... [challenge] every act of institutional racism in the country."

That defensive feeling about Trump among black people, deftly articulated by Abdul-Jabbar, led the popular black writer Ta-Nehisi Coates to a rash conclusion. He argued that Trump's victory was solely based on white resentment of President Obama as a black man in the White House. Racism, he explained, "remains, as it has since 1776, at the heart of this country's political life." Coates pointed out that Trump won white men and white women; he won whites with college degrees and whites without college degrees and whites overall. Trump won whites who earn less than $50,000, and he won whites who made less than $100,000 as well as whites making more than $100,000. "Certainly not every Trump voter is a white supremacist, just as not every white person in the Jim Crow South was a white supremacist," wrote Coates. "But every Trump voter felt it acceptable to hand the fate of the country over to one."

Amen to that point. It is a reminder that, for whites, the problem of racism is not the dominant issue. But for blacks it is the top issue.

Yet Coates is so fixed on exposing indifference among some white voters to Trump's racism that he blames all white people for Trump's victory. That analysis requires readers to ignore whites who voted for both Obama and Trump, a decisive group in swing states such as Michigan and Wisconsin. Coates also invites his readers to ignore the history of black-white alliances that successfully advanced equal rights for blacks to new heights. Certainly, there is a lot remaining to be done to lift the disproportionately high number of black people who remain in poverty. But the distance yet to be traveled to reach full equality includes work apart from combatting white racism.

For starters, there is a need for black people to speak honestly to each other about dysfunction in poor black neighborhoods. Growing income inequality has had a particularly punishing effect on the poor and poorly educated. Sadly, there are a lot of black and Latino people still in those categories. Black America also has to honestly deal with the damage done to children as a result of family breakdowns tied to high levels of single mothers. Also, there are people like Coates, black intellectuals, who excuse a lack of personal responsibility among the black underclass, even criminal behavior against other black people; most victims of the high rate of black crime are black people. Coates flies by these problems inside black America by pointing to the persistence of "systemic" white racism. That is weak.

Coates is highly critical of President Obama for asking black people to take responsibility in their own lives for moving up. The president also told black people to stop with the excuses that always come back to charging whites with racism. Yes, white racism is a fact of life, but so too is the stirring story of black Americans pushing forward on their own muscle to win economic and political empowerment.

But Coates sees people like Obama and me as talking down to black people. He doesn't like it when we emphasize the need for black Americans to do all they can to solve their own problems. He was particularly distressed when President Obama, speaking to Morehouse College in 2013, said:

> We know that too many young men in our community continue to make bad choices. Growing up, I made quite a few myself. And I have to confess, sometimes I wrote off my own failings as just another example of the world trying to keep a black man down.... But one of the things that all of you have learned over the last four years is that there's no longer any room for excuses.... We've got no time for excuses—not because the bitter legacy of slavery and segregation have vanished entirely; they haven't. Not because racism and discrimination no longer exist; we know those are still out there. It's just that in today's hyper-connected, hyper-competitive world, with millions of young people from China and India and Brazil... entering the global workforce alongside you, nobody is going to give

21

you anything you haven't earned....And moreover, you have to re-member that whatever you've gone through, it pales in comparison to the hardships previous generations endured—and overcame.

Coates's response to the president's intensely personal message to young black men was to accuse Obama of offering a mere "handwave at history, to speak as though the government he represents is some-how only partly to blame."

So is Coates proposing that black America wait? Does he want us to hold off on dealing with repairing families, nurturing children, improving neighborhoods and schools, until the government deals with all the wrong it has done to black people in the past? Does he want us to wait until all white people admit to the damage done by racism and apologize? That may be the case. Coates is a propo-nent of the government paying reparations to black America. That idea amounts to a pipedream. It has never found political traction in Congress, and no president has ever backed it. No major civil rights organization is pursuing that agenda.

But what troubles me most about Coates's view of black life in the age of President Trump is that he accepts a big chunk of Trump's argument against black people.

Coates unwittingly buys into the Trump idea that black Amer-ica is defined by the failings of the black underclass. It can only be described as bizarre to see Coates, a smart young black man whose writing is so wildly celebrated by white liberals, fail to see the reality of his own success as evidence that failure does not represent all black people. Coates is the product of a proud, resilient people—black Americans.

I agree with Coates that racism remains a problem in America. And I do think Trump is a racist—someone who believes black people are threatening and inferior when compared to other people. Trump has the same negative attitudes his father had toward black people. Time and again, his behavior demonstrates ignorance of the power-ful history of black America's struggle to overcome slavery and legal segregation. He doesn't seem to care about the disproportionate numbers of black men brutalized by overly-aggressive police officers. His comment about immigrants from Africa and the Caribbean coming from "shithole" countries offers a stark reminder of what he thinks of people from majority-black nations, especially when compared to the praise he generously heaped on largely white Norwegian immigrants.

A year into his presidency, the public perception of Trump as a racist had deepened. In February 2018, 57 percent of American adults, including almost half of the nation's white people, said the president is an outright racist, according to a poll by the Associated Press and the NORC Center for Public Affairs. That's even higher than the percentage of Americans who told YouGov he was a racist in 2016. The February 2018 poll numbers indicated that 85 percent of Democrats believe the president is racist; only 21 percent of Republicans agreed. It is shocking that one of every five Republicans is willing to admit to a pollster that their president, a man of their party, is a racist. But still, four of every five Republicans are plainly hesitant to speak to the elephant in the room and label the man a racist.

I can understand their fear. Hell, I've been condemned by another black man on live television as a "porch monkey" because I work for Fox News. Even liberal white critics have trouble with me for my criticism of black leaders such as Jesse Jackson and Al Sharpton. I've written that they often play racial politics for their own gain instead of working to solve the big problems in black America, such as the bad public schools that are an ongoing source of misery for too many black and Latino children. I even started the State of Black America, an annual program with the Aspen Institute to give a platform to people often without a voice who are looking for actual solutions to problems in black neighborhoods. I also wanted to amplify the voices of black people as well as Asians, Latinos, and recent immigrants who have a tradition of achievement, not despair.

I'm not the only black person who has been attacked by the black left. During the 2016 Democratic primaries some young black leaders took out the long knives to stab at the iconic civil rights hero John Lewis. They called the distinguished congressman an Uncle Tom and a sell-out for endorsing Hillary Clinton over Bernie Sanders.

White Democrats have also felt the sting of being called racist. Hillary Clinton was hit with charges of racism during her run for the Democratic nomination. Some black activists wanted her to apologize for having once described young drug-dealing thugs, some of them black, as "super predators." She stood her ground and defiantly told them she was not racist but expressing the same concerns coming from the Congressional Black Caucus in the 1990s about lack of attention to drug-related crime in black neighborhoods.

Showing no sign of being intimidated, Ms. Clinton rightly said the young activists could get apologies and other types of "lip service from as many white people as you can pack into Yankee Stadium"— complete with promises of changed hearts—but it wouldn't change anything. Then Clinton, who has strong support from black voters, challenged them to come up with plans to change laws and funding for better policies instead of looking for an apology.

So there is a lot of tension in the air on the left and the right— especially on the right—about opening yourself to charges of racism. But Trump's racism is far bigger than our current anxieties about expressing our thoughts on race. This is not about policy differences. This is not about slips of the tongue and ambiguous statements that are called out as politically incorrect. This is not about a lack of familiarity with concepts like "white privilege" or "micro-aggressions." No, Trump's track record of racism is much bigger than that, and it will not be denied.

It goes back to discrimination against black people when he was renting apartments. His bias was so extreme that he faced a federal lawsuit, and was forced to sign an agreement to change his rental practices. His own words diminishing black employees as undesirables at his casinos demonstrate how he felt about African Americans in general. So too are his years of work to undermine the first black president as a foreigner and a phony, not a real American. Trump's true colors as a racist were also on vivid display during his campaign. He made clear his desire to go back in time to the nation's social order after World War II, when black people lived as second-class citizens. All that and more reveal his genuine distaste for and distrust of black people.

Of course, Trump is not alone among politicians in knowing how to push racial buttons to win elections. Republican politicians from Barry Goldwater to Richard Nixon, Ronald Reagan, and Trent Lott energized their base of voters with racially loaded winks and euphemistic phrases ranging from protecting "states' rights" to calls for "law and order" to outright libels such as "welfare queens." But Trump is different from those Republicans. He is way beyond winks and loaded rhetoric.

Trump paid for full-page advertising to demand the death penalty for a group of black and Latino boys accused of rape (who were later exonerated). And in his victorious run for the presidency he lashed out against black people as a group living in hellish conditions without any acknowledgment of black achievement in the face of the awful history of racism in the United States. He never showed respect for black people as patriots who struggled to achieve equal rights despite centuries of bitter racism from their government and fellow citizens. But when black athletes knelt in protest of police brutality, he quickly labeled them unpatriotic "son[s] of…bitch[es]."

As president he has made a sport of picking on prominent black Americans, from Oprah Winfrey to Congresswomen Maxine Waters and Frederica Wilson. His bad behavior on race has led prominent conservatives as diverse as Jonah Goldberg, Charles Krauthammer, Paul Ryan, and Ben Shapiro to call out Trump for making racist remarks or emboldening the racist mix of the KKK and neo-Nazis that make up the "alt-right" movement. The willingness of at least a few conservatives to call out Trump's racism is just one small sign of progress on race relations.

Keep in mind that there have never been so many educated middle-class black people in America. Black Americans are the most affluent black people in the world. This is all thanks to black people's sacrifice and struggle. Black people made tremendous strides in the last half century. Those victories are a rebuke of the people who fly the Confederate flag.

Those people are losers and haters. Trump found them to be an audience looking for a political champion. His call to "Make America Great Again" reminds me and a lot of others, both black and white, of a latent anger among some whites who fear that black success somehow means less for them—losing a job or a seat in an elite school to a black person, a Latino, or an immigrant.

In his racially divisive speeches, tweets, and policies, Trump invites America to shift into reverse gear. He would have America go back to the "good old days," when a white majority did not have to face a rising minority population. He would turn away from celebrating the civil rights movement's success as a model for the struggle to deal with remaining racial inequality. Trump's promise is to return to a day when white people did not have to deal with these uncomfortable racial questions. Trump is willing to do a U-turn on racial progress without any appreciation for what it cost the nation to get to this point. That's why he never celebrates the civil rights movement and black progress. That is why he prefers disparaging black people as undeserving of admiration and emulation.

He never misses a chance to divide black and brown people from the rest of America. His unprovoked attack on NFL players who peacefully protest police brutality is just one example of Trump's repeated efforts to pull the scabs off of deep racial wounds.

Trump's distorted racial attitudes extend to Latinos. He started his presidential campaign by libeling Mexican immigrants as thieves and rapists. He promised to build a wall to keep out undocumented immigrants from Mexico and other Latin countries. He further pumped up racially fueled passions by calling attention to families—all white—hurt by crimes committed by undocumented immigrants. The truth is that undocumented immigrants have a lower crime rate than American citizens.

Just as he is turning back the clock on race relations, Trump is trying to turn back the clock on immigration, particularly from Mexico. He has proposed cutting legal immigration in half in addition to building a wall to keep out undocumented immigrants.

His effort to throw the nation into reverse on equal rights for all is contrary to the nation's ideals—one people out of many. And it comes at a time of increasing racial diversity and high rates of immigration. That's why a majority of Americans—including 15 percent of Republicans—say Trump is ripping the country apart. But the potential for greater division didn't stop Trump. His political strategy was to earn enough white votes by appealing to their fear that they are losing their dominant status. He was willing to turn back the clock on major civil rights victories, beginning with the provisions of the 1964 Civil Rights Act.

For example, what else but political gain can be at the heart of his administration's attention to voter fraud despite lack of evidence that there is any such problem? Trump is looking for a pretext to impose new, restrictive rules on voter identification as well as limited voting hours. These steps will suppress votes by people of color, most of them going to Democrats, to bolster chances for Trump and other Republicans to keep winning elections.

He is also doing away with agreements between police and black neighborhoods that were set up to end a constant stream of police killing and brutality.

There is a pattern here. In every case, Trump is willing to stir racial tensions and reverse major civil rights victories. He does not appreciate the price paid by Americans to achieve racial progress or the high cost of going back.

To the contrary, he finds political benefit in energizing the remnants of hate groups that have been fighting racial change since the 1950s. These are the people who launched massive resistance against school integration. They fought passage of the Civil Rights Act, the

1965 Voting Rights Act and the 1968 Fair Housing Act. And with Trump as president, they have new life.

As Americans fight to hold onto victories won at great sacrifice over many years, it is important to remember how much was sacrificed to get past the dark old days and what is necessary to keep us from losing the light of liberty for all Americans. In this book are factual, inspiring stories of people who put themselves on the front line of the fight for racial justice in America. They paid the price for progress. Using the Civil Rights Act of 1964 as a guide, I discuss six areas of civil rights success: voting rights, employment, education, housing, public accommodations, and the rising power of voices calling for equal opportunity. In every case, people facing great odds with far fewer resources than we have today somehow managed to sing "We Shall Overcome." They stayed in the fight, won their leg of the great race to the ideal of "justice everywhere." Now they have successfully handed the baton to a new generation and urge us to pick up the pace, before Trump invites our bitter history to wash over us again.

CHAPTER 1

VOTING RIGHTS

Less than three weeks after he beat Hillary Clinton in the biggest political upset in modern American history, President-Elect Donald Trump fired off a series of seemingly nonsensical tweets, questioning the results of the election he had just won:

"Serious voter fraud in Virginia, New Hampshire and California… big problem!" he wrote. Earlier he argued that in addition to winning the Electoral College he also won "the popular vote if you deduct the millions of people who voted illegally."

That was just the start.

At a meet-and-great with lawmakers just after his January inauguration, he made news by startling everyone in the room with the charge that five million immigrants voted illegally in November. Two days later, he tweeted about his plan for a "major investigation into VOTER FRAUD." He was at it again in a February meeting with recently defeated Senator Kelly Ayotte (R-NH). The new president told her that if Democrats hadn't illegally bused voters in from liberal Massachusetts she would have won reelection. He knew this, he said, because he would have won the state from Hillary Clinton without all the voter fraud. In May he was back on the topic, issuing

29

an executive order creating the Commission on Election Integrity, a federal panel to investigate voter fraud.

The real news here was Trump's decision to name his vice president, Mike Pence, to head the commission.

With Pence as commissioner, it became clear what the panel was designed to do. Pence served as a congressman from Indiana while the state passed a 2005 voter ID law that Judge Terence Evans of the Seventh Circuit Court called a "not-so-thinly-veiled attempt to discourage election-day turnout" from low-income and minority voters, who are less likely to have photo IDs. The judge said the Republican legislature was suppressing votes from people "believed to skew Democrat." The conservative majority on the US Supreme Court upheld the law in a 2008 case—*Crawford v. Marion County Election Board*. That ruling is now considered to be the opening act for the Republican Party's nationwide efforts to clamp down on voter fraud through the passage of state laws requiring voters to prove their identification. The new laws fit the design of Indiana's 2005 law, never finding actual fraud but always achieving maximum impact by decreasing votes coming from poor people and people of color.

Trump's selection for the vice chair of the commission raised even more eyebrows than his choice of Pence.

The job of day-to-day control of Trump's voter fraud commission went to Kris Kobach, the Kansas secretary of state. Kobach is "the most racist politician in America today," according to Kansas State Senate Minority Leader Anthony Hensley (D-Topeka). Hensley pointed to Kobach's false claim that President Obama ordered the Justice Department not to prosecute black criminals, a lie you'd expect to hear from a white supremacist or Klansman.

More alarm erupted about Trump's panel when it was revealed that Hans von Spakovsky, well-known for his unproven conspiracy theories blaming Democrats for promoting voter fraud, was on the commission. Most troubling, news reporters found that von Spakovsky proposed barring all Democrats and moderate Republicans from the voter fraud group.

"There isn't a single Democratic official that will do anything other than obstruct any investigation," von Spakovsky wrote in an email forwarded to Attorney General Jeff Sessions and released under the Freedom of Information Act. Von Spakovsky also argued that having "mainstream Republican[s]" on the Commission would be an "abject failure because there aren't any that know anything about this."

The commission got off to a controversial start when Kobach sent letters to every state in the nation demanding Social Security numbers, birthdates, addresses, and political party affiliations for every registered voter. By July 2017, twenty-one states had refused to give Trump's team any information. An additional twenty-seven states gave them only limited data. "We find it very difficult to have confidence in the work of this Commission," Massachusetts Secretary of State Denise Merrill said in a statement. Even in Mississippi, where Trump beat Clinton by eighteen percentage points, Delbert Hosemann, Mississippi's Republican secretary of state, told Kobach to "go jump in the Gulf of Mexico." The request also immediately drew lawsuits from the American Civil Liberties Union, Public Citizen, and the Election Privacy Information Center.

But Trump's panel continued its efforts, ignoring stop sign after stop sign as critics asked for proof of voter fraud. At one point Kobach's group announced they had found voter fraud in the 2016 race. They pointed to college students attending school in New Hampshire who voted there even though they were residents of other states. But state officials pointed out that New Hampshire's laws allow students residing in the state during the school year to legally vote in the state's elections.

At that point critics began to ask how far the president was willing to go with an Alice-in-Wonderland panel and a preordained outcome absent any evidence of voter fraud.

Finally, in early 2018, Trump signed an executive order disbanding the failing commission. He didn't admit that all the conspiracy theories about voter fraud had fallen flat. Instead, he blamed the states' lack of cooperation with the commission.

Allegations of voter fraud have an ugly history in American politics.

Black Americans, mostly slaves, had no right to vote until after the Civil War and the passage of the Reconstruction Acts, which gave them the vote in former Confederate states. Later, the Fifteenth Amendment guaranteed black men the right to vote around the country. When black men started voting and winning elected office, there was a backlash among whites in the Southern states of the former Confederacy. White power brokers in Southern states passed new laws to depress black voter turnout and stop the large black population in their states from controlling the region's politics. The new laws were justified as necessary to "reform and purify the electoral process, to root out fraud and poverty," writes historian Leon Litwack. These punishing Jim Crow laws were aimed at poor, uneducated black men and succeeded in scaring African Americans in the South away from the polls.

Fast-forward to the twenty-first century, as America is undergoing another major shift in race relations. As nonwhite citizens are on their way to comprising half of the nation, Republicans find their efforts to recruit voters of color are failing. Democrats, with their strong advocacy of civil rights and prominent black and Latino candidates, have made their party a home for most voters of color. Republicans, meanwhile, have become the party of older voters and evangelicals—and most of all, the party of white America.

After losing the 2012 presidential election, the Republican National Committee did an autopsy of the defeat. It called for putting more money into outreach to black and Latino voters. But Trump's insurgent campaign, fueled by white grievances, replaced any hope of a multicultural GOP in step with the country's demographics—a hope that had been elevated by the candidacy of Marco Rubio, a second-generation immigrant.

Republican state legislatures began party-line votes on measures to limit the power of voters of color. First came gerrymandering:

drawing congressional district lines to purposely corral black and Latino voters while spreading out white, Republican voters over a larger number of districts. Even where there are few white voters, the new district lines made them into a majority able to retain GOP dominance of elections for Congress.

Gerrymandering was paired with the new voter-ID laws championed by Mike Pence, Kris Kobach, and Hans von Spakovsky. The sudden new wave of laws threatened hard-fought voting rights, but in Southern states with a history of disenfranchising black voters, the federal government had the right to review any new voting procedures to protect racial minority groups from discrimination. That precaution suddenly ended in 2013, when the US Supreme Court, in a case known as *Shelby County v. Holder*, struck down central protections in the 1965 Voting Rights Act. Specifically, the ruling struck down a requirement for states with a history of suppressing the black vote to get federal approval for any changes to their voting laws. The court said this requirement was out of date and unfair to Southern states with no recent history of blocking black people from voting.

The ruling opened the way for Congress to update the Voting Rights Act based on more recent records of voting activities. But the Republican congressional majority never acted. Meanwhile, the Republican majorities in state legislatures saw a green light to pass new laws supposedly aimed at reducing voter fraud but with the side effect of decreasing the Democrat-leaning minority vote.

The Shelby County decision had an immediate and dramatic effect on voting rights in the United States. Between the 2012 and 2016 presidential elections, fourteen states successfully put in place new laws raising the bar on requirements for voter registration and limiting voting hours. Most of them were in the South, but several states outside the South joined the action. Republican political dominance in state legislatures allowed for new restrictions on voter registration in Indiana, Ohio, Kansas, Nebraska, Wisconsin, New

Hampshire, and Rhode Island. Following the 2016 election, more new laws, once again raising the requirements for voter identification, passed in North Dakota, Missouri, and Arkansas.

The first brake on these restrictive laws came in the summer of 2016. A federal court found that a North Carolina law requiring photo IDs and limiting early voting before election day clearly "target[ed] African Americans with almost surgical precision."

Then in August 2017 the federal courts struck down a similar Texas law. It had required people to produce government-issued photo IDs or bank statements and utility bills in order to register to vote. The federal court ruled it out of line because it "imposes burdens disproportionately on blacks and Latinos," a population with a disproportionate share of people in poverty and less likely to have their names on bank accounts or utility bills, in the words of the federal judge.

"We'll never know how many people were kept from the polls by these [new] restrictions," wrote voting rights scholar Ari Berman in the *Nation* following the 2016 presidential election.

What we do know is that in Milwaukee, home to seven out of ten African Americans in the critical swing state of Wisconsin, 52,000 fewer people voted in 2016 than in 2012. In Milwaukee County, a mostly Democratic area, dominated by young voters and people of color, the Democrats got 103,000 fewer votes than they did four years earlier in the 2012 election. In the end, Trump won Wisconsin by less than 30,000 votes.

After the November 2016 election the Leadership Conference for Civil Rights found that in 381 counties in the South, there were far fewer polling places than there had been in 2012. The counties were all located in in Southern and Southwestern states previously required by the Voting Rights Act to get "pre-clearance" or federal permission before making changes to voting procedures and polling places. The review found North Carolina closed 27 polling places, 12 closed in South Carolina, 66 in Alabama, 44 in

Mississippi, 103 in Louisiana, 212 in Arizona, and a shocking 403 in Texas.

The sad reality is that Republicans made these changes without evidence of voter fraud. Every review of voting by private and government agencies confirms that it remains an incredibly rare phenomenon. An American is far more likely to be struck by lightning than to see anyone impersonate a registered voter, according to a 2007 report published by the Brennan Center for Justice at New York University Law School. But in a hardball game of politics based on a pragmatic view that most people of color vote for Democrats, the Republicans state legislatures acted to gain political advantage by suppressing their vote.

The combined power of the Trump panel, closed polling places, and restrictive new voter registration laws takes the nation back in time. We have returned to a moment in history before passage of the 1964 Civil Rights Act and the 1965 Voting Rights Act offered protections for people of color's voting rights. The new attacks are in line with the long, sad history of segregationist tactics to keep black people from voting before the civil rights laws.

In the bad old days, the racists would ask black people trying to register to vote questions like these:

"How many bubbles are in a bar of soap?"

"How deep is the Alabama River?"

"How many jelly beans are in this glass jar?"

These are absurd questions—with no correct answer. A black American stumped by one of these bizarre questions was not allowed to register to vote.

In Mississippi the white registrars also had fun mocking black people by requiring them to explain any of the nearly three hundred sections of the state constitution. It was a system designed to ensure that no African Americans would be allowed to register. And even before a black person reached the registrar, there were threats to take away jobs, as well as letters from white-owned banks cancelling mortgage loans to blacks trying to vote.

If none of those tactics worked, there was always the old reliable use of violence. Black people standing in line to register to vote were often beaten by local police and sheriffs. Even white people trying to help blacks register faced constant threats of violence and, in some cases, death. That is what happened to three voting rights workers, two of them white, in 1964 Mississippi. Those young men literally gave their lives to protect the voting rights our president has now put in question.

A review of their sacrifice is necessary to understand the price paid to achieve racial equality in the recent past and the cost of President Trump's effort to reverse those gains with baseless allegations of frequent, nationwide fraudulent voting.

News of the disappearance of James Chaney, Mickey Schwerner, and Andy Goodman came on a Monday, June 22, 1964, while a group of college students gathered at Western College for Women, a small school in Oxford, Ohio—now part of Miami University of Ohio. They had been recruited by civil rights organizations for Freedom Summer, an effort to have young people, many from elite colleges including Harvard, Yale, Stanford, Princeton, and Berkeley, give up summer vacation and go into the muddy cotton fields and overheated sharecroppers' shacks in backcountry Mississippi to help local African Americans register to vote.

Freedom Summer was organized by a group of young, mostly black activists in a group called the Student Nonviolent Coordinating Committee (SNCC, pronounced "Snick"). Sending young white people to the South was a strategic effort to attract national attention to voter suppression in Mississippi. SNCC wanted federal government officials to be forced to see violent opposition to black voter registration from local white segregationists. The goal was to force the Justice Department to defend the constitutional right of black citizens to vote. And the activists wanted to increase public pressure on Congress to draft meaningful legislation in defense of black voting rights.

In early spring, SNCC workers had sent brochures and applications out to various Friends of SNCC satellite organizations that had been formed by contacts on college campuses around the country. "Students from the north making the necessary sacrifices to go south would make abundantly clear to the government and the public that this is not a situation which can be ignored any longer," read a SNCC Fact Sheet used to recruit students at West Coast colleges.

SNCC leaders toured campuses and delivered speeches to drum up excitement. SNCC's local headquarters in Jackson, Mississippi, received 736 applications. "We are pleased to have you participate as a member of the 1964 Freedom Summer in the Mississippi Project," read a stock letter to a successful applicant, who was asked to attend the orientation program at Western College, funded by the National Council of Churches.

Many of the volunteers still being trained in Ohio met Chaney, Goodman, and Schwerner before they left with the first wave of students into Mississippi. News of their disappearance reached the students in Ohio as a studious, young black New Yorker in horn-rimmed glasses, Bob Moses, was at the front of the room lecturing them on what to expect as they went into the South.

The students—who would total roughly seven hundred by the end of the summer—listened intently to the soft-spoken Moses, who had been traveling the deep South for nearly four years by this point. Moses and other SNCC leaders told the students about the hardships facing any black person trying to register to vote in Mississippi. Even among the states of the former Confederacy, the Magnolia State had the lowest percentage of black people registered to vote as a share of the state's entire black population.

Mississippi in the early 1960s remained a rural society with a plantation economy based on cheap labor provided by the most recent generation of people who a hundred years earlier were legally held as slaves. With no big cities, Mississippi did not have even the limited cosmopolitan atmosphere of Southern hubs like Charlotte,

Atlanta, and Nashville. The 1960 Census showed that Mississippi had the lowest per capita and median family income in the United States. "Never before in American history had one state been so far removed from the voting mainstream," wrote Joseph Crespino in his book, *In Search of Another Country: Mississippi and the Conservative Counterrevolution.*

To prepare the college students for their first trip to Mississippi, the SNCC workers led role-playing exercises. Screaming, threatening, and manhandling the students, they pretended to be racist Mississippi registrars, sheriffs, and judges. They taught the volunteers what to do if they were arrested or assaulted. The young people had to study maps of Mississippi, familiarizing themselves with escape routes along the highways they'd be traveling between the state's small towns.

Most important for the mostly white students was the straight talk from people like Moses. He had credibility as someone who had spent time in Mississippi. And he cautioned them not to expect to change Mississippi in one summer by laying out the limited scope of how many people they could expect to register in a political structure controlled by violent white segregationists. "The unreal world of the barbarous newsreel and the tabloid spread was suddenly becoming our world," wrote a journalist covering the event. He quoted one SNCC worker as telling the young people: "Now look man, this is the way it is.... Smith [College] ain't Mississippi."

Yet none of this prepared the white students for the news they heard from the twenty-nine-year-old Moses on June 22.

Moses was in the front of a classroom speaking when a SNCC worker came into the room and pulled him aside. He quickly gave him the news out of the students' earshot. Moses listened to the news, took a moment to stare into space, and then relayed the message to the volunteers gathered in the room: "Yesterday morning, three of our people left Meridian, Mississippi, to investigate a church burning in Neshoba County. They haven't come back, and we haven't had any word from them. We spoke to John Doar," an assistant attorney general in the Civil Rights Division of the Department of Justice and SNCC contact. "He promised to order the FBI to act, but the local FBI still says they have been given no authority."

Moses was too undone to keep the class going. A white Jewish twenty-year-old and Queens College graduate named Rita Schwerner who was just five feet and ninety pounds—came to the podium and erased the map of Mississippi that had been drawn in chalk on the board. On the blank board she used large letters to spell out the names of the three men who had gone missing: James Chaney, Andy Goodman, and Mickey Schwerner, her husband.

Mickey Schwerner, twenty-four years old, white, and Jewish like his wife, had driven from New York City to Mississippi with Rita in January as part of a project for CORE—the Congress of Racial Equality. The Schwerners were stars among the young people arriving for Freedom Summer because of their experience. They told stories about bunking in the black section of an eastern Mississippi town called Meridian. They were white, but the whites in Meridian would not have let any civil rights worker live in their midst. The local white newspapers described the civil rights workers as communists, Northern agitators, and troublemakers trying to destroy their supposedly peaceful Southern way of life by riling up the local blacks.

Schwerner was traveling with James Chaney, a black twenty-one-year-old Mississippi native. They had teamed up in January on a CORE voter registration project. Chaney had been plastering walls as a day laborer before the civil rights workers came to town. He was fascinated by the new white people like Schwerner who were boldly challenging Mississippi segregation.

The third man in their group was Andy Goodman, a white twenty-year-old, who knew Mickey and Rita because he had been her classmate at Queens College in New York.

Chaney and Schwerner planned to run a voter registration drive out of the Mt. Zion Methodist Church in Longdale, Mississippi, an all-black rural town in Neshoba County, thirty-five miles from Meridian. The church had agreed to host the Freedom School, a makeshift community center where local black citizens could learn how to answer the convoluted questions they might be asked during a registration test about the US and Mississippi constitutions. Andy Goodman, though he'd never been to Mississippi, had impressed Chaney and Schwerner at orientation and had been tapped to lead the Freedom School.

But local Klansmen who had learned of their plans to start a Freedom School set Mt. Zion Methodist Church on fire. Five days later, on a Sunday afternoon, Chaney, Schwerner, and Goodman decided to drive from their SNCC headquarters in Meridian to see what remained of the church in Longdale. They said they'd be home by late afternoon.

In Longdale they met with the local black community leaders who'd been at Mt. Zion for a church financial meeting the night it was set on fire. They told the three civil rights workers how Klansmen and the local police had intimidated them as they left the church, looking for the "white boy," meaning Schwerner, whom they'd been tailing since he first arrived in Mississippi that January. Their newsletters described him as a "Jew boy," a "mixer," and a "commie."

Chaney, Goodman, and Schwerner found Mt. Zion with "its ashes still giving off smoke five days after it was torched," as historian Carol George wrote in her book *One Mississippi, Two Mississippi: Methodists, Murder, and the Struggle for Racial Justice in Neshoba County*.

Back in their station wagon by late afternoon, Chaney, Goodman, and Schwerner began traveling the road back to Meridian. But local law enforcement and Klansmen had seen them. They were pulled over and arrested for speeding at around 4:20 p.m. by deputy sheriff Cecil Price and brought to the jail in Philadelphia, a nearby city in Neshoba County.

It wasn't uncommon for civil rights workers in Mississippi to be arrested on trumped-up charges. They'd be taken in for speeding, interfering with police business, disturbing the peace, or some other made-up offense.

This time was different. White Mississippians were expecting Schwerner. When word had gotten around that he was back in Longdale, local Klan leader Edgar Ray Killen drove from Philadelphia to Meridian to gather a group of Klansmen. James Jordan, a Klansman involved in the murders, later confessed that Killen had told the others to pick up gloves from the hardware store for what he promised would be a messy job.

That night at around 10:30, Chaney, Goodman, and Schwerner were released from prison. As they sped back to Meridian in their station wagon, they were stopped again by deputy Price. This time Price forced the three into his squad car and drove off to a side road, where they were met by three cars full of Klansmen. Schwerner was shot in the heart. They shot Goodman in the abdomen. Because Chaney was black, they beat him before shooting him three times, in the head and chest.

The three bodies were thrown into the same car they had been driving, taken to a farm owned by a wealthy landowner named Olen Barrage, and thrown into an unfinished earthen dam, where the bodies were then covered up with dirt by a bulldozer.

On Tuesday the twenty-third, the day after Moses got word of their disappearance, members of a local Native American tribe, the Choctaw, found the burnt-out station wagon on a logging path off a highway near Philadelphia.

News of the disappearance of Chaney, Goodman, and Schwerner created a national sensation with headlines about the mystery of their disappearance and fear that racial violence had killed them.

"Three Rights Workers Missing," blared the *Washington Post*. And for the following six weeks, the story of the hard, deep divide between the races got a compelling new story line in the form of questions about what happened to the three civil rights workers.

Broadcasting from her New York City apartment, with her husband and the parents of Mickey Schwerner, Carolyn Goodman—Andy's mother—spoke to the nation, urging Mississippi officials to take her son's disappearance seriously because she knew that even in

Mississippi there were parents "who like myself have experienced the softness, the warmth and the beauty of a child whom they cherish and love and want to protect." Carolyn Goodman, a psychologist, "spoke as a mother, whose second of three sons she may never see again," reported the *Boston Globe*, with every word "holding onto a dogged hope that their son and the other two young men would be found alive and well." The Schwerners and Goodmans said they had also spoken to the family of James Chaney down in Mississippi.

Part of the problem for federal agents looking for Chaney, Goodman, and Schwerner was that most white Mississippians denied that anything had happened. That Tuesday, President Lyndon Johnson phoned Senator Jim Eastland (D-MS) and asked, "Jim, we've got three kids missing down there. What can I do about it?" Eastland responded, "Well, I don't know. . . . I don't believe there's three missing. . . . I believe it's a publicity stunt." When local FBI agent John Proctor interviewed Price, the deputy sheriff denied that he knew anything, and the two drank moonshine together.

Local newspapers, meanwhile, wrote front-page stories suggesting that these murders were the result not of racist Klansmen but of the work of the civil rights movement itself. "Nothing has been said about how much wiser the missing young men would have been had they stayed home and minded their own business," noted an article in the *Pascagoula Chronicle*.

As many as four hundred navy sailors were assigned to comb Neshoba County for the bodies. "Searchers for three civil rights workers, missing since Sunday, began dragging the muddy Pearl River today for their bodies," reported the *New York Times* on June 28. Yet they were unable to determine where the bodies were until they were tipped off by an anonymous source that the FBI would call "Mr. X." The mystery man is believed to have been a highway patrolman named Maynard King, who knew the men who had committed the crime.

The FBI's discovery of the bodies on August 4, 1964, was documented with excruciating detail in a report filed eight days later on August 12. After a bulldozer cleared off land from the top of the dam at 9:00 a.m., the FBI used a dragline—meaning a heavy-duty crane with a bucket attached to the end of it—to dig up the land. As the hole grew deeper, the diggers smelt the "faint" and then the "pungent... odor of decaying organic material." The dirt was infested with blow files—or calliphoridae—an insect that dwells near rotting animal flesh.

At 3:00 p.m., the body of a shirtless man wearing boots and wrangler jeans, Mickey Schwerner, began to appear. At 5:07 they found Goodman's body. And at 5:14 p.m., they found Chaney. The FBI report also noted a wedding ring on Schwerner's left hand.

Bob Moses, the young man who announced their disappearance, didn't need an FBI report to find out what had happened to Chaney, Goodman, and Schwerner.

"The kids are dead," Moses told the volunteers at a speech on the final night of training in Ohio, still more than a month before the three bodies would be found. "When we heard the news at the beginning, I knew they were dead," Moses continued. "There may be more deaths." His blunt, cut-to-the-chase words stood in stark contrast with his nerdy, bookish demeanor. Moses was reserved, wore glasses, and had a steady, calming manner. This coupling of fearlessness and soft-spoken nature would come to be called the Bob Moses Mystique. It didn't hurt that his name referenced the man who led the Israelites out of slavery in Egypt.

Giving the white students a chance to bow out while still far away from the depths of Mississippi, Moses went on: "If for any reason you're hesitant about what you're getting into, it's better for you to leave." Referring then to the mission on which they were about to embark, he continued: "Because what has got to be done has to be done in a certain way, or otherwise it won't get done."

Later, the public would find out the murders of Chaney, Goodman, and Schwerner had been an entirely coordinated effort between local law enforcers, Klansmen, and wealthy landowners. The exact details of what had happened spilled out like family secrets over the following months and years.

But the evening that the three men were confirmed dead, students stayed up all night talking with their peers in the college laundry room. They also had to get on the phone with parents who were telling them to just come home—it was too dangerous. Overwhelmingly, the young people decided to stay, and got in cars heading down to Mississippi.

Why did they follow Bob Moses? How did he inspire such loyalty? Most importantly, why was he telling a group of white students to go to Mississippi knowing full well that they too could meet the fate of Chaney, Goodman, and Schwerner?

Robert Parris Moses was born in Harlem, the world famous black neighborhood in New York City, on January 23, 1935. On March 19, 1935, less than two months after he was born, a major race riot broke out in front of a Harlem convenience store after word spread that white police officers had killed a black Puerto Rican teen. During the riot that ensued, three black people were killed and sixty were injured, leaving $200 million worth of damaged property in an already poor neighborhood.

Reflecting on another Harlem race riot in 1943, this one caused by a white cop shooting a black soldier trying to defend a black woman arrested for disorderly conduct—and resulting in six deaths and six hundred arrests—Moses told an interviewer that he "knew what was going on" but, as an eight-year-old, "didn't have a clue about what it meant."

His family knew the pain of racial hatred. Moses's paternal grandmother, Julia Trent, was the descendent of a Virginia slave who had married the slave master's son. That threw generations of children into an unending identity crisis, forever unsure of whether they were black or white, descended from masters or slaves.

Moses's paternal grandfather—the Reverend William Henry Moses—had been a black Baptist minister in the South and vice president of the National Baptist Convention, a leading organization of black church leaders at the turn of the century.

Bob Moses grew up in a working-class Harlem family. His father, Gregory, was a janitor—a "good job in the thirties," Moses later said—and his mother was a homemaker. They lived in a housing project. Yet things were as tough for the Moseses as they were for any black family in the community. Every few weeks he, his mother, and his older brother, Gregory—another brother, Roger, would be born in 1941—walked from Harlem to the closest A&P, a chain of discount grocery stores, located several miles away in the Bronx. The "little 'mom and pop...grocery stores" even in Harlem were too much for what Moses' dad made as a janitor, Moses later explained. And the 1943 Harlem riot taught Moses about the frustration, anger, and sometimes violence that resulted from years of poverty and structural racial inequality.

Yet Moses also witnessed the unique talent of blue collar black folks living in poor neighborhoods. His father was never satisfied with his job as a janitor. Yet he was charismatic and willing to engage in debate with friends and colleagues: a sort of "working-class public speaker," Moses later explained.

When Jackie Robinson, the first black man in major league baseball, began playing at Ebbets Field in 1947, Moses's dad stopped rooting for the Harlem-based New York Giants and became a fan of their crosstown rivals, the Brooklyn Dodgers, where Jackie played through the 1950s.

As he grew up, Moses found an intellectual home in New York's left-wing political circles. A friend's father operated a printing press, and he gave Moses the latest newsletters and magazines featuring black progressive thinkers and activists. One year he even attended a communist-run summer camp in New York—a "red diaper baby summer camp," as he later described it—which he didn't particularly like because there was too much singing and not enough discussion of race relations.

Bob Moses excelled in New York City schools, and at age fourteen he was admitted to Peter Stuyvesant High School, a highly selective public school known then and now for its gifted students who wouldn't have been able to afford private school. Going to Stuyvesant was Moses's "entry into the white world," he would later say. Though the school was integrated, "there were maybe a handful of [blacks and Latinos] in a school with about three thousand students."

Moses earned admission to honors classes and served as class president. He then went on to Hamilton College, a highly regarded school in upstate New York, where he studied math and philosophy. He played basketball at both Stuyvesant and Hamilton, and graduated from college with honors in philosophy.

Moses's first real connection to the civil rights movement developed through his interest in pacifism. At Hamilton, Moses was considering registering as a conscientious objector to the draft. Aware of his interest in pacifism, a professor urged him to join the American Friends Service Committee (AFSC), which led Moses to meet civil rights organizer Bayard Rustin.

At a 1953 meeting held in Rustin's New York City apartment, Moses and several young men discussed plans to avoid the draft. For Moses, what was more important than anything he heard from Rustin was the fact that he dared to be there. "In showing up I became somebody because I was the only black kid coming in," he later wrote.

Moses's interest in pacifism went beyond avoiding military service. During the summers of 1955 and 1956, he participated in month-long Quaker service projects organized by the AFSC in Belgium, France, Germany, and Japan: building mental hospitals and summer camps for poor children.

When he came home to New York, Moses found a new community at the folk concerts, or hootenannies, he attended in downtown Manhattan. He got to watch singer-songwriters such as Pete Seeger perform songs calling for racial justice. Seeger and other singers pushed their audience to confront the reality of black people being lynched in the South. "Seeger was always talking about the South," Moses recalled. Seeger, of course, would become famous for turning a gospel hymn by Charles Albert Tindley (1851–1933) entitled

"I'll Overcome Someday" into the civil rights anthem "We Shall Overcome."

After college, Moses went to Harvard, where he received a master's degree in philosophy in June 1957. He was planning on working toward a PhD, but when his mother died of cancer in the winter of 1958, Moses returned to New York to comfort his father and got a job as a math teacher at Horace Mann, a wealthy white private school in Riverdale. Teaching math to rich white teens, the civil rights sit-ins, bus boycotts, and Freedom Rides were just the stuff of newspaper headlines.

Moses's thinking about race got another boost when he took a side job as a tutor for the teenage black jazz singer Frankie Lymon. On tour with Lymon as he traveled to Chicago and Detroit and other cities with large black populations, Moses discovered black ghettos even more poor and hopeless than Harlem.

With his mind focused on race relations, Moses was primed for action but unsure what to do. Then he heard about the Greensboro, North Carolina, sit-in movement in 1960. Like many black Northerners, Moses was shocked and inspired by the stories and pictures of courageous black people sitting in at Greensboro lunch counters even as they were beaten and spit on. "They had a certain look on their faces—sort of sullen, angry, determined," he later explained. "They were kids my age, and I knew this had something to do with my life."

Moses's uncle, Bill Moses, taught at the Hampton Institute, the historically black school in Virginia, and headed the Hampton NAACP chapter. During Moses's spring break from teaching in 1960, he decided to see his uncle and get a better sense of the movement being created by young black people in the South.

Once in Hampton, Moses jumped headfirst into the civil rights movement. He joined in as a group of activists picketed a Woolworth's store in the nearby city of Newport News, Virginia. He also attended a rally headlined by the Reverend Wyatt Tee Walker, an early organizer for the Southern Christian Leadership Committee. Walker told Moses the SCLC was opening an office in Harlem.

When the young teacher got back to New York from his trip to the South, a lot had changed. The movement to fight for civil rights was catching fire in the North. After teaching every day, Moses volunteered at the Harlem SCLC office led by his old friend Bayard Rustin. When Moses returned South after the semester to volunteer at the SCLC offices in Atlanta for the summer, Rustin wrote a letter introducing him to SCLC leader Ella Baker.

The civil rights movement was in the midst of a transition when Moses got to Atlanta in 1960. Baker, one of the few women in a leadership role in the movement, was telling young people they needed to take charge and stop waiting for established leaders in the NAACP or even the popular Dr. Martin Luther King Jr. to set the direction for the fight against the segregationists. "Strong movements don't need strong leaders," she would say.

Moses immediately agreed with Baker, and wanted to take action. But when he got to the Atlanta SCLC office in July, no one was even working. In fact, the only person there was a young white woman named Jane Stembridge, addressing envelopes for a brand-new organization created in April 1960 called the Student Nonviolent Coordinating Committee. Baker had given the new group some space for their effort to organize the young, college-centered energy sparked by the sit-in movement. Stembridge was from Georgia. The daughter of a Baptist minister whose progressive views on race relations got him fired from jobs at several churches, she was doing graduate work at Union Theological Seminary when, like Bob Moses, the sit-ins inspired her to go back South to work on civil rights.

Stembridge and Moses quickly became friends. Asked by the SCLC to draft a tedious fundraising letter, Moses was bored. His attention was on the young, grassroots, insistent calls for energy and action being stirred up by SNCC. But SNCC's leaders didn't know Moses, the graduate of white schools in the North. Moses's bookish demeanor, his interest in philosophy, and the simple fact that he was from New York made them suspect that he was a communist or

Soviet sympathizer. "We thought he was a communist because he was from New York and wore glasses and was smarter than we were," explained Julian Bond, an African American born in Tennessee who had joined SNCC that April.

Ironically, Moses's outsider status among SNCC activists is exactly what allowed him to gain their respect.

SNCC workers were making plans for a major October conference in which student activists from around the country could come together and articulate their goals for SNCC. Unlike the top-down approach of the older civil rights groups, SNCC's young leaders wanted their movement to be led by students and regular people around the nation, not older people huddled in Atlanta.

The problem was that SNCC had few connections in rural Mississippi, Alabama, and Louisiana. And everyone feared being sent into the rural South to set up civil rights programs in those areas. No matter how bad things were for black people in the urban South, they were worse in the countryside, the land of black sharecroppers and white Klansmen. They heard stories of black people like Emmett Till, lynched in 1955 for supposedly whistling at a white girl. Tactics like sit-ins were too dangerous in Mississippi, where black employees would simply be fired for uttering even a word of protest.

"I'd never been to Mississippi," explained Julian Bond. "And I didn't want to go to Mississippi."

White Mississippians had a complicated relationship to the state's black population. There were as many blacks as whites in the state. So whites knew blacks as servants in their homes, as workers, as neighbors. And at the core of the white Southern attitude toward black people was the assumption that local African Americans were perfectly happy with the way things were: that they had no need for integration and voting rights because they lived separate yet equal lives.

An August 1954 article by the editor of the *Jackson Daily News*, a local Mississippi paper, argued that the "great masses of Negroes in

Mississippi" were "happy and contented in their schools, churches, and social activities," and therefore, "why not let them have what they want?"

"The difference between the north and the south," explained an article in another local paper, the *McComb Enterprise Journal*, in July 1948, "is the white people and the colored of the South feel kindly toward one another."

Elliot Trimble of the *Natchez Democrat* echoed this sentiment in August 1954, writing that there was "no basic conflict between whites and negroes on the issue of segregation."

A white Mississippi planter interviewed for a 1963 documentary about SNCC entitled *The Streets of Greenwood* described a sort of intimate relationship between him and his black sharecroppers: "A lot of the [black] people we got on the place now are people that have been here a long time. . . . They've been good to me. We've been good to them. There's a sort of closeness there, really."

Mississippi whites' disregard for the struggles of African Americans grew out of the brutal sharecropping system, which was the basis of the local economy. White Southerners sustained a seemingly impenetrable racial caste system as a matter of economic self-interest, protecting a unique source of cheap labor—subservient black workers.

Moses didn't understand the Deep South psychology of covering up explosive feelings. "I didn't know enough to be afraid," he later said, when he volunteered to travel by bus through Alabama, Louisiana, and the Mississippi Delta, recruiting young people to join SNCC. Moses's willingness to go to rural counties, where veteran civil rights workers feared being attacked if not killed, won him a lot of respect from his fellow SNCC activists.

Traveling through the rural South, the Mississippi Delta specifically, Moses experienced poverty the likes of which he'd never seen before. When invited into a rickety house, he soon had personal knowledge that nine out of ten black people in the state had no toilets. More than half had no running water. In a letter to

SNCC leaders Moses described how, after he had finished eating a bowl of stew, a black farmer he had never met reached into his bowl to eat a piece of bone whose meat Moses had already chewed off. Even the black Mississippians who were lucky enough to work were employed as sharecroppers, subject to the whims of white planters.

Moses stayed at the home of local black NAACP leader and activist Amzie Moore. He became a guide to rural Mississippi. Almost fifty years old, Moore ran a gas station, worked at the post office, and pretty much knew the name, location, and occupation of every African American in the Delta. Moore was no sharecropper; he was middle class and had traveled the world, having fought in Asia during World War II.

Moore took Moses around the region, introduced him to the locals, and even had Moses deliver some speeches about the civil rights movement at black churches in the area. Moses befriended Moore. They had late-night conversations about Mississippi history.

Moses told Moore that SNCC leaders in Atlanta believed that direct action, pickets, and sit-ins were the most effective strategy to achieve their goal of racial equality through racial integration. Moore had a different point of view. He believed poor black people in the state, lacking electricity and running water, didn't really care about integration. They had other concerns—most of all the harsh poverty weighing down on them in a subsistence economy.

And making racial integration with white people the bottom line flashed a bright red for Moore; it would spark violence. And there was the problem of money. Moses said Moore explained to him that maybe the two of them could afford to go to a desegregated restaurant in Mississippi, but how about "the Jackson Negro who might get fired for it[?] ... How about the Negro who makes fifteen dollars per week?"

In the words of Moses's biographer, Laura Visser-Maessen, the young man from New York who was reporting to people in Atlanta was finding out that "Mississippi blacks had different objectives than the Atlanta students, who were primarily interested in access to seg-regated public facilities that many Mississippi blacks could not even afford to patronize."

Moore wasn't opposed to integration but told Moses to tell his bosses in Atlanta "it was not going straight to the heart of what was the trouble in Mississippi." The trouble, he said, was that more than 95 percent of black Mississippians were not registered to vote. "Somehow, in following [Moore's] guidance there," Moses later said, "we stumbled on the key—the right to vote and the political action that ensued."

Those conversations led Moses to plan a major voter registration drive for rural Mississippi for the following summer, 1961.

Moses and Moore immediately faced several high hurdles.

First, there were practical issues. Following Reconstruction, Southern lawmakers set up a system of poll taxes and citizenship tests that made it nearly impossible for African Americans to even register to vote. Moore and Moses would need to teach local blacks to pass these tests.

The tests, according to Lawrence Guyot, a CORE activist working in Mississippi, were "clearly devised...to make sure illiterate whites would be registered but no Negro, regardless of how literate, would be registered."

The second hurdle facing Moses and Moore was even bigger: the awful emotional scars left on so many people by oppression. Moore and Moses needed to inspire confidence in black Mississippians who lacked the belief that it was their right to go to the polls and vote. So many sharecroppers, after generations of abuse, poverty, and a gen-eral lack of access to the goods of the government, were accustomed to their status as second-class citizens. Voting had become a distant star. They knew about it. But it was an abstraction in their gritty, sub-sistence lives. To them gaining the vote wasn't something to seriously think about, let alone fight for. They didn't see how it would make their lives better.

Moses had to change that attitude. He and Moore came up with a plan to make the good that could come from voting real for Mississippi's black residents. With a state map pinned to the wall, they settled on two congressional districts in western Mississippi. The strategy called for one hundred SNCC volunteers to hold voter education classes, with the ultimate goal of teaching two hundred thousand blacks about voter registration. Moses reported back to the Atlanta office, telling them of a major voter registration drive that he and Moore were planning for the following summer.

When Moses returned to Mississippi the next summer—he had gone back to New York to finish the last year of his teaching contract—he again teamed up with Moore. The lack of interest in voter registration from SNCC leaders in Atlanta was still a problem, but it did not discourage them. At first, however, they found the work slow going, and the lack of progress made it hard to justify investing more time in it. Then everything changed.

Moses received an unexpected letter from a black man he did not know, a barber and retired rail worker named C. C. Bryant. He was the NAACP chair in Pike County, several hundred miles south, on the Louisiana border.

Bryant had read of SNCC's plans to work on voting rights in the magazine *Jet*, specifically an article by Ed King, a white chaplain at Tougaloo College, a black school just outside Jackson. King's writing called for black Southerners to step up to the power of their right to vote. Bryant recommended that Moses and Moore bring their drive to Pike County—specifically the town of McComb, where he lived—and register black voters.

It's hard to overstate the rag-tag nature of the 1961 McComb voter registration drive. As Moses later explained, "I didn't go [to SNCC] and say, 'Here's my plan....Can I get your permission? I hooked up with Amzie [and told SNCC]. I want to...work on that."

This time, Moses moved into Bryant's home. There he was joined by local NAACP leaders Webb Owens and Jerry Gibson, and a handful of black high school students fascinated by this highly-educated visitor from the fabled Harlem, New York. In early August Moses and the students began going door-to-door, telling residents about the registration drive.

Moses's grassroots approach earned him the trust of the sharecroppers whose houses he and the students entered. These weren't foreigners coming to town to start trouble. They were teens from the neighborhood. They knew their parents. Moses and the students purposely dressed in workmen's overalls as they knocked on doors, went inside, and asked people if they'd like help registering to vote. They talked about voter education classes being held at a black Freemasons temple above a supermarket the way they'd talk about a family gathering.

Classes began on August 7. The next day, Moses took four people to register in the town of Magnolia, the Pike County seat. Three out of the four blacks were accepted. The next day, Moses brought three more, and two were accepted. By day three, the registrar picked up on what Moses was doing and passed only one of the nine people Moses brought to Magnolia.

But something big was happening. Word spread about the African Americans trying to register to vote in McComb. Black farmers in nearby Amite County and Walthall County reached out to Moses, asking him to bring the voter education project to them.

Things intensified on August 15, when Moses led two black women and one black man to register in the town of Liberty, the Amite County seat. The registrar failed all three, and the white townspeople, so angry that an African American had the audacity to even come to the courthouse, sent a highway patrolman to pull Moses and the others over as they were driving away.

Are you that "nigger that came down from New York to stir up a lot of trouble?" the police demanded of Moses.

He did not flinch, telling the patrol he was the "negro who came down from New York to instruct people in voter registration." After ordering Moses to "get in the car, nigger," the cop took him to the McComb police headquarters and charged him with interfering in police business. He was found guilty and given ninety days in jail with a $50 fine.

Moses's sentence was converted to just a $5 fine when the officers heard Moses making his one permitted phone call to John Doar, assistant attorney general in the Civil Rights Division at the Department of Justice whom SNCC leaders, fearing just such a moment, had told Moses to call if the Mississippi police grabbed him.

The call to Doar may also have saved Moses from getting lynched. It was later rumored that local Klansmen, working with the police, planned to take Moses from the jail and kill him. But after the call to Washington they called it off, not wanting to attract federal attention.

Then Moses defied the rules of logic and safety. He refused to pay the $5 fine that would have allowed him to go free. Moses believed the whole affair to be unjust. He announced he would rather stay in police custody than pay the fine. He insisted on going to a jail in Magnolia. It was only after an NAACP lawyer came to the prison and paid his $5 fine that Moses agreed to leave jail.

Once he was out Moses went right back to work, setting up voter education classes at a distant dairy farm. But two weeks later, Moses drove back into town with two African Americans, a farmer named Curtis Dawson and a minister, Alfred "Preacher" Knox. He planned to register both men.

As the trio made its way to the courthouse, they were accosted by three white men demanding to know where they were headed. Moses responded, "To the courthouse." Assuming that they were going to register to vote, the leader of the white group struck Moses with the butt of his knife.

He "swung and swung again," recalled Moses, "hitting me in the head as I tried to shield myself by stooping with my head between my knees."

An all-out brawl began, with Preacher Knox launching his own attack on the knife-wielding white man and the other two whites joining in the fight.

These weren't random townspeople who attacked Moses. The leader, Billy Jack Caston, was the son-in-law of E. H. Hurst, the local state representative and the cousin of the county sheriff. Caston was known to local black people to be a violent man.

Caston and his friends beat Moses into a "semiconscious heap," as Moses later described his condition. His white shirt was covered with blood, and he'd later need eight stitches for three wounds he had taken to the face.

But Moses was so determined after the fracas that he did not stop, despite the sight of his own blood. "We've got to go on to the registrar," he told Knox and Dawson.

Continuing to the courthouse, Moses saw a highway patrolman and told him what had happened. He even pointed out Caston and his buddies, who were still standing by, cursing them. The officer did nothing, and Moses continued.

They reached their destination. When they got to the courthouse, the registrar was so disturbed by the sight of Moses—his bloodied shirt, his lacerated face and head, and maybe the sight of his black skin—that the registrar's office simply shut down for the rest of the day. Tired and angry, the three men left Liberty.

Yet even then, Moses persisted. After getting his face stitched up, he decided to press charges against Caston, making him the first African American in Amite County ever to press charges against a white.

White Mississippi segregationists tried to scare him off by bringing more than a hundred men with guns to the trial. Moses did not fold even when Caston told the judge that Moses had started the fight. According to Caston, Moses had "brushed his shoulder and spun around into a boxing stance on the sidewalk." Moses took the stand and told his story.

The all-white jury evidently believed Caston's blatant lie more than the evidence of Moses's still bruised face. Caston was acquitted. Waiting outside the courthouse while the verdict was announced,

Moses heard guns being fired off in glee from the white audience members.

And again, Moses persisted.

On September 5, less than a week after getting beaten by Caston, Moses and SNCC activist Travis Britt took four more African Americans to the very same courthouse. Again, Moses was confronted by whites, this time telling him that he "should be ashamed coming down here from New York stirring up trouble, causing poor innocent people to lose their jobs and homes."

One of the white men started beating on Britt, choking and hitting him. Moses and Britt, who knew that the Klan would probably try to kill them if they retaliated, did not fight back. Moses made a futile attempt to alert the sheriff to what was happening.

Just two days later, on September 7, a Nashville activist named John Hardy, who had come to help Moses with registration efforts in Walthall County, brought two people to register at the courthouse in Tylertown, the county seat, and got smashed in his face by the pistol-wielding registrar.

That was just the start of the violent white reaction to black voter registration in the summer of 1961. The violence peaked with the murder of Herbert Lee on September 25.

Lee, a successful middle-aged black dairy farmer, lived next door to an African American named E. W. Steptoe. Moses conducted his voter education classes in Amite County at Steptoe's house. Lee got involved with the classes because he and Steptoe were longtime friends. And they even had a white ally: Billy Jack Caston's father-in-law, Mississippi state representative E. H. Hurst.

But Hurst and Lee's relationship had frayed. He found out that Lee, who was illiterate, had started attending Moses's voter education classes. On the night of September 25, 1961, Hurst followed Lee into the parking lot of a cotton gin, screaming that Lee owed him $500.

At this point, according to Hurst, Lee took out a tire iron from his car, and Hurst got out his pistol to defend himself. The pistol accidentally went off, Hurst said, killing Lee in an act of self-defense. At least this is what the coroner's jury reasoned.

The story did not add up to Moses, who spent the next few nights driving through the county interviewing black residents about the murder. Moses was scared out of his mind, knowing that he too could be killed. "You were afraid of every headlight that came up," Moses explained later.

Moses learned that Hurst was a liar. A black logger who had witnessed the murder confided to Moses that he had been pressured to corroborate Hurst's story. "At the coroner's jury," Louis Allen told Moses, "they asked me about the piece of iron. I said I hadn't seen no iron. 'Is this the piece of iron?' I said, 'Yes.'"

Allen told Moses that he wanted to come clean at an upcoming grand jury reviewing the results of the coroner's jury. He said he would tell the truth if he could be promised protection. Moses asked John Doar at the Department of Justice if they'd be able to guard Allen if anyone tried to attack him after he came clean. Doar said they could not. Fearing for Allen's life, Moses told him that it would be too dangerous to tell the truth.

Word had gotten around that Allen had told the FBI what really happened, and for the next two and a half years he endured perpetual abuse from local law enforcement. Fed up, by January 1964 he was planning on moving to Milwaukee. Instead, he was shot in the head three times and died in his driveway.

To date, no one has been prosecuted for the killing of Louis Allen.

The deaths of Lee and then Allen haunted Bob Moses for the rest of his life. At Lee's funeral, his widow approached Moses and screamed at him, "You killed my husband! You killed my husband!" Years later, in his 2001 autobiography, *Radical Equations*, Moses described feeling the same way: "If we hadn't gone into Amite to organize, Herbert Lee wouldn't have been killed. I was sure of that."

The murder of Lee ended the summer 1961 voter drive—"stopped it cold," Moses later wrote. But the following summer he was back in

Mississippi, this time moving back to the Mississippi Delta, the area where he had initially met Amzie Moore two summers earlier.

By now SNCC's leaders had a newly positive attitude about voter registration and even gotten money for it. The funds came from the Voter Education Project (VEP), a philanthropic organization endorsed by the Kennedy administration. The president's top aides had an interest in common with SNCC: they wanted fewer front-page stories about protests. Their goal was to lower political pressure on the president from both sides of the fight. In addition to VEP, Moses also had more helping hands from the NAACP and CORE. Both groups had recently joined with SNCC to form the Council of Federated Organizations (COFO) in order to put VEP money to the best use in Mississippi.

Moses continued with the grassroots strategies he had implemented the summer before. New SNCC volunteers, many students from Mississippi historically black colleges like Tougaloo, Rust College, and Jackson State College, moved into Delta cities and towns like Holly Springs, Ruleville, and Clarksdale. Moses was the leader. He floated from one town to the next, advising the young people who had come to help with voter registration.

Per Moses's instructions, the volunteers didn't barge in and tell the local blacks to go register. First, they got to know them. Often the SNCC workers helped the black sharecroppers with chores and farm work. This helped earned the locals' trust as well, making them feel comfortable enough to come to the classes.

Frank Smith, a Morehouse student and SNCC activist, employed the strategy in Holly Springs by "just loafing around" looking for "the most trusted and respected leaders." A black priest from town let him use his Catholic church for meetings with interested community members. In July, they canvassed the town and got 150 African Americans to take the registration test.

Mississippi whites punished local blacks for registering. The new voters had their taxes raised and allotted cotton acreage reduced.

That summer, Sam Block, a twenty-three-year-old Air Force veteran who was a family friend of Amzie Moore, volunteered to lead registration efforts in Greenwood, Mississippi, just eight miles south of Money, Mississippi, where Emmett Till had been killed less than a decade earlier for allegedly whistling at a white woman.

When Block got to Greenwood and black "people found out what I was there for, they said it was best for no one to have anything to do with me," Block recalled. Not even the local black ministers who thought a voter registration drive was a good idea.

When Block was able to rustle up eight people to go with him to the courthouse, the town sheriff confronted him: "Nigger, where you from?"

"Well, I'm a native Mississippian," responded Block, knowing that the sheriff was trying to frame him as an outside agitator.

"Yeh, yeh, I know that, but where you from?" demanded the sheriff, frustrated with Block's cheeky response.

"Well, around, some counties," Block responded.

"Well, I know that," went the sheriff. "I know you ain't from here, cause I know every nigger and his mammy."

When Block suggested that the sheriff might know "the niggers," but wondered whether he knew "any colored people," the sheriff spat in his face and told him to get out of town.

At around midnight on August 16, Block called Moses from his office in Greenwood in a panic, saying that a group of whites armed with guns and chains had gathered outside the building.

It took Moses and colleague Willie Peacock some time to arrive in Greenwood, which was about an hour away from where they were stationed in Cleveland, Mississippi. When they did get to the office at around 3 or 4 in the morning, they saw that the door had been kicked in. They later learned that a frightened Block, joined by activists Lawrence Guyot and Lu Vaughn Brown, had climbed out of the window, jumped to a neighbor's roof, and climbed down their TV antenna.

Despite the recent violence there, Moses, on the tail end of an all-nighter, decided to take a nap. Peacock later told other SNCC workers about Moses's strange decision to fall asleep in a room just torn apart by bloodthirsty Klansmen. The nap became a legend.

But of course it did not stop the turmoil. In one case Moses, Amzie Moore, and several other SNCC activists were driving back to Ruleville from the courthouse in Indianola with seventeen people who wanted to register to vote.

The officials at the Indianola courthouse had refused to register any of the black people. And they sent a highway patrolman to stop Moses's bus and ask questions. The officer fined the bus driver for the ridiculous crime of having too much yellow on the bus—meaning that they were impersonating a school bus. And in the following weeks the local white leaders printed the names of the people on the bus in local media outlets.

The Williams Chapel Missionary Baptist Church, where SNCC had recruited voters in Ruleville, had its water shut off and tax-exempt status revoked.

Meanwhile, Fannie Lou Hamer, one of the sharecroppers trying to register, was evicted from the land she worked for a white farmer. The farmer said he was under pressure from local Klansmen to oust her. "They gon' worry me tonight," the plantation owner told Hamer. "They gon' worry the hell out of me, and I'm gon' worry the hell out of you."

One day, a threatening white man asked Moses and Moore as they were walking down the street whether they were "the folks getting the people to register" because "I've got a shotgun waiting for you. Double-barrel."

Several black townspeople—a sanitation worker named Lenard Davis, a driver named Fred Hicks, and the Surney family, who owned a dry cleaner—were fired or had their business shut down after a family member had tried to vote.

And on September 10, whites shot into three different black homes: that of Mary Tucker, who had quartered Hamer a few days earlier; Joe McDonald, who housed SNCC workers; and Hattie

Sisson, who'd attempted to register. Instead of hitting Sisson, the bullets struck her granddaughter, Vivian Hillet, and her friend Marylene Burks. The young ladies were visiting Sisson on their way to Jackson State College. One was hit in the head and neck, and the other in the arms and legs.

Following yet another bloody summer in 1962, Moses knew he needed to work faster and think bigger. He needed to keep mobilizing poor blacks on a local level; grassroots empowerment had always been key for Moses. But grassroots mobilization needed to be met with federal action.

Moses had been encouraged by the words of President Kennedy, who, at a September 13 press conference following the shooting in Ruleville, proclaimed that "the United States Constitution provides for freedom to vote, and this country must permit every man and woman to exercise their franchise. To shoot [guns at people trying to register], as we saw in the case of Mississippi . . . I consider both cowardly as well as outrageous."

"The right to vote is very basic," the president continued, "and if we are going to neglect that right, then all of our talk about freedom is hollow." He promised that "if it requires extra legislation and extra force, we shall do that."

Moses heard the president's words and adopted a newly defiant attitude. He called for the president to back up his stand that people have a right to vote, including black people. Speaking at a SNCC conference that Easter, Moses said federal government action was necessary but doubted the president would follow through: "I don't for one minute think that the country is in a position or is willing to push this down the throats of white people in the Delta, and it will have to be pushed down their throats."

In the fall of 1963 he began planning the 1964 Mississippi Summer Project, which everyone immediately called Freedom Summer. The idea was to have students from around the country come to Mississippi, link up with the activists Moses had been training for the last several years, and force the president, the Justice Department, and the FBI into action to protect black people trying to register to vote. Moses and SNCC spent the winter and spring of 1964 recruiting volunteers for Freedom Summer. Moses spoke to college students, urging them to spend their summer volunteering in Mississippi. Recruitment posts, or Freedom Centers, were set up on elite college campuses.

The famously subdued Moses had developed an edge as he toured colleges recruiting students. When someone made a joke about outhouses in Mississippi during an event at Queens College, where he recruited Andy Goodman, Moses shouted: "Don't laugh! This is for real—like life and death."

Moses encouraged the roughly seven hundred students who did sign up to avoid going in with a savior complex; to not "come to Mississippi to save the Mississippi Negro," he warned. "Only come if you understand, really understand, that his freedom and yours are one."

The training for Freedom Summer began in mid-June, and it was at one of the early classes that Moses, Rita Schwerner, and several hundred volunteers learned that James Chaney, Andy Goodman, and Mickey Schwerner had tragically disappeared.

Yet the volunteers had little time to grieve the loss of these three friends. The morning after Moses's final speech, several hundred students got on buses and headed down to Mississippi. Over the following ten weeks the students and SNCC workers spread throughout the state to launch their voter registration drive for black Mississippians. This was on a scale never seen by the state's white dominated politics and culture.

"On a normal day we roll out of bed early in the morning," wrote a volunteer named Robert Feinglass to his father in Illinois: "We study the map of the county, decide where we will work for the day.... We drive from farmhouse to farmhouse. I have averaged almost 200 miles a day in the car."

The black families they canvassed were understandably suspicious of volunteers' motives. "There are always children out front," Feinglass continued. "They look up and see white men in the car" with "those terrified eyes," having been "well-taught in the arts of avoiding whites."

Their parents were suspicious too, knowing that being associated with these outside troublemakers could cause them to lose their home and livelihood.

This was understandable. Mississippi whites had done everything they could to make the local black residents stop joining these "outside agitators." In a June 1964 article, a local paper, the *Meridian Star*, referred to Dr. King as "the unspeakable Martin Luther King." That July, the *Jackson Daily News* labeled the nonviolent Baptist minister an "extremist agitator."

Ben Bagdikian, a journalist who traveled with SNCC, later recalled that he was "urged to listen only to the 'real' leaders, who were saying that 'their' Negroes were happy with things as they were," rather than "giving voice" to leaders like Dr. King and the famous NAACP lawyer Thurgood Marshall.

A June 1964 article printed in the *Greenwood Commonwealth* predicted that "the long heralded summer of racial agitation" would be met with "the indifference, and probably in some instances the hostility, of the people they have come to 'free.'"

Even when local blacks agreed to register, volunteers had to coach them to make the trip to the courthouse. "At about 9:30 two of us COFO workers drive to the house" and ask how the potential voter felt, one volunteer recalled. "Usually he says 'fine,' but then offers some small excuse for not going [to the courthouse] ... [like] meeting some unexpected guests." The volunteer responded: "Well how long will it take to get ready? We can pick someone else up and be back for you in ten minutes.... All their excuses usually disappear.... I wait at the house and we all drive to the courthouse together."

As part of Freedom Summer, forty-seven Freedom Schools were established across Mississippi, attended by 2,500 people. Local blacks of all ages learned practical math and writing skills that could help them fill out job applications, but they also had political and philosophical discussions. And sixteen community centers, established

across the state, offered day care programs for children and job training and health consultations for adults.

The immediate, quantifiable results of Freedom Summer were anti-
climactic. Fairly few black Mississippians became registered voters that
summer. Only 1,600 of the 17,000 who attempted to register that
summer were accepted.

Yet the full impact of Freedom Summer was felt across the nation when Moses created the Mississippi Freedom Democratic Party
(MFDP), another leg of the summer project. The new political party
led by blacks and whites was an alternative to all-white control of the
state's Democratic Party. Volunteers would help Mississippi blacks
"freedom register" for their own party, elect delegates, and then demand at the national party's convention that the integrated political
party be seated to replace the segregationists from Mississippi who
arrived at the 1964 Democratic National Convention in Atlantic
City.

It was easier to convince someone to freedom register than go to
the courthouse, take a citizenship test, and risk getting arrested, pistol-
whipped, and lynched. All that was required was for people to fill out
a registration form. By mid-August, sixty-three thousand people registered as members of the Mississippi Freedom Democratic Party. More
than eight hundred delegates attended the new party's state convention
in Jackson. There, forty-four delegates were chosen to attend the DNC.

Independent of whether the DNC allowed the new, interracial
Democrats from Mississippi to attend—and Bob Moses doubted
that they would—they'd be able to tell their story to all the media in
Atlantic City, exposing the injustice of voter suppression in Mississippi to a national audience.

The twenty-hour bus ride from Mississippi to New Jersey was an
emotional affair. These were rural blacks. Most had never been north
of Atlanta. They were hurt when, along the way, they heard that President Lyndon Johnson did not want them at the convention. He
worried that the MFDP would alienate the Southern Democrats he
needed to win election.

On August 22, 1964, Fannie Lou Hamer, the poor Mississippi sharecropper, was slated to speak at a hearing before the DNC Credentials Committee. She planned to make the claim that Mississippi's seats at the DNC belonged to the new party. The drama attracted the attention of national TV news programs.

In a last-ditch effort to sabotage the MFDP, President Johnson decided to hold a press conference just as Hamer was speaking. He knew how powerful her story was and didn't want it to be aired on TV.

In the end, the Credentials Committee ruled against Hamer and the MFDP. They were offered two at-large seats to the DNC convention. But MFDP delegates felt that these were token seats only meant to shut them up. They unanimously rejected the deal, leaving Atlantic City without attending the convention. SNCC leaders were disillusioned with the Democrats. They were also frustrated with established black leaders, especially Congressman Adam Clayton Powell, who thought they were being ridiculous for not taking the offer of the two seats.

Smeared as a radical fringe group, SNCC faded into obscurity. As did Moses, who fled to Montreal in 1966 to dodge the draft; Moses was fervently antiwar. In 1969 he moved to Tanzania, where he stayed until 1975 and taught math at a secondary school.

Yet Bob Moses, SNCC, and the Mississippi Freedom Democratic Party evidently struck a chord in the national conscience.

Ironically, President Johnson's attempt to drown out Fannie Lou Hamer's testimony drew more attention to her speech. Over the next few days, major news outlets played sound bites from Hamer's testimony: Hamer narrating her attempt to register to vote in Indianola, describing how the planter she worked for forced her to leave her home, and telling how local townsmen had shot at a friend's house because they believed she was living there.

Speaking in her backcountry Mississippi accent, Hamer asked the crowd, "Is this America, the land of the free and the home of the brave, where we have to sleep with our telephones off the hooks because our lives be threatened daily, because we want to live as decent human beings, in America?"

"She had Mississippi in her bones," Moses explained years later. "Martin Luther King or the SNCC field secretaries: they couldn't do what Fannie Lou Hamer did. They couldn't be a sharecropper and express what it meant, and that's what Fannie Lou Hamer did."

On August 25, three days after his attempt to silence Hamer, President Johnson told Hubert Humphrey and Walter Reuther, "We're hearing them.... We passed a law back there in '57 and it said it was the first time in eighty-five years that everyone was going to have a chance to vote.

President Johnson made these remarks only after the crisis of seating the MFDP at the convention had been averted. But he was sincere, and did work to enhance the 1964 Civil Rights Act's protections for voting rights by backing the 1965 Voting Rights Act. After he won election in November 1964, he told his new attorney general, Nicholas Katzenbach, to "write me the goddamnedest, toughest voting rights act you can devise."

The Voting Rights Act outlawed the use of tests that have the "purpose" or "effect" of denying someone the right to vote "on account of race or color." It required that the federal government approve any change in voter laws in "state[s] or political subdivision[s]" with histories of voter suppression. And it authorized the federal government to appoint "federal examiners" to register voters and observe practices in states and/or political subdivisions with cases of voter suppression.

The Voting Rights Act brought about urgent and dramatic change in the American South.

In 1964, just 6.7 percent of Mississippi's black population, or 28,500 people, were registered to vote. Three months after the law was signed, 57,000 people were registered. By September 1967, 59.8 percent of Mississippi's black population had signed up to vote.

Change was not limited to Mississippi. Between March 1965 and September 1967, the share of eligible African Americans registered to vote in Alabama rose from 19.3 to 51.6 percent. In Georgia it rose from 27.4 to 52.6 percent, in Louisiana from 31.6 to 58.9 percent, in South Carolina from 37.3 to 51.2 percent, and in Virginia from 38.3 to 55.6 percent.

The Voting Rights Act was directly responsible for many of these changes. For instance, nearly one third of the 181,233 African Americans in Mississippi who signed up between 1964 and 1967 were registered by federal examiners. But "the remarkable effect of the act is that it has a preventative effect," the SCLC leader and former aide to Dr. King, Andrew Young, later noted. There was a sudden change in attitude among county political officials. For the first time "local registrars began to register black voters so that federal examiners would be kept out."

With more votes came more representation.

In 1967, Robert G. Clark Jr. became the first African American since Reconstruction to serve in the Mississippi state legislature. The grandson of a slave, Clark was a well-known community member, athletic director at a junior college, and former public schoolteacher fired for his support for integration following *Brown v. Board of Education.* By 1987, there were twenty African Americans serving in the Mississippi House of Representatives. In 1969, Charles Evers—brother of the slain Medgar Evers—became the first African American since Reconstruction elected mayor of an integrated town in Mississippi.

In Alabama, the number of African Americans in the state House of Representatives rose from 0 to 19 between 1967 and 1987. Also in Alabama, between 1969 and 1987 the number of African Americans elected to serve on school boards, municipal, and state governments rose from 70 to 448.

And in November 1972, Andrew Young and a lawyer named Barbara Jordan became the first African Americans elected to Congress from the South since Reconstruction, in Georgia and Texas, respectively.

African Americans around the nation understood the importance of the 1972 elections. After the elections, in his syndicated column appearing in black newspapers such as the *Pittsburgh Courier*, Louie

Martin observed: "The growing number of blacks in the Congress is threatening" the hundred-year "unholy alliance between Dixiecrats and Tory Republicans [that] has served to kill or emasculate most efforts to move America forward in a liberal direction." The paper continued: "No longer can the racists play the old anti-black games and escape notice and retaliation."

In his *Chicago Daily Defender* column Benjamin Mays wrote: "The use of the ballot is a sign of freedom."

Over the next several decades, a class of powerful African Americans would earn positions in Congress from states where black people had been systematically disenfranchised just decades earlier: Harold Ford Sr. and Jr. in Tennessee; Mickey Leland, Craig Washington, Eddie Bernice Johnson, Sheila Jackson Lee, Al Green, Marc Veasey, and Will Hurd in Texas; Mike Espy and Bennie Thompson in Mississippi; Sanford Bishop, John Lewis, Cynthia McKinney, Denise Majette, David Scott, and Hank Johnson in Georgia; William Jefferson, Cleo Fields, and Cedric Richmond in Louisiana; Earl Hilliard, Artur Davis, and Terri Sewell in Alabama; Jim Clyburn and Tim Scott in South Carolina; Eva Clayton, Mel Watt, Frank Ballance, G. K. Butterfield, and Alma Adams in North Carolina; Corrine Brown, Alcee Hastings, Carrie Meek and her son Kendrick Meek, Allen West, Frederica Wilson, Val Demings, and Al Lawson in Florida.

This post–civil rights movement class of black members of Congress, coupled with the black "firewall" of support for Democratic candidates, helped pave the way for the coalition that elected Barack Obama, the nation's first black president in 2008.

And yet this story of Southern black enfranchisement sits beside the story of ongoing white resentment toward black gains during the civil rights movement.

Civil rights veterans spoke out angrily when then-Republican presidential candidate Ronald Reagan decided to deliver an August 1980 speech about states' rights at the Neshoba County fair. That is the same county where Chaney, Goodman, and Schwerner were killed sixteen years earlier.

"What 'states rights' would candidate Reagan revive?" asked Andrew Young, in an article published in the *Washington Post*. "Do the powers of state and local governments include the right to end voting rights of black citizens?"

Nearly forty years after Reagan's Neshoba County Fair speech, and over fifty years since Bob Moses led white students to fight for black voting rights in Mississippi, President Trump's phony allegations of voter fraud force us to ask Andrew Young's question yet again. When President Trump promises to "Make America Great Again," we must ask what "Great America" is our president trying to revive?

CHAPTER 2
EDUCATION

ONLY A FEW WEEKS into his presidency, President Trump met in the Oval Office with the presidents of several black colleges. The fallout from the meeting revealed how much black people have to lose with Trump as president when it comes to education.

The White House staged the event to produce pictures of the newly inaugurated president graciously reaching out to black America, even though 90 percent of blacks voted against him.

The black educators agreed to come to the White House despite strong objections from their students and alumni. The critics warned the black college presidents they might end up as nothing more than smiling props as Trump signed an executive order related to black colleges. But Trump promised the educators to "do more for [historically black colleges and universities, or HBCUs] than any other president has done before."

It was a not-so-subtle dig at his African American predecessor, President Obama, for not doing more for the financially struggling black colleges. Trump picked up that some black educators felt distant from President Obama. The nation's first African American president attended elite white schools, Occidental and Columbia for his undergraduate work and Harvard for law school. The week of the meeting, the Trump White House's website republished an article from McClatchy, "President Trump Seeks to Outdo Obama in Backing Black Colleges."

Trump's desire to outshine Obama was a bright lure to the black college presidents. They saw a chance to take advantage of Trump's boast to "do more." They wanted increased federal funding for their schools, and added tax breaks for companies that donate to black colleges or sponsor scholarships.

The black college presidents did not get what they were promised—far from it. After the meeting, Trump signed an executive order with no extra money or tax benefits for black higher education. "Instead of the long awaited executive order containing or signaling [more funding and scholarships], the key change is a symbolic shift of the White House HBCU Initiative from the Department of Education to the White House," Morehouse College president John Wilson Jr. later admitted in a statement of disappointment to his Morehouse students. In other words, Trump gave them a symbolic gesture and no real help.

The Root, a popular website focused on news about black people, headlined their story on the meeting, "We Got Played." The only thing the educators got from Trump, the article concluded, was a "lousy Instagram photo."

"The budget doesn't match" Trump's promise to make HBCUs a priority, concluded Walter Kimbrough, president of Dillard University, an HBCU in New Orleans, when he realized that Trump did not offer any added financial help to the schools in his 2018 proposed budget.

In fact, Trump later proposed a tax plan that took away tax deductions for interest paid on student loans. He also proposed a tax on college endowments that would have hurt some of the financially struggling black colleges.

Another wave of contempt fell on the black college presidents when Trump's secretary of education, Betsy DeVos, put out a statement after their White House meetings. She twisted the history of black colleges to make them appear as grandparents of the Trump-backed movement for school choice. The controversial reform effort supports alternatives to traditional public schools, from charter schools to vouchers that give students options to escape failing schools. Small-government Republicans, opposed to public school bureaucracy and the power of teachers' unions, are big boosters of the school choice movement.

DeVos wrote: "Historically Black Colleges and Universities... started from the fact that there were too many students in America who did not have equal access to education. They saw that the system wasn't working, that there was an absence of opportunity, so they took it upon themselves to provide the solution." She continued, "HBCUs are real pioneers when it comes to school choice. They are living proof that when more options are provided to students, they are provided greater access and greater quality. Their success has shown that more options help students flourish."

What happened to the racist bans on former black slaves attending white schools? That is the primary reason for the creation of black colleges and universities. In a bold stroke, she had whitewashed that ugly history of racism and put black college presidents into position as cheerleaders for the school choice movement. It was a slick political move.

DeVos's statement prompted snickering and head shaking.

"HBCUs were not created because the 4 million newly freed blacks were unhappy with the choices they had," Morehouse president Wilson said in his statement. "They were created because they had no choices at all. That is not just a very important distinction, it is profoundly important."

In one White House meeting the black educators lost control of their most precious story—the triumphant history of how black Americans made their own way when white Americans closed the school doors on black children.

Black colleges and universities were created just years after it was a crime for black people in America to get an education. During the early nineteenth century, when black people were still legally held as slaves, white planters were scared out of their minds by the thought of the large population of slaves starting to rebel. A violent slave revolt in Haiti in the late 1700s, led by Toussaint-Louverture, was successful and became a source of deep pride among slaves. But that revolt also stirred deep fear among slave owners. Subsequent rebellions in the American South prompted outright alarm among plantation owners. One of the most celebrated attempts at a slave insurrection was led by Denmark Vesey, a Charleston, South Carolina, slave who could read.

Preventing slaves from learning how to read and write became a strong tool for every slave master intent on suppressing slave revolts. During the decades before Emancipation laws forbidding the education of slaves were passed in nearly every Southern slaveholding state.

Slave masters regularly cut off the fingers of slaves who learned to read and write. Charley Mitchell, a man born in slavery in 1852, later explained to a federal history project interviewer: "Course, I didn't get no schooling. The white folks said niggers don't need no learning. Some niggers learnt to write their initials on the barn door with charcoal, then they try to find out who done that, the white folks, I mean, and say they cut his fingers off if they just find out who done it."

On some plantations, merely holding a book could cause you to get whipped or sold. "Lawd, you better not be caught with a book in your hand," Louisa Adams, who was born in slavery in North Carolina, told the history project. "If you did, you were sold." Another former slave, Jack Maddox, confirmed the story: "If a nigger was caught with a book, he got whipped like he was a thief."

The violence never stopped the slaves' desire to read.

"The ability to read exists on probably every plantation in the state, and it is utterly impossible for even the masters to prevent this," claimed an 1835 petition signed by a group of 123 whites seeking the repeal of a South Carolina law preventing South Carolinians from teaching slaves to read religious scripture.

Frederick Douglass, the celebrated speaker and newspaper editor, learned to write by copying down various letters written on the pieces of timber in the shipyard where he labored as a young slave. In order to learn additional letters, he would then brag to "any boy who I knew could write" that he too could write. When they told him to prove it, he wrote down the letters he knew. He challenged them to write down more letters than he had. Douglass would then study the letters they wrote, learning additional letters of the alphabet each time.

For Douglass and countless other slaves, learning to read and write disproved the idea that they lacked intelligence. It was a personal, defiant rejection of theories of black racial inferiority. The power of black literacy made the black slave autobiography—taking the risk of writing down one's life—into a celebrated genre in the black literary tradition. The best known example is *The Narrative of the Life of Frederick Douglass, an American Slave,* which was key to turning white public opinion against slavery and made Douglass one of the leading black abolitionists of the late 1800s.

The desperation for educational opportunity among black Americans continued during the Reconstruction Era following the Civil War. The federal government tried to help. Three thousand schools staffed mostly by white female teachers from the North were set up across the former Confederacy to educate former slave children. The Freedmen's Bureau, a federal government agency created to help the former slaves, organized these schools, which had more than 150,000 students just four years after the end of the war. In 1890, the Second Morrill Act required the former slave states in the South to either allow black students into the all-white colleges or give out land grants to create black colleges. This was the real background that led to the creation of most HBCUs. It was not about school choice.

But even as black people crowded the schools, the white view of spending money to educate black people remained negative. In 1899, long after the Civil War, future Mississippi governor James K. Vardaman said that education for black people "only spoils a good field hand and makes a shyster lawyer or a fourth-rate teacher. It is money thrown away."

That attitude led the all-white state governments in the South, many controlled by former Confederate segregationists, to limit funding for black schools. Teachers in black schools were paid less and had fewer credentials. Schools were overcrowded. Typically, the black schools lacked paper, pencils, chalk, textbooks, and chairs. The schools themselves were often cheap and makeshift, created from broken-down churches and abandoned shacks. In the 1930s in Mound Bayou, Mississippi, black parents had to buy the school-teacher's groceries to allow the local school to stay open for more than four months per year. In 1950, the state of Mississippi spent more than three times as much money on each white student as it did on each black student.

As a crippling result, black Americans remained trapped between no schools and poorly funded schools. Whites stigmatized them as stupid and lazy, but the only schools available to black people offered low-level educational training, far behind the schools for white Americans. In 1950, before *Brown v. Board of Education* and the civil rights movement, black men over twenty-five years old had completed a median of just 6.4 years of formal schooling, with white men having completed a median of 9.3 years. Black women completed a median of 7.2 years of school, with white women completing a median of 10 years.

By 1950, just 7.5 percent of men of color (blacks and other non-whites) had finished high school, and 2.9 percent had finished some college. Women of color (black women and other nonwhites) did somewhat better, but not by much. In 1950, only 9.2 percent had four years of high school, and 3.2 percent had begun college.

The big advance in black education came in 1954. The Supreme Court ruled in *Brown v. Board of Education* that separate and equal education was unconstitutional and damaging to black citizens. "Segregation of white and colored children in public schools has a detrimental effect upon the colored children," read the majority opinion. "The impact is greater when it has the sanction of the law, for the policy of separating the races is usually interpreted as denoting the inferiority of the negro group. A sense of inferiority affects the motivation of a child to learn." The Supreme Court's ruling stirred massive resistance among white Southern politicians. But it gave birth to optimism among civil rights leaders. The year after Brown saw a surge in protest, including the start of the Montgomery Bus Boycott, which brought Rosa Parks and Dr. Martin Luther King Jr. to national attention. The movement for racial equality in employment, in housing, and in public accommodations from hotels to lunch counters found new energy with the court's breakthrough ruling to end legal school segregation. Rising expectations for rapid change brought more black and white people into the protest movement.

In the decades following the Brown decision, the centerpiece of all civil rights efforts remained the fight to improve education for black people. In 1980, for the first time in US history, the average black man and woman finished high school. And by 1979, less than 2 percent of black people were illiterate. That was a big jump from 1910, when 30 percent of people of color could not read or write.

Additionally, more and more blacks and other nonwhites were going off to college. By 1970, 6.8 percent of men of color had completed four or more years of college. By 1980, it was up to 11.9 percent. And by 1991, 17.8 percent, nearly one-fifth of all men of color, had finished four years of college. Black women also saw great improvements in their graduation rates. In 2014, black people made up 14 percent of all college students in the United States— roughly on par with the black share of the total United States population.

The current state of black education is still not what it should be. But the progress made could easily be undone by a hostile president like Donald Trump. And even with meager progress, there is still a lot to lose.

The risk is large because, sad to say, the improvements in black education have been uneven. As a group, black students, especially poor black children, still lag behind their white peers in reading and math skills. According to a 2016 report by Child Trends based on 2015 data from the National Assessment of Educational Progress, only 18 percent of African Americans are deemed "proficient" in reading by fourth grade, whereas 46 percent of white fourth graders are proficient in reading. Early reading and math skills are good indicators of who is likely to graduate or drop out, go off to college or remain in the cycle of poverty that plagues too many black communities.

And for all the progress made, most black Southern children still go to schools that are racially segregated. In 2011, for example, nearly half of black Mississippians still attend schools in which 90 to 100 percent of students are of color.

Things are just as bad and often worse in supposedly more progressive Northern cities. In New York, segregated neighborhoods and vast income inequality allow white parents to send their children to parochial or private schools, leaving African American and Latino students in public schools with high poverty rates and troubling drop-out rates while struggling to match the test scores of white students. In 2011, 64.6 percent of New York black students attended schools where nine out of ten students are also people of color. And things have gotten worse over time. According to a UCLA study, the share of black students attending predominately nonwhite schools in Northeastern states rose from 42.7 percent in 1968 to 51.4 percent in 2014.

Troubles in black family life have added to the problem. As of 2016, according to the Annie E. Casey Foundation, 66 percent of black children live in single-parent homes, compared to 24 percent of white kids. This means fewer black parents available to read to their kids, help them with homework, drive them to afterschool activities, and offer financial support for college.

EDUCATION

From President Jimmy Carter, who created the US Department of Education, to President Bush's No Child Left Behind program, there has been a consistent effort over the last half century to remedy the damage done to black people by segregated schools, segregated neighborhoods, and the corrosive effect of high poverty rates. President Obama picked up the fight by offering added federal dollars to school districts trying new strategies to improve education, with a special emphasis on black people and other people of color.

President Obama also called for corporations and charities to privately help black and Latino students get better education and job training. The plan, called My Brother's Keeper, began by targeting young black and Latino men who needed help graduating from high school, landing a spot in college, and getting a job. Some needed references or just a number for an employer to reach them.

In 2014, under President Obama, the Department of Labor also gave $76 million to YouthBuild, a program that gives job training to young people who have dropped out of school or been in the criminal justice system—disproportionately blacks and Latinos.

This is the next step in the epic, ongoing story of a nation working to deal with the deep injury caused by allowing black people to be held as slaves, robbed of their labor and the chance for a better life through a good education. In its current form this tragic history can be seen in the statistical difference between the odds of a black student and a white student going to college. As of 2016, according to the Bureau of Labor Statistics, 69.7 percent of white recent high school graduates but just 58.2 percent of black recent high school graduates are enrolled in college. In 2015, the average black score on the math portion of the SAT was more than one hundred points lower than the average white score.

For all its power, the struggle to deliver quality education to black America and the problems that poor quality education continues to produce for black people—from high black unemployment to high rates of crime and low rates of marriage—is a story of little consequence to President Trump and Secretary DeVos.

They are much more interested in shrinking the budget for the Education Department so it has less power to interfere with local school boards. DeVos has also made a priority of attacking "political correctness" on college campuses which, she believes, lean politically to the left. She is also busy changing sexual harassment policies for college campuses that she argues do little to protect men who face unfair charges.

Her priorities do not include pressing for black students and other students of color to get better educational opportunities. In their first year in office DeVos and Trump showed more concern for the charge from hard-right provocateurs on the radio that the nation's education system is being taken over by liberal professors, Democratic-leaning teachers' unions, and radicals in the Black Lives Matter movement.

One white grievance frequently aired on conservative programs is the complaint that white students are losing out to black students and other students of color when it comes to college admission because of affirmative action or preference given to nonwhite students.

As a white student at Stanford in the 1990s, Candice Jackson, now Trump's acting head of the Office for Civil Rights at the Department of Education, wrote that affirmative action policies aimed to promote academic achievement among students of color instead "promote racial discrimination" against whites.

Another Trump administration official, Attorney General Jeff Sessions, at a 1997 senate hearing called affirmative action "a cause of irritation" that "makes people unhappy if they lost a contract or a right to go to a school or a privilege to attend a university simply because of their race."

In August 2017 the *New York Times* printed parts of an internal Justice Department memo that indicated Sessions remains more interested in identifying any possible discrimination against white students in college admission than trying to open colleges to blacks. The memo called for "investigations and possible litigations related to intentional race-related discrimination in college and university admissions."

A spokesman for the Department of Justice confirmed the contents of the memo. But his spin was that Sessions was acting on allegations from Asian American students that they faced higher standards for admission to Harvard University than other racial groups because the university did not want a disproportionate number of Asian students despite their qualifications.

But the point still holds. Trump's administration has no appetite to join in the long-standing struggle to improve educational opportunities for blacks. Their attention to the grievances of Asian students came across as political expediency: a convenient substitute for the grievances of white students, who object to colleges giving preference in admission to black students. That charge of a racial double standard requires turning a blind eye to the great obstacles faced by blacks, from lack of good schools to lack of money, to achieve the level of education needed to enter a school like Harvard.

In fact DeVos has either eliminated or recommended eliminating a number of programs intended to improve education for black Americans. In March 2017 she cancelled the Opening Doors, Expanding Opportunities grant program, which outgoing Secretary of Education John King created in 2016 to allow low-income students to transfer to better schools, usually with higher-income students. This grant program was a response to federal studies, which indicated that public schools have grown more racially and economically segregated over the last thirty years. The Obama-era program had a small budget of $12 million and was already approved by Congress.

Critics pointed to twenty-six school districts that had taken steps to apply for the money and described the cancellation as a "slap in the face." Congressman Bobby Scott (D-VA) called it not only "disappointing" but "shortsighted" to cancel such a small, low-cost program. "Just last year, the Government Accountability Office found that our nation's public schools are more segregated by race and class now than they were in 1968."

Richard Kahlenberg, an education researcher at the Century Foundation, told the *Washington Post*: "I'm very concerned that if the Trump Administration is not willing to continue even a small program for school diversity, then it's clearly not much of a priority for them."

In the spring of 2017, Trump's 2018 budget blueprint recommended cutting NASA's education program, which would have meant abolishing the Minority University Research and Education Program. This initiative is meant to get more college students of color involved in math and science and prepare them for the STEM-related fields crucial to today's economy.

One key component of former president Obama's agenda was a program called Rethink School Discipline, which called for school officials to cut down on using police to arrest students for bad behavior, as well as curtailing the disproportionately high rate of suspensions and expulsions for black students. In January 2014, former attorney general Eric Holder and Secretary of Education Arne Duncan began efforts to help educators replace zero-tolerance policies with new programs to help teach students how to behave better: "A routine school disciplinary infraction should land a student in a principal's office, not in a police precinct," Holder argued in a statement.

Secretary DeVos had a different view. Instead of compensating for the long history of racial bias against black students in education, she identified black students as a primary source of bad behavior in schools. She hired a politically polarizing lawyer, Hans Bader, to serve in the Education Department's Office of General Counsel. In June 2014 he wrote a column for the conservative website the *Daily Caller* making the case that "higher black suspension rates reflect higher rates of misbehavior among blacks." Bader dismissed poverty, broken families, and racial bias as part of the problem. He gave no thought to helping black students stay in school, graduate, and go on to college or get a job. His is an unsympathetic view of all black students as a group of bad actors.

Unfortunately, this is a view that President Trump found politically appealing. Following the February 2018 shooting in Parkland, Florida—where nineteen-year-old Nikolas Cruz killed seventeen people at Marjory Stoneman Douglas High School—Trump didn't limit his policy recommendations to increasing the police presence at schools and help for young people with mental illness. Those are the usual conservative talking points following a school shooting, intended to avoid any question of gun control. Instead, Trump announced the creation of a commission to "repeal...the Obama administration's 'Rethink School Discipline' policies."

Critics were confused. Why was the president using the tragedy in a mostly white suburban school to eliminate a program meant to help students of color, especially in big cities with mostly minority student populations? Sherrilyn Ifill, president of the NAACP's Legal Defense and Educational Fund, noted that "yet again, the Trump administration, faced with a domestic crisis, has responded by creating a commission to study an unrelated issue in order to advance a discriminatory and partisan goal."

If Trump's commission does end up making it easier to throw black and Latino children out of school, the results will be especially felt in big cities, where overly harsh punishment for students often results in children of color getting thrown into the school-to-prison pipeline. This kind of ignorance is just one example of an answer to the question candidate Trump proposed when he asked black voters, "What the hell do you have to lose?"

The polar opposite of Trump's infamous phrase, "what the hell do you have to lose," has been used in the past by open racists acting in defense of white supremacy by defending school segregation. On August 5, 1962, the *Meridian Star*, a Mississippi newspaper known for its fierce criticism of the civil rights movement, published the following battle cry for white segregationists: "We have too much to lose." Their immediate fear was one black man, James Meredith, an Air Force veteran who wanted to enroll in the University of Mississippi, the state's flagship school.

For a year and a half, Meredith and his allies in the NAACP and the Kennedy administration had been fighting the white Mississippi establishment, led by the segregationist Mississippi governor, Ross Barnett, who refused to allow any black student to attend the school.

An article published in the Jackson *Daily News* on May 18, 1954, the day after the Supreme Court handed down *Brown v. Board of Education*, declared that "white and negro children in the same school will lead to miscegenation. Miscegenation leads to mixed marriages and mixed marriages leads to mongrelization."

That fear gained political standing as white governors and all-white state legislatures in the Southern states engaged in massive resistance against the court order to integrate public schools. During his gubernatorial campaign in 1959, Barnett warned that Mississippians could not "let our country become as mongrelized as Egypt, where a cultural nation allowed itself to integrate with inferior races that brought about its downfall." Barnett was referring to the black Nubians who, white supremacist legend had it, once destroyed the previously white ancient Egyptian civilization.

To governors of the former Confederate states, James Meredith's potential enrollment in Ole Miss was perceived as an all-out assault on the future of the white race—an assault that needed to be immediately defeated.

"Mississippi, it is time to move," said Edwin Walker, a retired major general for the US Army and white supremacist, on a Louisiana talk radio program in September 1962. "We have talked, listened, and been pushed around far too much by the anti-Christ Supreme Court," he said, referring to Associate Supreme Court Justice Hugo Black, who, earlier that month, upheld a circuit court decision compelling the all-white school to admit Meredith. Walker issued a call for his followers to resist racial integration: "Rise... to a stand beside Governor Ross Barnett at Jackson, Mississippi. Now is the time to be heard. Thousands strong from every State in the Union. Rally to the cause of freedom. The Battle Cry of the Republic." As if preparing for a battle, he told listeners to "bring your flag, your tent and your skillet. It's now or never." All that apocalyptic rhetoric had one aim: keeping black students out of Ole Miss.

White supremacists around the nation heeded the retired general's call to arms, vowing to defend the state of Mississippi in the name of "states' rights" to resist federal overreach. Private airplanes, taking off from Jackson, Mississippi, papered Saturday afternoon football games across the South with postcards written by the Mississippi Sovereignty Commission. The cards, addressed to President Kennedy, expressed resentment against "the unnatural warfare being waged against the sovereign state of Mississippi." Governor Barnett's office was inundated with telephone calls from Americans who vowed to "bring our guns and fight," one of Barnett's office assistants later told historian William Doyle. The sheriff of Jackson County, Mississippi, James Ira Grimsley, brought a bus of fifty-two armed men to head to Oxford to stop racial integration at the school, at one point promising to "show them goddamned niggers that they weren't going to take Mississippi."

Americans began speaking of a second civil war between the federal government and the state of Mississippi over Meredith's application to the university. The *Guardian*, a British paper, called the standoff between Mississippi and the Kennedy administration "one of the most serious clashes between Federal power and state authority since the Civil War." The *Christian Science Monitor* warned there would be a "minor new Civil War." The *Hartford Courant* accused Governor Barnett of "doing his best to start another Civil War." Victor Wilson of the *New York Herald Tribune* called it the "gravest constitutional crisis since the Civil War." A few days beforehand, Governor Barnett himself, speaking to a television audience, called it the "greatest crisis since the War Between the States."

What took place on the campus of Ole Miss in the fall of 1962 was in fact a terrifying battle that one World War II veteran described as scarier than Pearl Harbor.

Tellingly, James Meredith saw himself less as a civil rights activist and more as a warrior. In his 2012 memoir, *A Mission from God*, he writes: "I am a warrior. . . . I considered myself an active-duty soldier. I was at war, and everything I did I considered an act of war."

Others saw him as a religious figure: "If I know what a mystic is, then James Meredith is a mystic," David Sansing, an Ole Miss historian, once said of Meredith. "He doesn't think like we do. He doesn't act like we do. He doesn't even hear the same sounds we hear." According to Jack Greenberg, an NAACP lawyer, Meredith "acted like he was an agent of God."

James Howard Meredith—as a child called "J. H.," "J-Baby," but mostly "J-Boy"—knew how to follow a divine mission. He began as a soldier. Prior to enrolling in Ole Miss, he had spent nine years in the US Air Force. The discipline required to serve in the air force likely appealed to Meredith. From a young age, he had been taught that personal responsibility was the only way to combat white supremacy in rural Mississippi.

Meredith's paternal grandfather, Ned, was born a slave in Neshoba County, Mississippi, in 1850—the site of Chaney, Goodman, and Schwerner's murder during Freedom Summer a century later. After the Emancipation Proclamation and the end of the Civil War, many former Mississippi slaves found themselves trapped, with no choice but to become sharecroppers, subject to the same cruelties and grim life they led as slaves and often under the same white plantation owners.

But Ned's son, Moses Arthur (James's father), saved up enough money to buy an eighty-four-acre plot of land in 1925 in nearby Attala County—northwest of Neshoba—close to the city of Kosciusko. Owning a property that size in rural Mississippi was rare for a white family and nearly unheard-of for blacks. But Moses Arthur, nicknamed Cap—short for Captain—was able to grow his own cotton, in addition to working full-time at a cottonseed oil mill. Though he was hardly wealthy, his house always had a fresh coat of paint and window screens. He acted like "a king in his own domain . . . a sovereign state," Meredith wrote in an earlier memoir, *Three Years in Mississippi*, published in 1966. In his 2012 memoir he described his father as a "regal man with the carriage of a king" who did not bow down to white people. At one point a powerful white man also nicknamed Captain demanded to know why Cap didn't call him Captain "like the other niggers." According to Meredith family legend, rather than apologizing Meredith shot back: "Why should I call you by my own name?"

Born on June 25, 1933, James Meredith, like his father, showed no trepidation about speaking frankly to white people. When a white kid in a moving school bus shouted at Meredith as he walked to school, calling him a "nigger," young Meredith threw a rock that hit the kid who had taunted him. When the white child's father confronted Cap that night, Meredith's father responded plainly: "Don't mess with my children." In her book, *James Meredith: Warrior and the America That Created Him*, author Meredith Coleman McGee— James Meredith's niece—writes that "no one yelled out of the bus afterward."

Without money for college, Meredith enlisted in the air force in July 1951, first attending basic training in New York, then taking classes at Western New Mexico College to become a military clerk in the newly integrated military after World War II. He ended up at Nebraska's Offutt Air Base. At age nineteen he was made a sergeant. His rapid rise in rank was explained by a white colleague as the result of Meredith's intense focus on any job he was assigned: it was not a matter of race, but of Meredith's uncompromising drive to prove himself. "Meredith was not the most popular supervisor. Not because he was colored, but because he was interested in getting the job done through hard work; an interest shared by few and viewed as an offense by many." In October 1955, he reenlisted for another four years and was sent to Kokomo Air Force Base in Kokomo, Indiana. During his time serving, Meredith took college courses at the University of Kansas, the Armed Forces Institute, Washburn University in Topeka, and the University of Maryland. He even served as an education officer, advising his black and white colleagues on the best courses to take while serving.

In 1957, he was sent to Tachikawa Air Force Base, near Tokyo, for three years—a trip that had a major effect on his sense of himself as a black man in America. In Japan, Meredith was considered different not because he was black but because he was an American.

"It's the only place in the world where I was near free," he told a journalist in 1963. He explained what he meant in more depth in in his 2012 memoir: "For three years, when I was off duty, I traveled the cities and small towns of Japan, I walked its country lanes, visited its museums, climbed its mountains, breathed its air, ate its food, and savored the company of its people." Away from the United States, Meredith realized that the Jim Crow racial caste system of the South was not the natural way of life but an artificial system set up by Southern whites.

"It was in Japan that I got to fully realize that white supremacy and the inferior position of blacks in America was a man-made construct, not a natural construct." He concluded that "the concept of 'white supremacy' in such a civilization was so nonexistent as to seem completely absurd."

While Meredith was stationed in Japan, the big news in the United States was the attempted integration of a Little Rock, Arkansas, high school. In September 1957, a mob of angry whites led by Arkansas governor Orval Faubus blocked a group of nine black students from enrolling in Central High School. President Dwight D. Eisenhower was forced to deploy a thousand members of the 101st Airborne to surround the school and escort the students—the Little Rock Nine—as they began classes.

Southern politicians immediately began to stir up the remaining bitterness of a civil war that had ended less than 100 years previously. "My fellow citizens, we are now an occupied territory," Governor Faubus said on TV. Senator Olin Johnston (D-SC) promised, "If I were Governor Faubus, I'd proclaim a state of insurrection down there." But where Southern politicians saw Armageddon, James Meredith, watching from Japan, saw opportunity. In a 2000 interview he explained that the events in Little Rock led him to think seriously about how he could do his part to further the cause of civil rights: "Little Rock was a very, very big factor in my whole desire to break the system of white supremacy." He also saw that the federal government was willing to use military force to defeat segregationists and back up the Supreme Court's ruling on school integration.

He said that he "genuinely believed that the only way that we would get our full rights of citizenship was to get a greater military force on our side than Mississippi had, and there was only one force in the world bigger than that, and that was the U.S. armed forces. So, when Eisenhower, who had been the biggest general in our history, committed the troops to support the rights of citizenship, that was what my objective was in the whole Mississippi scheme."

Meredith and his wife, Mary June Wiggins—whom he had met while stationed in Indiana and married in 1956—got immediately involved with politics when they landed back in Mississippi in 1960. Having received half of the credits he needed to graduate from college through courses he had taken while in the air force, Meredith decided to enroll in Jackson State College, an HBCU, in the fall of 1960 to get a degree in history and political science.

They began by attending NAACP meetings, where they met the local chapter's field secretary Medgar Evers, who later became a national martyr when a white racist assassinated him. But listening to Evers led Meredith to begin talking about completing his undergraduate degree at the whites-only University of Mississippi.

Evers and Meredith knew what had happened to African Americans who attempted to attend all-white institutions in the South. When Autherine Lucy Foster was admitted to the University of Alabama in February 1956, a thousand whites rushed on campus, chanting, "Keep 'Bama White," burning crosses, swinging Confederate flags, and chucking eggs and rocks at her. When Clyde Kennard, a black man from Hattiesburg, Mississippi, had applied to the University of Southern Mississippi, in 1959, he was sentenced to seven years in Mississippi State Penitentiary for stealing chicken feed. The conviction was later revealed to be a setup by the white Sovereignty Commission to send him to jail and keep him out of the university.

For a black man, to get into the University of Mississippi was a much bigger deal than integrating any of those schools. Ole Miss was a bastion of the Old South, an institution designed to ensure that white supremacy was jealously defended. The university was founded to protect young Mississippians from the antislavery movement taking hold in Northern schools. In 1837, a newspaper in Vicksburg, Mississippi, printed a story about a Mississippian who was verbally attacked by an abolitionist while dropping his daughter off at school in Philadelphia. The article asked why slave-holding plantation owners would want "an education for their children among a people... who encourage a system of the most flagitious falsehoods." In an 1839 letter to the Mississippi state legislature, Governor Alexander G. McNutt wrote, "Those opposed to us in principle cannot safely be entrusted with the education of our sons and daughters." Albert G. Brown, governor from 1844 to 1848, continued the argument, claiming in his first inaugural address that Mississippians could no longer be "sending our youth abroad, where they sometimes contract habits [and] false prejudices against our home institutions and laws."

In the decades following the Civil War, the University of Mississippi became a leading defender of "Lost Cause" mythology: the notion that the Civil War had been not about slavery but rather about states' rights and the genteel "Southern way of life." It was argued that African Americans were happy as slaves, that things were simpler back then, that slaves loved their masters and that their masters, in turn, loved them.

In 1897, the college yearbook was named Ole Miss, the name that slaves would use when referring to a master's wife. By 1907, a Confederate veteran set up a student essay contest, awarding a prize to the student who could write the best argument justifying the South's secession from the union. The Ole Miss sports teams adopted the nickname The Rebels in 1936, and, soon after, the Confederate flag and the song "Dixie" became unofficial symbols of the school—connecting Ole Miss to the growing mythology of the kind-hearted slave-owning South.

Black students were strictly forbidden from attending Ole Miss, with university chancellor John Newton Waddell promising in 1870 that the university faculty would "instantly resign should the trustees require them to receive negro students." School leaders also made very clear that the school taught only praise for the Confederate cause. In the 1920s, the university's chancellor, Alfred Hume, claimed that "a history professor in this section believes that Robert E. Lee was a traitor and teaches men so. Ought not that chair of history to become instantly vacant?"

Outside the classroom, Ole Miss culture reflected the culture of the Old South. The school celebrated football, Southern belles, and generations of the same family sending their children to campus. Sororities and fraternities produced a loyal network of alumni intent on preserving Ole Miss traditions. Students went to Ole Miss to learn "the evils of work; how to relax at all times under stress and strain; the history of the plantation aristocracy in Mississippi, and which families to marry into," a former student put it in the *Meridian Star* in 1962.

As a Mississippi native, Meredith understood what Ole Miss meant to whites in the state. Nonetheless, he had been inspired by the NAACP and the election of President John F. Kennedy. The Democrat's platform called for "an affirmative new atmosphere in which to deal with racial divisions and inequalities which threaten both the integrity of our democratic faith and the proposition on which our nation was founded—that all men are created equal." Meredith later explained that his "objective was to put pressure on John Kennedy and the Kennedy administration to live up to the civil rights plank in the Democratic platform," by creating a crisis that would force the new president to follow President Eisenhower's example and send the military to defend school integration.

And so, on January 21, 1961, Meredith wrote to the university requesting application materials. He received a stock response from the university: "We are very pleased to know of your interest in becoming a member of our student body. If we can be of further help to you in making your enrollment plans, please let us know."

As instructed, he sent in his application for the spring 1961 semester. But he also added the following lines at the bottom of his application: "I sincerely hope that your attitude toward me as a potential member of your student body...will not change upon learning that I am not a white applicant. I am an American-Mississippi-Negro citizen. I certainly hope that this matter will be handled in a manner that will be complimentary to the University and the state of Mississippi."

Ole Miss had hoped to end things right then and there, telling Meredith in a February 4 message that his application was too late for the spring semester. "We must advise you not to appear for registration," the letter concluded. Meredith knew that was a cop-out: the university was looking for an excuse to reject his application.

Thankfully, he had already gone to Medgar Evers, and the NAACP leader had put him in touch with Thurgood Marshall, the head of the NAACP's Legal Defense Fund. On January 29, Meredith had written Marshall, telling him that he wanted to enroll in Ole Miss but anticipated problems, and requested help from the LDF. After speaking on the phone with Meredith, Marshall sent Constance Baker Motley, a trailblazing black woman lawyer who had risen to become his associate counsel, to Mississippi. Meredith also got advice from William Higgs, a white liberal lawyer, who urged Meredith to reach out to Burke Marshall, the assistant attorney general in Washington, DC. In a February 7, 1961, letter to the Justice Department, Meredith wrote: "What do I want from you? I think that the power and influence of the federal government should be used when necessary to insure compliance with the laws as interpreted by the proper authority." Meredith, working with Motley, filed a lawsuit in late May against the university in US district court in Meridian, Mississippi. He asked the court to grant him immediate admission to

Ole Miss, claiming that the university had rejected him only because he was black.

But, on December 12, 1961, the district court ruled that Meredith was denied admission because of problems with his application and not because of his race. The local press rejoiced and took potshots at Meredith. A June 1961 article in the *Meridian Star* explained: "Some misguided people ask what difference it makes if only a few Negroes go to a white school. The difference is that the first Negro is only the opening wedge for a flood in time to come."

But Motley appealed the case to the Fifth Circuit Court of Appeals. And in June 1962, the appeals court ruled in Meredith's favor. The majority opinion explained that ever since Ole Miss "discovered Meredith was a Negro they engaged in a carefully calculated campaign of delay, harassment, and masterly inactivity." Dissenting judges on the Fifth Circuit Court delayed the court's injunction all summer long with four different stays, forcing Motley to appeal to the Supreme Court.

By now, Meredith's name was known around the country. In late June, the UPI reported: "After 13 months of legal battling, James Meredith, 29, appears on the threshold of becoming the first Negro student to enter the University of Mississippi." The black press gave front page treatment to Meredith's case. A July 7 article in the *Baltimore Afro-American* was headlined, "Mississippi Fighting 'Lost Cause.'" Also that month, Roy Wilkins, the executive director of the NAACP, wrote in the *New York Amsterdam News*: "The State of Mississippi seems to have its back up against the wall." That proved to be exactly right. On September 10, 1962, Associate Supreme Court Justice Hugo Black, who had jurisdiction over the Fifth Circuit Court, ordered the dissenting judges' stays to be vacated. Ole Miss would be required to admit Meredith at once.

After the Supreme Court's ruling, Governor Barnett delivered an impassioned TV and radio address: "The powers not delegated to the United States by the Constitution nor prohibited by it to the States are reserved to the States respectively or to the people. These are not my words. This is the tenth amendment to the Constitution of the United States. Ladies and gentlemen, my friends and fellow Mississippians: I speak to you as your Governor in a solemn hour in the history of our great state and in our nation's history. I speak to you now in the moment of our greatest crisis since the War Between the States."

He vowed to forbid Ole Miss from being integrated under his watch, despite the views expressed in the "unfriendly liberal press"— words that bear an eerie resemblance to President Trump's tirades about "fake news."

At Ole Miss, whose fall semester was about to begin, crosses were burnt in front of the dorm where Meredith would be living if enrolled. An effigy of Meredith was burnt on a streetlight in front of the student union. A sign read, "Hail Barnett. Our Governor will not betray Mississippi." Meanwhile, Meredith was charged with lying about his address on his voter registration form. And the legislature immediately passed a law forbidding anyone charged with moral turpitude from applying to a college or university in the state.

Over the following two weeks, a series of events transformed an already-tense situation into an all-out national crisis.

On the one hand, the Kennedy administration wanted to avoid conflict at all costs. Attorney General Bobby Kennedy began a series of phone conversations with Governor Barnett, who promised that, while the state of Mississippi would continue to fight Meredith's entry through legal means, there'd be no violence.

The Justice Department didn't believe things would remain peaceful. Beginning the week of the seventeenth, US marshals began flying into Memphis, an hour north of Ole Miss. The US Army began scouting the area around Oxford, finding equipment for their troops, figuring out their command structure and communication pathways. If necessary, they'd be used as reinforcements.

On Thursday, September 20, 1962, Meredith, accompanied by US marshals and a Justice Department lawyer, St. John Barrett, entered campus. They were met by roughly a thousand protestors—some students and some not—and Governor Barnett. The crowd chanted "Glory, Glory, Segregation—The South Shall Rise Again," and "Two, four, six, eight, we don't want to integrate." When Meredith walked by, they shouted, "Go home, nigger." When Meredith entered the auditorium, Governor Barnett asked him, "What can I do for you?" to which Meredith replied simply, "I want to register." Barnett refused. Unsuccessful, Meredith retreated from the turbulent campus.

That weekend, the Justice Department filed charges against the registrar, chancellor, dean, and school trustees for failing to carry out court orders. And the Fifth Circuit Court of Appeals in New Orleans made it clear that Meredith would have to be registered. In a dramatic phone call Tuesday morning between Bobby Kennedy and Governor Barnett, the governor threatened that if Meredith attempted to register again, he'd be denied again. Kennedy asked the governor, "Do you consider yourself a part of the Union?" Barnett told Kennedy, "We have been part of the United States, but I don't know whether we are or not.... It looks as if we are being kicked around." True to his promise, later that day two thousand spectators collected in front of the Woolfolk Building, a government office in Jackson where the Ole Miss trustees' office was located. Meredith, accompanied this time by John Doar, the assistant attorney general for civil rights, walked up to the board of trustees office, where Governor Barnett was holding court. Yet again Barnett, standing in the doorway, told the men, "I hereby now and finally deny your admission to the University of Mississippi."

Behind the scenes, however, Barnett was negotiating with federal officials about how Meredith could be enrolled. The question was how he could save face with all the segregationist fury in the state. After all, he'd campaigned for governor as a strict segregationist. Meredith's entrance into Ole Miss would need to be planned so that it looked like Barnett had not caved in, but had absolutely no choice but to let Meredith into school.

According to historian Charles Eagles, "either communication or cooperation had broken down," because the plan failed miserably. The plan was for Meredith to go to campus again in mid-week, protected by a group of federal marshals, and finally register. But Meredith was met by a barricade of highway patrol cars and sheriffs' deputies led by Lieutenant Governor Paul Johnson. Doar, the assistant attorney general, told the lieutenant governor, "We want to register this man." But the lieutenant governor did not go along. He replied, "I do not accept the papers." Johnson then ignited the anger on campus when he told Doar, "We are going to block you.... If there is going to be any violence, it will be on your part and the U.S. marshals."

The lieutenant governor and James J. P. McShane, the chief US marshal, stood eye to eye with fists raised. The federal officials, realizing the danger of forcing the issue, had McShane back away. They retreated from campus as the crowd of white Mississippians roared.

The Kennedy administration returned to negotiating with Barnett, who, according to several accounts, asked that the federal government have its officials pull out guns so they could say they were forced to register Meredith.

A day later Meredith returned to campus. This time a crowd of thousands of students blocked him from registering. Federal officials kept Meredith nearby as they looked for their next opportunity. On Sunday morning, September 30, President Kennedy signed an executive order, "Providing Assistance for the Removal of Unlawful Obstructions of Justice in the State of Mississippi," giving the secretary of defense the power to enforce the court order at Ole Miss, as well as federalizing the Mississippi National Guard. Additionally, army troops were put on alert at Fort Bragg in North Carolina, Fort Dix in New Jersey, and Fort Benning in Georgia.

It was also at this point that retired General Edwin Walker called on white supremacists from around the country to descend on Oxford, Mississippi.

On Sunday, September 30, at 4 in the afternoon, a group of several hundred federal marshals organized their central command post at the Lyceum, the central campus building where Meredith would be registering the following morning. They carried riot clubs, gas masks, helmets bearing the words "U.S. Marshal," and .38 revolvers. It was a weird sight—a militarized university campus—and by 5:30 over four hundred students, faculty, and townspeople were milling around the Lyceum to gawk at it all.

The crowd was rowdy, and trouble began as more and more people spilled onto campus. At first, they taunted the federal marshals. "Go ahead and shoot me, you nigger-loving son of a bitch," said a boy to a marshal. "Go home, Yankees," shouted other protestors. Confederate flags flew from dormitory windows. Some people put "Kennedy Go Home" stickers on the marshals' trucks and chanted "Two, one, four, three. We hate Kennedy." They smashed the marshals' windshields and threw Molotov cocktails.

William D. Trahan, an Ole Miss student at the time, later explained his fellow students' rowdiness like this: "Most of us were unreconstructed rebels.... One hundred years after the War we felt like we were still being treated like a conquered province."

During the mayhem of early evening, federal marshals snuck Meredith onto campus and escorted him to Baxter Hall, where he'd be spending the night.

Local highway patrolmen had been sent to campus to calm things down. But they were just as angry at the federal marshals as the crowd was and had no intention of protecting the marshals. "What are you going to do if one of those marshals starts pushing you around?" one highway patrolman asked his partner. The other promised that: "I'm gonna break his damn jaw if I can hit it hard enough." A federal marshal named Felix M. Aycock later reflected: "When we asked them to hold the crowd back, the patrolmen just stood there and laughed at us." When another marshal told a patrolman to help him out, he was told, "To hell with you, you son-of-a-bitch, I didn't invite you down here." Indeed, the patrolmen helped the mob by shining their flashlights at the marshals, so they would have better targets for their rocks, eggs, and bricks.

The mob attacked reporters too. A cameraman named Gordon Yoder and his wife, both white, cowered inside their station wagon as rioters smashed Yoder's cameras and called Yoder's wife a "nigger loving bitch." Dan McCoy, a photographer from *Newsweek*, was surrounded, punched, and kicked by a group of rioters led by an Ole Miss football player. When McCoy yelled, "For God's sake, get me out of here," to a group of patrolmen watching the whole thing from a sheriff's car, they did nothing.

At this point most of the rioters were not Ole Miss students. Adults from surrounding towns and out of state made up most of the mob. "You goddamn, Jew-looking Yankee son of a bitch. Come night and we're going to kill you," one rioter screamed at a federal marshal.

Marshals began shooting tear gas into the crowd. According to journalist Richard Starnes, "the campus became an indescribable nightmare." Rioters broke into the chemistry building, ransacked the place for dangerous chemicals, and hurled them at the federal marshals. According to one marshal, a World War II vet named Willard McArdle, "I was more frightened at Mississippi than I was at Pearl Harbor..." Others had the same thought: Deputy Marshal James Kemp later said, "I was a gunner's mate in the Navy, and after my ship went down, I was in the Atlantic Ocean for an hour." But the Battle of Oxford "was the worst thing I've ever been in."

Tragedy struck a little before 9 p.m., when a thirty-year-old New York–based reporter for Agence France-Presse was shot in the back, and the bullet reached his heart. Paul Guihard bled to death. To this day, no one has been prosecuted for his murder.

That night the segregationist General Walker, who'd been lying low for the first few hours of the riot, arrived on campus. Standing by a Confederate monument on campus, the general delivered a roaring speech. He praised the rioters, telling them to "stand by your governor." With his blessings, they began building barricades of garbage cans and loose construction material. They broke into the campus fire house, hijacking a fire truck, and driving it wildly while they sprayed the marshals with fire hoses. Gene Same, a deputy marshal, was shot by a sniper with a .22 rifle. The bullet went down his throat and lodged in one of his ribs. Bill Crider, a forty-five-year-old AP reporter was clubbed to the ground and shot in the back. Two Atlanta federal prison guards were shot, one in the stomach and forehand, and another in the head and chest. And a border patrolman named Dan Pursglove was shot in the thigh, later telling William Doyle, author of *An American Insurrection: James Meredith and the Battle of Oxford, Mississippi, 1962,* "You've spent four years in the marine corps, a year in Korea, and ten years in the border patrol, now some fellow Americans are going to be your demise."

Klansmen were arriving on campus by the busload. A popular local radio was playing Confederate war music. A highway patrolman manning the phone lines at headquarters later remembered that: "People were calling in from across the nation wanting to volunteer.... They asked where to report, where to bring their arsenals and weaponry to join the revolt. There were serious people who wanted to join the 'Rise of the South.'"

Tragedy struck for a second time at around 11 p.m., when Ray Gunter became the second casualty of the night. A twenty-three-year-old jukebox repairman, Gunter had been watching the riot with his friend Charlie Berryhill. They had no intention of joining in, and just planned to watch the chaos. But when they decided it was time to get back in their car and leave the premises, Berryhill realized Gunter was slumped over on the ground. In horror, he saw that Gunter had been shot in the forehead. To date, no one has been charged with the murder of Ray Gunter.

Up until this point, the rioters had faced only federal marshals. The Mississippi National Guard, whom President Kennedy had federalized in his executive order earlier that day, had not yet been called in. At around 9:50 that night, the Second Squadron of the 108th cavalry regiment of the Mississippi National Guard, all of seventy-one men, was ordered to take control of the campus.

The National Guardsmen were all white. They were from the surrounding area. They were nearly all segregationists who disapproved of federally enforced integration as much as any other white Mississippian. Yet the Battle of Oxford also gave some Americans a chance to demonstrate tremendous acts of courage and respect for their country. As one member of Troop E, also an Ole Miss student at the time, later reflected: "We were on the side of the students in the university. We thought we were being invaded." Yet as soon as the seven truckloads of men got to campus, they were attacked by rioters, who hurled slabs of cement at their vehicles, just as they'd been attacking the marshals and reporters for hours. The national guardsmen quickly put politics aside and began forcing the rioters off the campus.

At around midnight, they were joined by another 165 national guardsmen from Troop G, Second Squadron of the 108th.

Nineteen army helicopters also landed at the Oxford airport, carrying 177 military policemen, each armed with semiautomatic weapons and chemical gas grenades. When they arrived on campus at 1:35 a.m., they were met by a wall of fire; the rioters had poured gasoline on the ground and then ignited it. And yet the MPs walked through it. "Keep going through the fire! We're gonna go marching through it," a lieutenant yelled out.

Now there were over eight hundred men—federal marshals who'd been there from the beginning, the guardsmen, and the MPs from the 503rd—fighting the rioters.

At one point, a white Alabama-born sergeant from B Company threatened to shoot a group of twenty rioters who were throwing liquor bottles at a fifty-year-old black woman cowering in the street as she tried to make her way to work. As the sun rose, the federal troops had control of campus. As if this was the aftermath of the liberation of Europe, women and children began cheering when the military police swept faculty housing to make sure none of the rioters remained.

Amazingly, James Meredith slept through the entire night in Baxter Hall. At about 8 a.m., Meredith, with McShane, the federal marshal, and Doar, the assistant attorney general, entered the registrar's office to sign up for courses. This time he succeeded.

On his first day of classes, students taunted him, asking him, "Was it worth two lives, nigger?" After the chaos of the previous night, only 30 percent of students attended classes. The tear gas on campus was so thick that Meredith's first math class had to be cancelled. Rocks were thrown at his dorm room window in Baxter Hall. When he entered the on-campus grill, all but one student immediately left the cafeteria. The words "Whites Only" were placed above the water fountain he used. Meredith was accompanied by federal marshals wherever he went: to class, to eat, to sleep.

Almost a year later, on August 19, 1963, he graduated from the University of Mississippi, in front of an audience of 2,500 people with no protest, no violence, neither booing nor cheering. The chancellor of the university, John Davis Williams, politely shook Meredith's hand as the school's first black graduate crossed the stage to receive his diploma.

Half a century later, it seems as if a chorus should have erupted in song. Meredith's heroic struggle to break down racial segregation at the University of Mississippi opened doors for students around the nation and particularly in the South.

The numbers tell the story of what America has reaped from Meredith's sacrifice.

In 2015, 13.4 percent of undergraduates at the University of Mississippi were African American. In fall 2016, just under 11 percent of students at the University of Alabama—meaning over four thousand students—were African American. In 1962, they had no black students. And 15.9 percent of students at the University of South Carolina are African American. They had no black students until 1963.

Today, Ole Miss students can major and minor in African American Studies and take classes on the "History of Jazz," the "Rise and Fall of American Slavery," "Readings in U.S. Black Feminism," and even the "Experiences of Black Mississippians."

Since the 1954 *Brown* decision and Meredith's historic stand in 1962 at the University of Mississippi, black students in public elementary and high schools have also seen major changes.

Across the South, the share of black students attending hyper-segregated schools, where 90 to 100 percent of students are black and Latino, decreased from 77.8 percent in 1968 to 34.2 percent 2011. Black high school drop-out rates also fell dramatically. According to the Pew Research Center, between 1964 and 2015, the share of African American adults ages twenty-five and older who've graduated high school rose from 27 to 88 percent, and the share of black people twenty-five and up who have at least a bachelor's degree rose from 4 to 23 percent.

Celebrating that good news is very different from saying the fight to repair the long history of denying education to black Americans is finished.

Blacks still are behind in college graduation rates. And in 2015, the Brookings Institute reported that black students are only 4 percent of students at top colleges, where a "top college" is defined by how much money former students are making by mid-career.

Unfortunately, these problems reach way back to the skills that students are taught early on. According to Child Trends, as of 2015 black fourth graders still scored an average of twenty-four points lower than white fourth graders on the National Assessment of Educational Progress (NAEP) math assessment, and black eighth graders scored an average of thirty-two points lower than white eighth graders on their NAEP math assessment. In other words, there is still work to be done in order to ensure that every student, of every race, has equal access to a quality education.

Despite the remaining obstacles facing blacks, a growing numbers of white Americans began to feel that it was they, and not African Americans, who were being discriminated against: that their children were being denied spots in America's top colleges because admissions offices were filling quotas with underqualified black students; that, in turn, this country no longer belonged to them. These feelings festered and grew, and were acknowledged, legitimated, and furthered by their friends, their favorite talk radio hosts, their elected politicians, and Supreme Court justices.

These forces created a situation in which, according to a 2017 poll organized by National Public Radio, Harvard University, and the Robert Wood Johnson Foundation, 55 percent of white Americans believe that "there is discrimination against white people in America today." The same survey found that 11 percent of white Americans say that "they have been personally discriminated against because they are white...when applying to or while at college." A poll conducted in 2016 by the Public Religion Research Institute and the Brookings Institute found that "approximately six in ten (57%) white Americans and roughly two-thirds (66%) of white working-class Americans agree that discrimination against whites is as big a problem today as discrimination against blacks." According to a 2016 Pew Research Center survey, 41 percent of white Americans, and 59 percent of white Republicans, believe that there is "too much...attention paid to race and racial issues in the U.S. today." This is the country that elected Donald Trump president.

Carol Anderson, a professor of history at Emory University, said this phenomenon—which she has termed "white rage"—is at least in part the result of an ingenious marketing strategy deployed by Presidents Richard Nixon and Ronald Reagan, as well as countless other white politicians. They tapped into white sentiment that slavery is long in the past and that successful, even wealthy blacks can be seen on television, in sports, even in corporate board rooms and politics.

President Nixon certainly believed that the black freedom struggle had ended. He wrote in his memoirs, "With the passage of the Civil Rights Act of 1964 and the Voting Rights Act of 1965, almost every legislative roadblock to equality of opportunity for education, jobs, and voting had been removed."

Sometimes speaking in a kind of racial code, and other times using openly discriminatory language, many conservative politicians told white Americans that they—the whites—were not the problem anymore. Rather, the problems faced by people of color in America were the result of their inability to take responsibility for their actions. In his memoir, *The Haldeman Diaries: Inside the Nixon White House*, Nixon's chief of staff, R. H. Haldeman admitted, "[Nixon] emphasized that you have to face the fact that the whole problem is really the blacks." A decade later, President Reagan managed to redefine welfare recipients as welfare queens who used government money to buy fancy cars—not poor black men and women struggling to make ends meet. Even though the majority of welfare recipients were white, not African American, President Reagan was able to twist at reality so that the national conversation centered on the idea that most of these people were undeserving minorities ripping off white taxpayers.

White Americans responded well to these strategies, with all but 15 percent of white Americans telling pollsters William Brink and Louis Harris in 1966 that "the pace of civil rights progress was too fast."

Furthermore, many white Americans growing up in the decades after the civil rights movement didn't hear about the gallant battles waged by men like James Meredith. Instead, white politicians hammered black activists like Jesse Jackson and Al Sharpton, charging them with being "race hustlers" who "played the race card." They pointed to Louis Farrakhan, the controversial leader of the Nation of Islam, as living proof that blacks can be racist against whites, too.

In place of support for repairing past discrimination against blacks came calls for a colorblind nation. Gradually, support for race-conscious policies, such as busing students to integrate public schools and affirmative action admissions programs on college campuses, lost public support, and the conservative majority on the Supreme Court began limiting efforts to make up for past racist policies in education.

In *San Antonio Independent School District v. Rodriguez* (1973), a group of parents in a lower-income Texas community, where 95 percent of people were either Hispanic or African American, took their school district to court, alleging that lower property tax revenues had allowed for a system in which their children were forced into significantly worse schools than white students in wealthy Texas neighborhoods. They said the school's financing system was unjust.

The high court ruled against them, explaining that "there is no fundamental right to education in the Constitution." Justice Thurgood Marshall, the man who, as a lawyer, argued *Brown* before the court nearly two decades earlier, saw a dangerous development. He called the court's decision "a retreat... [from a] commitment to equality of educational opportunity." Justice Marshall struck a similarly anxious chord a year later in his dissent in *Milliken v. Bradley* (1974), when the court struck down a busing plan to desegregate Detroit's predominately poor and black schools. He called the majority decision an "emasculation of our constitutional guarantee of equal protection."

The Supreme Court's reversal of black gains continued through the seventies. In the landmark case *Regents of the University of California v. Bakke* (1978), the court ruled that the quota system at the University of California, Davis, which assured sixteen spots for black students in its medical school, was unconstitutional. In an ominous foreshadowing of things to come, in a 2003 Supreme Court case involving a white applicant who alleged that the University of Michigan law school's affirmative action program had cost her a spot at the school, Justice Sandra Day O'Connor wrote, "The Court expects that 25 years from now, the use of racial preferences will no longer be necessary to further the interest approved today."

Affirmative action took a blow yet again in *Schuette v. Coalition to Defend Affirmative Action* (2014), upholding a ban on affirmative action policies in Michigan's public universities. But in 2016 the high court, in a 4–3 vote, agreed to allow schools to consider race "in service to student body diversity," but warned such action is a danger to the Constitution's "promise of equal treatment." Justice Samuel Alito, writing in dissent, called the decision "wrong" and evidence of "affirmative action gone berserk."

The arguments in all these cases steadily shifted the national focus from the work necessary to repair the damage done to black communities by denial of equal education. Now the focus was on the idea that such efforts are unfair to whites. That story has become more and more prominent, as white conservatives have been inundated with story after story telling them that affirmative action policies have created a nation in which *they*, and not African Americans, are the new minorities. A 1986 article in the *Wall Street Journal* entitled "Real-Life Costs of Affirmative Action" by a sociologist at Brooklyn College named William Beer noted, "We now know that it is legal for white males to be subject to racial and sexual discrimination in favor of people who have never personally suffered from it." In 1987, syndicated conservative columnist George Will called affirmative action "an ethnic and racial spoils system." A 1991 article in the *Wall Street Journal* by scholar Frederick Lynch entitled "Tales from an Oppressed Class" begins with the question: "How many white men have been affected by affirmative action[?]" And so it went, with white Americans—particularly middle-class white Americans living in areas where there are few people of color to begin with—being told every which way that, at a time when the black freedom struggle had supposedly ended, they were now facing discrimination against white people.

The appearance of the first black president, a Harvard Law graduate, only fed into the narrative that white men had become the new minorities. In her 2016 book *Strangers in Their Own Land: Anger and Mourning on the American Right*, Berkeley sociologist Arlie Hochschild describes her trips to Lake Charles, Louisiana, to better understand the mindset of the people who lived there, the Tea Party's strongest supporters, a group that felt they'd been uniquely left behind by twenty-first-century America.

Interestingly, what she found in Louisiana wasn't a group of racists. They were well-intentioned white Americans who felt they were losing ground—their inherited status as the dominant group in US society. They also saw that black Americans, formerly at the bottom of the barrel, continued to rise economically and in political power. Many of the whites she met with suspected that Barack and Michelle Obama had been the beneficiaries of affirmative action and government support. "Did Obama get there *fairly?*" these Louisianans pondered. "How did he get into an expensive place like *Columbia University?* How did Michelle Obama get enough money to go to *Princeton?* And then *Harvard* Law School, with a father who was a city water plant employee?...The federal government must have given them money."

Trump exploited these fears. Here's the president speaking with the Associated Press in 2011:

"I heard he was a terrible student, terrible," Trump said of President Obama. "How does a bad student go to Columbia and then to Harvard....Let him show his records."

According to Hochschild, white conservatives feel they are being passed over while people of color receive help in the form of welfare and affirmative action. This is part of the reason why, according to the 2017 NPR/Harvard poll, 55 percent of white Americans feel "there is discrimination against white people in America today." These white conservatives somehow close their eyes to the students of color stuck in failing schools. They have likely never visited the world where just 18 percent of African Americans are considered "proficient" in reading by fourth grade.

President Trump, who was born in Queens, New York, grew up within shouting distance of poor minority neighborhoods. But throughout his life, he purposely shunned association with the poor, blacks, and immigrants. He saw them as a problem.

Indeed, he once argued that blacks have been given too much, telling black TV personality Bryant Gumbel on NBC in 1989 that "a well-educated black has a tremendous advantage over a well-educated white in terms of the job market. And, I think some-times a black may think that they don't really have the advantage or this or that but...if I was starting off today, I would love to be a well-educated black, because I really do believe they have an actual advantage today."

This is not an isolated incident. Trump has repeatedly shown a clear disrespect for the black experience of being deprived of educa-tion and opportunity. In the late 1980s he told a white executive at his white Atlantic City casino that "laziness is a trait in blacks." He also said, "The only kind of people I want counting my money are short guys that wear yarmulkes every day."

President Trump's campaign speeches featured racial dog whistles—phrases that, though they never mention race explicitly, embrace the hot resentment of whites who feel *they* have been given a raw deal because of government policies and PC rhetoric that sup-posedly privilege African Americans, Latinos and women.

At a July 2015 rally in Phoenix he claimed to speak for the "silent majority" of Americans.

At the 2016 GOP convention, Trump promised to speak for the "people who work hard but no longer have a voice."

At a Dimondale, Michigan, rally in August 2016 he foreshadowed "a victory for all of the people whose voices have not been heard for many, many years. They're going to be heard again."

During a September 2016 rally in Iowa, he showered praise on the "hard-working American patriots who love your country," the "mothers and fathers, soldiers and sailors, carpenters and welders."

Over and over, in speech after speech, Trump talked about "the forgotten men and women of our country," as he said during his inaugural address.

As former President Bill Clinton said during a September 2016 rally for presidential candidate Hillary Clinton in Orlando, "if you're a white southerner you know exactly what" Trump's slogan—Make America Great Again—means. It means putting whites "back on the social totem pole and other people down." "Make America Great Again" is meant to indicate a world before all these Black Lives Matter activists were invited to speak on prestigous college campuses, a world before busing, affirmative action, and desegregation—a world before James Meredith.

This is the reason why white supremacists like David Duke, Richard Spencer, and the folks at the *Daily Stormer* backed Trump. It is why Trump refused, time and again, to denounce them. It's why race baiters like internet troll Milo Yiannopoulos—who runs a scholarship fund that is, according to its website, "exclusively available to white men who wish to pursue their post-secondary education on equal footing with their female, queer, and ethnic minority classmates"—so readily endorsed Trump. In Trump's imagined "War on White Men"—a phrase not used by Trump but frequently employed by his supporters on the "alt-right"—black students are guilty of taking advantage of white people. The reality of racial discrimination and the painful history of the people who battled against racism in schools as well as at work, and when facing brutal policemen, is now forgotten.

When asked about the civil rights movement, Meredith rarely speaks about the sit-ins, protests, and civil disobedience that, for many, characterize the era. Instead, he speaks of war, resistance, and revolt. When asked whether he would participate in the fiftieth anniversary of his integration of Ole Miss, Meredith said he would not, telling the Associated Press, "I ain't never heard of the French celebrating Waterloo.... I ain't never heard of the Germans celebrating the invasion of Normandy.... I ain't never heard of the Spanish celebrating the destruction of the Armada." The point was that the civil rights movement, experienced by Meredith, was not at all peaceful or civil. It was civil war.

For Trump, Meredith's war led to the defeat of white tradition and heritage. His racist view was supported when the former confederate states, with the exception of Virginia, voted for Trump. He promised to take them back to a time before Meredith, a time when a good education was a white privilege, and a time before the Supreme Court and James Meredith came along—a time when blacks accepted their inferior segregated schools. For black people, that's a lot to lose.

CHAPTER 3
PUBLIC ACCOMMODATIONS

IT'S NO SECRET THAT Donald Trump's campaign theme, "Make America Great Again," fell flat with black voters.

Given its popularity with Trump's openly racist supporters in the "alt-right" movement of Klansmen and neo-Nazis, the slogan became code for a return to a time after World War II when black people knew their place, women stayed home, and immigrants were whites from Western Europe. Lots of black people have not forgotten that when America was a 90 percent white country, racial segregation was common at water fountains and lunch counters as well as in racially segregated neighborhoods and schools. As a rule, black people knew not to apply for jobs as police officers or fire fighters, or in the all-white trade unions. Particularly in the Southern states, black Americans were also subject to daily denigration in the form of explicit insults.

There was nothing great about being black in that America.

The first step taken to change that awful situation came at the end of World War II with a presidential order to desegregate the military. Then a lightning bolt hit the American racial landscape. The 1954

Supreme Court declared public school segregation by race to be unconstitutional and illegal in *Brown v. Board of Education*. The power of the ruling went beyond words. Nine white men on the nation's highest court declared in plain, straightforward words that keeping black children in broken-down schools and separate from whites "generates a feeling of inferiority as to their status in the community that may affect their hearts and minds in a way very unlikely ever to be undone."

That deep pain was long known to black people. Now for the first time it was acknowledged by powerful white people. The decision stirred hope for a new day. It gave black people reason to think that if they spoke up, they could be heard. There was now a reason to resist racist customs, to believe that if they protested segregated seating on buses—as was done a year later by Rosa Parks and Dr. Martin Luther King Jr. in the Montgomery, Alabama, bus boycott—that the federal courts and the Supreme Court would stand with them, upholding the promise of equal rights.

With *Brown* as the launching pad, the movement took off. There were bus boycotts, protest marches, and lunch counter sit-ins that led to calls for new federal laws to guarantee equal rights to black citizens. But there was little progress made to pass a law mandating equal rights for all in public accommodations and employment. Even after the 1963 March on Washington and the assassination of President Kennedy, Congress refused to act on major civil rights legislation. Congress was filled with Southern segregationists who saw a strong civil rights bill as a threat to their idea of a "Great" America, a nation in which white control and dominance of black people was the unwritten law.

Many black and white people—famous artists, athletes, and religious leaders as well as civil rights activists—put pressure on Congress to pass a civil rights law, something capable of leveling the racial playing field. It became the brass ring for the civil rights movement, the prize for thankless years of sacrifice by people who insisted on their rights, from James Meredith to Rabbi Joshua Heschel to Chaney, Goodman, and Schwerner.

They all dreamed of a powerful federal law to fulfill the promise of the Emancipation Proclamation and the post–Civil War amendments to the Constitution. They wanted, in Dr. King's words at the March on Washington, to "cash a check...a promissory note" written by the Founding Fathers, based on the idea that "all men—yes black men as well as white men—would be guaranteed the unalienable rights of life, liberty and the pursuit of happiness." King concluded in 1963 it was still the case that "America has defaulted on this promissory note insofar as her citizens of color are concerned."

A breakthrough came with passage of the Civil Rights Act of 1964. It radically shifted the course of American democracy. Signed on July 2, 1964, by President Lyndon Johnson, the new law banned discrimination on the basis of "race, color, religion, or nation origin" in hotels, restaurants, retail stores, gas stations, movie theaters, sports stadiums, and all other public accommodations, as well as any program that received federal funding. It made it *illegal* for an employer to hire or treat employees differently based on their race, religion, sex, and country of origin. And it gave the federal government the tools to prosecute anyone who broke this law.

With the Civil Rights Act in place, no longer were the president, federal judges, and the FBI allowed to become bystanders as brutal sheriffs, the KKK, and white citizens' councils imposed their racist will on black people. No longer could federal officials look away as state and local governments kept blacks and whites indulged in the poisonous lie of "separate but equal" public accommodations, the legal standard established in the 1896 *Plessy v. Ferguson* Supreme Court decision. No longer could the federal government twiddle its thumbs as black applicants were denied jobs for which they were perfectly qualified. Under the new law the federal government gained legal power to shift direction and become a force to ensure that *all* Americans, of all races, had access to American institutions. The Civil Rights Act reminded people of America's founding principles of equal rights. And as President Barack Obama said at an event commemorating the fiftieth anniversary of the bill's passage, the new law reminded people "what the hell the presidency was for."

The man most qualified to speak about the enormous changes brought about by the 1964 law is Congressman John Lewis, a Georgia Democrat. Lewis was a keynote speaker at the 1963 March on Washington, as the chairman of the Student Nonviolent Coordinating Committee. He later had his skull fractured in a beating by Alabama state troopers using batons when he marched for voting rights. Now near eighty, the bald congressman with the hoarse Southern drawl has come to personify the generation of men and women who fought for equal rights for black people and specifically the Civil Rights Act.

Lewis found himself defending the 1964 Civil Rights Act just before President Trump was inaugurated in January 2017. Speaking at the Senate Judiciary Committee's confirmation hearings for Senator Jeff Sessions, then a nominee to be attorney general, Lewis repeated three short words: "law and order."

This was the term used by President Nixon to steal the moral high ground from the civil rights protestors, the poor blacks who rioted in cities across the country during the "Long Hot Summer" of 1967 and in the wake of Dr. King's 1968 assassination. During his 1968 campaign, Nixon's promise to restore "law and order" was a euphemistic appeal to whites tired of marches and loud demands for equal rights.

"Law and order" is also the phrase that candidate Donald Trump used during his 2016 presidential campaign, after alarming suburban whites with horrific portrayals of crime in black neighborhoods. And it's a term that has been used by former senator Sessions (R-AL), one of the few lawmakers who wholeheartedly endorsed candidate Trump during the Republican primaries.

This history was on Congressman Lewis's mind when, at Sessions's confirmation hearing, he asked whether "Senator Sessions' call for 'law and order' will mean today what it meant in Alabama, when I was coming up back then." He explained that segregationists dressed up their racism as legitimate by using local laws "to violate the human and civil rights of the poor, the dispossessed, people of color."

Back in Alabama, where Lewis and Sessions both grew up in the 1940s, "law and order" meant getting "arrested and taken to jail" for not "mov[ing] to the back of the bus" if a white person needed a seat, for not "cross[ing] the street when a white person walked down the same sidewalk," for drinking "from the white water-fountain," and for looking "a white person directly in their eyes."

"Segregation was the *law* of the land that *ordered* our society," Congressman Lewis explained to the all-white Judiciary Committee. And to those who fought the unjust laws of segregation during that era, "law and order" meant a federal government that stood idly by as Southern states banned black people from their schools, jobs, and voting booths, while black activists were "beaten, tear-gassed, left bloody, some of us unconscious," and others lying on the ground, almost dead. This is what happened on March 7, 1965, when Lewis, then chairman of SNCC, led a group of six hundred demonstrators in an "orderly, peaceful nonviolent fashion to walk from Selma to Montgomery, Alabama, to dramatize to the nation and to the world that we wanted to register to vote." They were stopped and beaten back on Edmund Pettus Bridge, a day now memorialized as Bloody Sunday.

"Law and order" meant a federal government that stood aside while Southern states enforced laws that segregated schools, restaurants, hotels, trains, and entire neighborhoods. It meant a federal government that did nothing while, as of 1967, sixteen states explicitly forbade black and white people from marrying each other. It meant a federal government that did nothing as blacks were systematically blocked from white schools and skilled jobs, doing dangerous factory work (if you were lucky enough to get a factory job), or working endless days in the fields as a sharecropper, unable to gain any wealth or open doors for your children. And "law and order" incredibly meant the acceptance of white racists lynching black people.

That is what happened to Laura and L. D. Nelson, a black mother and her son, kidnapped from prison and hanged from a bridge in Oklahoma in 1911 after they argued and exchanged shots with a local deputy sheriff, who was killed. It was also what happened to fourteen-year-old Emmett Till, who was beaten until he was disfigured, then shot and thrown into a Mississippi river in 1955 for allegedly whistling at a white woman. And under Southern "law and order," James Chaney, Andy Goodman, and Mickey Schwerner were shot by local police and buried in a dam for the crime of registering voters in rural Mississippi during Freedom Summer. All in all, 3,446 African Americans were lynched between 1882 and 1968. In other words, "law and order" meant a federal government that could do nothing as state governments, local governments, and individual whites barred blacks from white schools, jobs, and public spaces—terrorizing them, sometimes killing them, if they dared to disobey.

Congressman Lewis warned the Judiciary Committee that a "clear majority of Americans" are "afraid this country is headed in the wrong direction." He said he was testifying against Sessions for millions of black and white Americans "concerned that some leaders reject decades of progress and want to return to the dark past, when the power of law was used to deny the freedoms protected by the Constitution, the Bill of Rights, and its Amendments."

Sessions won confirmation. But Lewis spoke for black America and its allies in questioning whether Trump's pick for attorney general was the right man to ensure that the Civil Rights Act of 1964 is enforced in the twenty-first century. Indeed, Jeff Sessions has a history of treating civil rights protections for black people as a nuisance. When President Reagan appointed him to serve on a federal court in the 1980s, Sessions was denied by the Senate Judiciary Committee because of a series of racist comments he had made throughout his career. As it turns out, Sessions once said he thought the KKK was "OK until I found out they smoked pot," and referred to a black lawyer, a colleague, as "boy," a term that whites used to address blacks in order to remind them that they were not, and could never be, men. He also was on record calling civil rights organizations such as the NAACP and the ACLU "un-American" and "communist-inspired." He charged them with trying to shove "civil rights down the throats of people."

President Trump's selection of Sessions revealed how much the two have in common. Trump, too, has a history of dismissing the Civil Rights Act as nothing more than a bother, something hindering his business decisions, ranging from the people he allowed to rent his apartments to the people working in his casinos. When Trump and his then wife Ivana walked through their Atlantic City casinos, the black employees would be taken out of the room so as to not upset the Trumps. In 1991 Trump was fined $200,000 by the New Jersey Casino Control Commission under state antidiscrimination laws for taking black and female workers off of the casino floor whenever a hotshot gambler named Robert LiButti—a known racist and a misogynist—came to play cards. A 2016 investigation by the Associated Press wasn't able to find one black person working as a senior vice president for the Trump Organization over the last several decades. Randal Pinkett, a black man who got a job with Trump after winning the TV show *The Apprentice*, told the AP, "It was quite commonplace for me to be the only person of color in the room for meetings at the executive level."

Given the president's clear disrespect for the rights of black people, it was no surprise that the Trump administration went out of its way to diminish the Civil Rights Act, the backbone of protections for people of color against discrimination.

Under President Obama, a younger generation of African American activists, led by the Black Lives Matter movement, had put enormous pressure on the federal government to use the 1964 Civil Rights Act to address racial disparities in the criminal justice system. They rallied against the disproportionate numbers of black people stopped and frisked by police officers, sent to jail for longer amounts of time, and, at points, unjustly killed by law enforcement officers—as was the case with Michael Brown, Freddie Gray, Alton Sterling, Eric Garner, and Tamir Rice, to name just a few.

In response, Eric Holder and Loretta Lynch, Obama's attorneys general, drew up several consent decrees, or legally binding agreements, between local police departments and the federal government. The deals put in place specific reforms to protect communities of color against repeated use of excessive force and outright police brutality.

Attorney General Sessions and President Trump reversed the Obama administration's actions. After only three months as the head of the Justice Department, Sessions sent out a memorandum to his top aides and US attorneys around the nation announcing that he'd be reviewing all "existing or contemplated consent decrees." According to Sessions, stopping crime, maintaining public safety, and "respect[ing] the civil rights of all members of the public" are "first and foremost, tasks for state, local, and tribal law enforcement." Consent decrees already initiated in Cleveland, New Orleans, Newark, and Los Angeles—fourteen police departments in total—were put on hold. All of the consent decrees currently being considered for more police departments also were put in limbo.

Sessions actually tried to stop a consent decree from going into effect in Baltimore: the city where a twenty-five-year-old black man named Freddie Gray died from spinal cord injuries after being roughed up and dragged into the back of a police van by three officers in April 2015. Gray, with a long record of arrests, had been seen carrying a knife. In a brief to the US District Court of Maryland, a Trump Justice Department representative wrote that "the United States seeks the extension of time to assess whether and how the provisions of the proposed consent decree interact with the directives of the President and Attorney General." The attempt to undo the decree failed. US District Judge James Bredar ruled, "The time for negotiating the agreement is over."

Sessions and Trump often talk about how they—unlike President Obama—will let police do whatever they need to do to get the job done. In an April 17, 2017, op-ed in *USA Today*, Sessions argued that "too much focus has been placed on a small number of police who are bad actors rather than on criminals." He claimed that "too many people believe the solution is to impose consent decrees that discourage the proactive policing that keeps our cities safe." And he pledged that, under his leadership, the Justice Department "will not sign consent decrees for political expedience that will cost more lives by handcuffing the police instead of the criminals." The implication was that Obama's police reforms were meant for "political expedience"—petty attempts to gain black votes—and not heartfelt federal initiatives to end race-based discrimination.

And yet the irony here is that even as President Trump claims to be standing up for police departments, lots of police chiefs want no part of Trump and Sessions's attempts to advocate for them. When Sessions tried to stop Baltimore's consent decree from going into effect, Kevin Davis, then Baltimore's police commissioner, told the *Baltimore City Paper*: "We need a consent decree in Baltimore to fundamentally change the police department for decades to come."

In speech after speech, Trump and Sessions continued to suggest that black people, not the police who brutalize them, are the problem. The president and attorney general remained entrenched in their position even when the overwhelmingly majority of African Americans—84 percent, according to a 2016 survey by the Pew Research Center—said that they are treated "less fairly than whites...in dealing with the police." Pew also found 75 percent of black people believe that black people are treated worse by the courts.

The facts support these expressions of black concern. In 2014 black people, who make up about 13 percent of the population, made up 34 percent of the 6.8 million people currently incarcerated in the United States. In Trump's eyes, the disproportionate rate of black incarceration has nothing to do with the nation's history of discrimination. He sees it as the result of disrespect for law and order, and the fact that cops feel they need to tread carefully around criminals so they don't get accused of being racist or using excessive force.

During a July 2017 speech on gang violence in Long Island, Trump suggested that police officers were too gentle when making arrests. He told them to stop protecting peoples' heads when they put them in the backseat of a squad car. "Please do not be too nice," he said, for a cheap laugh.

In Trump's worldview, the Obama administration didn't respect police officers at all, telling the crowd in Long Island, "We have your back 100 percent. Not like the old days. Not like the old days."

And again: "I will always have your back—100 percent, like you've always had mine," he promised in late March at a listening session with the leadership of the Fraternal Order of Police, a law enforcement union with over three hundred thousand members that endorsed Trump. John McNesby, the president of the Philadelphia branch of the Fraternal Order who was present at the listening session, referred to Black Lives Matter protesters as a "pack of rabid animals" at an August 2017 speech.

In September, at an Alabama rally for then Senate primary candidate Luther Strange, President Trump struck similar chords of bitter racial politics when he demanded an end to football players protesting police brutality by not standing for the national anthem: "Get that son of a bitch off the field right now," he proposed as his remedy for any player who kneeled. "He's fired. He's fired!"

The players' protests began the year beforehand, when Colin Kaepernick, a quarterback, said he was "not going to stand up to show pride in a flag for a country that oppresses black people and people of color." Kaepernick was not signed for the following season, but the protests picked up support among players, especially after the white supremacist rally in Charlottesville, Virginia. Michael Bennett, a defensive player, said, "I can't stand right now—I am not going to be standing until I see the equality and freedom."

During the Alabama rally, the new president promised NFL team owners, none of whom are black, that if they took his advice to punish the league's mostly black players, they would be celebrated by his supporters. "For a week," he said, the owner who fired the protestors would be feted as "the most popular person in this country. Because that's a total disrespect of our heritage," he said using language reminiscent of Jim Crow's defenders. "That's a total disrespect for everything we stand for."

The Trump administration's withdrawal from previous administrations' attempts to prevent excessive use of force by police also extends to bipartisan congressional efforts to reduce mandatory sentences for drug and gun crimes. The 2015 bill won the support of thirty-seven sponsors in the Senate and seventy-nine members of the House. But Sessions, as a member of the Senate Judiciary Committee, voted against the bill. "Sessions was the main reason the bill did not pass," Inimai Chettiar, the director of the justice program at the Brennan Center, told the *Washington Post*. "He came in at the last minute and really torpedoed the bipartisan effort," she continued.

President Trump and his attorney general brought the hostile hard-line opposition toward any consideration of racial bias to debates over undocumented immigrants. On August 25, 2017, Trump pardoned Joe Arpaio, former sheriff of Maricopa County, Arizona, who'd previously been found in contempt of court by a district judge for failing to comply with previous court orders to stop engaging in racially motivated policing meant to trap undocumented immigrants. Arpaio has since declared his candidacy for the US Senate.

In an April 2017 statement about so-called sanctuary cities—local governments that do not hold undocumented immigrants in their jails for deportation unless federal agents have a detainer or warrant—Sessions claimed: "Many of these jurisdictions are also crumbling under the weight of illegal immigration and violent crime." His words hit hard at Latinos, the group of immigrants with the highest percentage of undocumented people in the country. But his words also provoked memories of Trump's campaign tirades against black neighborhoods—such as when he talked about "American carnage" in his inaugural address. Session amplified that theme when he excoriated the nation's biggest city, New York, for allowing "gang murder after gang murder, the predictable consequence of the city's 'soft on crime' stance."

New York officials didn't take kindly to Sessions's distortion of the facts or his assessment of their work. "I like to think of myself as a pretty calm and measured person," New York police commissioner James P. O'Neill said at a press conference that day. "But when I read that statement by DOJ this afternoon, my blood began to boil. I've been lucky enough to be a cop in this city for 35—almost 35 years. I've seen the hard work that's done every day by the 36,000 men and women that go out there, and patrol the streets, and keep it safe.... Since 1993, murders down 82 percent; shootings down 81 percent; overall crime is down 76 percent....To say we're soft on crime is absolutely ludicrous."

In its first months in Washington, the Trump administration also reignited the War on Drugs. That Reagan-era program quadrupled the American prison population in thirty years, leaving "mostly black men strapped with lengthy prison sentences—10–20 years, sometimes life without parole for a first drug offense," the *Washington Post* reported. As the newspaper story indicated, the Reagan plan was very damaging to poor black neighborhoods. It gave heightened energy and funds to Wild West–style policing of street drug traffic in poor minority neighborhoods. That led to a high number of arrests of young people of color, especially young men. And that resulted in a spike in mandatory sentences for drug crimes. The fallout for black Americans went beyond the impact for whites, despite statistically higher levels of drug use among whites. Sentencing for possession of crack cocaine—an inexpensive version of cocaine, often associated with the black underclass—was far more punishing than sentences for possession of powdered cocaine, more expensive and often associated with white socialites and businessmen. Black civil rights leaders as well as academics made the case that the laws put in place as part of the War on Drugs in the 1980s were hurting black communities by hammering young men doing little more than trying to pick up a few dollars with small-time drug sales. Once caught in the courts and jails, the young men lose time at school and find their future chances to get a job burdened by the presence of a criminal record.

The Obama administration tried to ameliorate the problem by allowing state and local governments to decriminalize medical and recreational use of marijuana. Then in 2010 Congress tried to fix the racial imbalance over penalties for cocaine use by passing the Fair Sentencing Act. It threw out the "mandatory minimum" sentence of five years in prison for possession of crack cocaine. Also, the new law lessened the difference in penalties for possession of crack and powder cocaine. In August 2013, President Obama's attorney general, Eric Holder, sent a memo to US attorneys instructing them to limit harsh sentences for people caught with drugs who are not major dealers, gang leaders, or part of a major criminal cartel. Holder's approach was to avoid charging common, low-level drug dealers with high-level offenses that left judges with no alternative but to impose lengthy mandatory sentences.

Yet again, in another example of what black people, Latinos, and the poor have to lose with Trump as president, Sessions "rescinded" Holder's 2013 memo.

The Trump Justice Department in a May 2017 memo urged federal prosecutors to "charge and pursue the most serious, readily provable offence" for any and all crimes. This means low-level drug users will be charged with crimes that result in the harshest punishments possible. During a March 2017 speech in Virginia, Sessions said, "I think we have too much tolerance for drug use—psychologically, politically, morally."

Then Sessions appointed Steve Cook, a federal prosecutor from Tennessee known for his single-minded, punishing approach to drug use, to become one of his top assistants at the Justice Department. Cook referred to Obama's approach to low-level drug use as "soft on crime." In every case Cook had prosecuted, he pushed for the harshest possible sentences for drug offenders. He told the Associated Press he is sick and tired of people who "see these drug traffickers as the victims." Cook seems to think that there is nothing wrong with US courts giving minor drug offenders harsh sentences. At an event hosted by the *Washington Post* last year, he said, "the federal criminal justice system simply is not broken. In fact, it's working exactly as designed."

The Trump administration also is trying to step away from the Obama administration's efforts to eliminate the use of private prisons, which have been widely criticized for being far less safe and producing higher rates of recidivism than public prisons. In August 2016, nearing the end of Obama's term, Deputy Attorney General Sally Yates instructed the head of the Bureau of Prisons to begin phasing out its contracts with private prison companies. And yet, as early as February 2017, Sessions sent a memo to the Bureau of Prisons "rescinding" Yates's instructions. He wrote that Obama's policy "impaired the Bureau's ability to meet the future needs of the federal correctional system." With historically low crime rates, it is hard to see Sessions's goal as anything but keeping up the prison population for the nation's growing number of prisons—even private ones.

The administration's approach to crime is just one window into its approach to law and black America. Sessions has made it clear that he will be taking a far more limited reading of the Civil Rights Act itself. Title VII of the law makes it illegal for an employer to discriminate against an employee based on his or her race and sex. The Obama administration argued that transgender Americans are to be considered a protected group under the Civil Rights Act, with former vice president Joe Biden saying in October 2012 that "transgender rights are the civil rights issue of our time."

Trump apparently feels differently. In an October 2017 memorandum, Sessions nullified a December 2014 memorandum from Holder to US attorneys indicating that the Obama Justice Department would begin considering transgender people a protected group under the Civil Rights Act. Sessions's memo piggybacked on Trump's own decision in July to ban transgender people from the military (though the ban itself has thus far been blocked by the courts). This new, much more restricted reading of civil rights legislation also applies to LGBT rights. In October 2017 during an event at the Heritage Foundation, Sessions spoke in defense of the Colorado bakery that refused to bake a wedding cake for a gay couple—*Masterpiece Cakeshop v. Colorado Civil Rights Commission*. "Although public accommodations laws serve important purposes," he explained, "they—like other laws—cannot be interpreted to undermine the individual freedoms that the First Amendment guarantees."

Sessions's position is an injury to the unprecedented effort made in the Civil Rights Act to ensure that the federal government would protect the civil rights of all Americans independent of race, sexual orientation, or national origin. In every case Trump and Sessions are deconstructing the hard-fought victories for individual rights won with the passage of the Civil Rights Act itself.

Those victories came from real people taking very real risks to push through resistance among the nation's white majority. That opposition ranged from indifference to anger at being asked to think about tangled, emotional issue like racism and white privilege. Of course, it also meant dealing with people who defended racial segregation as part of their way of life, their heritage and tradition.

Senator Everett McKinley Dirksen, a sixty-eight-year-old Republican, was the kind of ally that Trump and Sessions would excoriate if he were serving the country today. Unexpectedly, when his moment in history arrived, Dirksen turned out to be a white man willing to take the risk to face up to racial injustice—willing to take a stand with little prospect for political reward and obvious political downside.

Dirksen did not fit the typical profile of a champion for black rights. He didn't know any black people growing up. His hometown, Pekin, a small city just south of Peoria, Illinois, had almost no black people. It became a major Klan headquarters in the 1920s, and was known as a sundown town, where it was quite frankly unsafe for African Americans to be outside after dark. Even today, African Americans make up just over 2 percent of Pekin's population. In fact, Pekin was featured in scholar James W. Loewen's book *Sundown Towns: A Hidden Dimension of American Racism*, which tells the stories of small American towns that remain deeply scarred by American racism. "We have friends who live in Pekin, and they don't want us to drive through alone," a black teen from a neighboring town admitted to Loewen in 2004. In 2006, the city high school went so far as to switch to a sports league with teams that had fewer black players.

Yet Dirksen didn't identify with his hometown's harsh insistence on keeping black people out. Instead, he took pride in Illinois's *Republican* legacy. Born on January 4, 1896, Dirksen was given the middle name McKinley in honor of the Republican president William McKinley, who would take office the following year. Dirksen and his family were Republican to the bone. After dropping out of a prelaw undergraduate program to fight in World War I, he and his brother operated a wholesale bakery selling bread to local businesses; he was also an active member of the American Legion. Dirksen's world was "the Republican fold," in the words of historian Elliot Rosen. "Dirksen came from a world that revolved around the small town, the American Legion, the Loyal Order of Moose, family, free enterprise, individualism, and hard work."

Elected to the Pekin city council in 1927, then to the House of Representatives in 1932, and to the US Senate in 1950, Dirksen was often asked to speak publicly about the historical figure he admired most, Abraham Lincoln.

"Lincoln came into a controversy-torn Washington," Dirksen said in a February 9, 1935, speech commemorating Lincoln Day. "He settled down to be a president. He was. When the question of freeing the slaves was paramount, he acted without fear. When questions arose concerning important decisions during the civil war, he acted without fear of the consequences."

In notes that Dirksen used for a February 1941 Lincoln Day address, Dirksen wrote, in red upper-case letters, that it was "TIME TO EMULATE [Lincoln's] COURAGE AND RESOLUTION."

During a 1951 Lincoln Day speech, Dirksen praised President Lincoln's quiet determination to lead on difficult questions facing the nation: "How modest he was at Gettysburg where he delivered that deathless challenge long ago."

Dirksen was more like Lincoln than a man of the twentieth century. He was old-fashioned. His life consisted of "Sanka, cigarettes, Maalox, and bourbon whiskey," writes historian Todd Purdum. He was flamboyant, with a patch of "carefully tousled hair," remembers William Safire, a Nixon speechwriter. Dirksen loved to make long, schmaltzy speeches on the Senate floor. His high school yearbook claimed that he may have suffered from a case of "Big-Word-Itis." And as a lawmaker, he was called the Wizard of Ooze. People would cry "Ev's up!" when he was about to make a speech. At an oratorical competition he participated in as a high school student in 1913, he had met William Jennings Bryan, possibly the most famous orator in American history.

During the 1950s Dirksen developed a relationship with Irene McCoy Gaines, an African American woman, and president of the National Association of Colored Women's Clubs, which had 50,000 members by that point. Gaines was an active Illinois Republican, which is how she came to know Dirksen. And upon her request, beginning in 1956, he began proposing congressional resolutions that would allow the president to proclaim a week in February Negro History Week, which had been informally acknowledged by Congress since 1926 but never made into law. His proposed resolutions all failed.

Gaines's influence led Dirksen to introduce a Senate bill (S. 3415) to "establish a federal commission on civil rights and privileges;

promote observance of civil rights of all individuals and aid in discrimination in employment because of race, creed, or color." That April, he also introduced S. 3605, which would have "establish[ed] a bipartisan commission on civil rights in the executive branch of government."

Dirksen was a strong supporter of the 1957 Civil Rights Act. He condemned the Southern segregationists for crippling its enforcement power before passing it. At one point during debate on the act Dirksen said, "Seldom in my long legislative experience have I seen . . . so many ghosts discovered under the same bed, but I am confident that if the civil rights bill is enacted, the heavens will not be rent asunder, the waters will not part, the earth will not rock and roll, and we will go on."

Dirksen's progressive stand on racial issues was possible because he was enormously respected across the aisle, particularly by President Johnson. Dirksen was a senator's senator, with a deep love of the Senate and its rules, and secure enough in his power to stand above petty feuds in a closely divided Senate.

And it was for these reasons that after a breakfast meeting with Senate Democrat leaders on February 18, 1964, President Johnson cornered Senator Hubert Humphrey (D-MN), the majority whip, and gave him his marching orders on the civil rights bill.

"The bill can't pass unless you get Ev Dirksen. You and I are going to get Ev. It's going to take time. We're going to get him. You make up your mind now that you've got to spend time with Ev Dirksen. You've got to let him have a piece of the action. He's got to look good all the time. . . . You get in there to see Dirksen. You drink with Dirksen! You talk with Dirksen! You listen to Dirksen!"

Johnson, a legendary master of Senate politics from his years as Senate majority leader, knew how to count the votes needed to pass a bill. Johnson had had a hand in watering down previous civil rights bills to win votes. The bills were tepid to the point where they might as well have been defeated. But he crafted them to keep southern segregationists votes. Now as president and facing demand for a civil rights bill with muscle, Johnson knew he needed Republican votes to make up for the projected loss of votes from segregationist Democrats. Through Johnson's strategic eyes he saw Dirksen as the power-broker, a man with the stature to hold together Republican support of the Civil Rights Act.

There was a long history of failed civil rights acts before Dirksen pushed the 1964 bill. Congress passed civil rights acts as far back as the 1860s, but these fell short of protecting the liberty of freed slaves from bitter Confederates still fighting the new reality of black people as full American citizens.

After the Civil War federal troops occupied the former Confederacy to establish a new political order without slavery. Congress passed three constitutional Amendments in the Reconstruction era. The Thirteenth, Fourteenth, and Fifteenth Amendments respectively banned slavery, made black people full citizens with "equal protection of the laws," and finally allowed black men the right to vote. The federal government also created the Freedmen's Bureau to help former slaves with schools, food, and shelter as they became self-sufficient.

The 1875 Civil Rights Act banned segregated public accommodations, requiring that "all persons within the jurisdiction of the United States...be entitled to the full and equal enjoyment of the accommodations, advantages, facilities, and privileges of inns, public conveyances on land or water, theaters, and other places of public amusement...applicable alike to citizens of every race and color, regardless of any previous condition of servitude."

Reconstruction turned out to be brief and the exception instead of the new rule for life in the South. It ended almost as soon as it began, as angry and racist white Southern Democrats, aided by a conservative Supreme Court and apathetic Northern politicians tired of fighting with Southern leaders, allowed the states of the former Confederacy to reconstitute their all-white, segregated political rule.

The former Confederates put in place written laws and unwritten customs to keep black people in perpetual second-class citizenship.

This oppressive system of laws became known as Jim Crow, named after the white actors who painted their faces black and caricatured black people as lazy, untrustworthy, and idiotic. The power to keep black people in submission resided not only in Jim Crow laws but in the daily threat of violence. For example, in Louisiana, a disputed 1872 state election between the Republican Party (supported by free black men) and the Fusion Democrats (the white former Confederates) emboldened militant white segregationists threatening to kill newly freed black people across the state who had dared to cast a vote.

Several hundred African American men responded by setting up a fortress at a courthouse in a central Louisiana town called Colfax. On April 14, 1873, a white militia approached the courthouse, captured a black man, gave him a torch, and told him to set the courthouse on fire or they'd kill him. The lone black man set the courthouse on fire, forcing the besieged African Americans out of the blazing building. Between 150 and 280 African Americans died from gunfire as they tried to get out of the building during the Colfax Massacre, which historian David Blight has called an "American My Lai."

And yet, shockingly, in *United States v. Cruikshank* (1876), the Supreme Court ruled that it could not charge the ringleaders of the Colfax Massacre with anything because the Fourteenth Amendment—passed less than a decade earlier to guarantee African Americans citizenship rights—only forbade *states* from denying individuals life, liberty, and property. It could do nothing to block *individuals* from denying others their right to "life, liberty, and property." In other words, the federal government had no power to block a group of white vigilantes from slaughtering upwards of three hundred African Americans.

That meant there was no legal basis in federal law to prosecute the Texans who lynched 339 African Americans between 1885 and 1942, the Mississippians who lynched 539 African Americans between 1882 and 1968—Americans overall who lynched 3,446 African Americans between 1882 and 1968.

"In the name of federalism," wrote historian Eric Foner, "the decision rendered national prosecution of crimes committed against blacks virtually impossible." Suddenly, the Supreme Court effectively said that there could be no federal mechanism to prosecute whites who killed blacks for violating local race protocols set by night-riding terrorists and even white men with badges who cracked down on any black person stepping out of line.

During the 1874 midterm elections, Democrats opposed to Reconstruction gained a House majority, as well as nine Senate seats. Meanwhile, twenty-three of the thirty-five state legislatures holding elections that year also went to supporters of racial segregation. Then in 1877 the last of the federal troops stationed in the former Confederacy were ordered to pull out. For the first time since the Civil War, white segregationist Southerners "now... no longer [had] to feel like aliens in their native land," explained Blight.

The US Supreme Court also did its part to end the Reconstruction era. And in a group of cases known as the Civil Rights Cases, the Supreme Court ruled in 1883 that it was constitutional to keep black people out of inns, hotels, theaters, and first-class train travel. Five lawsuits had been filed by black plaintiffs against racial discrimination in public accommodations under the 1875 Civil Rights Act. The court decided that the 1875 act was unconstitutional. In his majority opinion, Justice Joseph Bradley wrote that while the Fourteenth Amendment did indeed "nullif[y] and make void all state legislation, and state action of every kind, which impairs the privileges and immunities of citizens," the federal government had no power to prevent individuals who owned a hotel or other public accommodations from barring black people. In other words, while the federal government could negate a *state* law requiring segregated accommodations, it could do nothing about individual innkeepers, restaurateurs, and conductors who used a racist standard to keep blacks out of their facilities.

By 1896 all federal protection from racist state laws ended with the Supreme Court's *Plessy v. Ferguson* decision. That case centered on an Afro-Creole Louisianan man named Homer Plessy who bought a ticket for the whites-only railroad car in defiance of the 1890 Louisiana Separate Car Act mandating "equal, but separate" train cars for blacks and whites. The Supreme Court ruled that "separate but equal" accommodations for different races were perfectly legal.

Though Frederick Douglass, who died in 1895, didn't live to see the *Plessy* decision come down from the court, he had already concluded decades before that "today, in most of the southern states, the fourteenth and fifteenth amendments are virtually nullified," with citizenship rights having become "practically a mockery," as he wrote in his autobiography, *The Life and Times of Frederick Douglass.*

With the end of the great promises of federal protection for black rights, the former Confederate states passed more laws relegating blacks to separate and inferior schools, restaurants, hotels, and railroad cars. Black children could not play in white parks, and black voters were kept away from the voting booths.

That separate and racist reality persisted despite the amendments to the Constitution. Equal rights activists failed again and again to pass meaningful civil rights legislation in the face of opposition from white Southern Democrats.

The politics of Congress passing a civil rights bill with power changed during the Great Migration of the 1920s and 1930s; millions of black people left the rural South and headed north for factory jobs and higher wages in cities like Chicago, Detroit, and Philadelphia. Their numbers created new black neighborhoods and made black votes a political factor in those cities for the first time.

During and after World War II, American presidents were buffeted by new political pressure from the growing presence of black residents in the nation's big cities. Their increasing population in the North led to the creation of black-owned newspapers that gave a platform to the black perspective and political voice. Black Northerners also elected black politicians.

The end of the war also saw black soldiers returning home, wearing their uniforms with pride and expecting to be treated as heroes. When a black soldier was turned away from a lunch counter or forced to the back of the bus, the NAACP, the nation's top civil rights organization, splashed the episodes across the front pages of black newspapers. The point was to stir outrage at white political leaders for not protecting the rights of black service members who had fought to defend American democracy.

Membership in the NAACP tripled between 1933 and 1944. African Americans, at least in the North, also became politically organized, emerging as a key voting bloc. As a result, congressmen, senators, and American presidents found themselves in a new political dynamic. They now had to balance the demands of white segregationists in the South with demands from civil rights groups for federal legislation with real teeth to protect their freedoms.

As early as 1941 A. Philip Randolph, the president of the Brotherhood of Sleeping Car Porters, one of the first successfully organized black labor unions, had enough political pull—both inside the labor movement and among civil rights leaders—to force President Franklin D. Roosevelt to pay attention to black demands. Randolph called on the president to open the way for black workers to get jobs in factories making munitions and supplies for the defense industry. To pressure the president, Randolph threatened to organize a massive African American March on Washington. The prospect scared Roosevelt and much of Congress. They openly feared the capital would be under siege from a mass of black people. Roosevelt opted to calm the situation by signing a 1941 executive order integrating the defense industries.

By 1947 President Harry Truman, speaking at the thirty-eighth annual NAACP convention, said black civil rights were as important at that moment as the Constitution and the Bill of Rights were to the

Americans of the early Republic. Citing laws written by the Founding Fathers to ensure that their government would not become like the tyrannical British Empire, Truman argued for individual rights across color lines. "The extension of civil rights today," Truman explained, "means not protection of the people against the government, but protection of the people *by* the government." On July 26, 1948, Truman signed Executive Order 9981, which desegregated the military.

Yet nearly all attempts at meaningful legal reform were met with white segregationist defiance. Even a presidential panel created by Truman refused to compel military leaders to integrate for fear, they said, of destabilizing the military with racial unrest. It took until 1954 for the army to do away with its last segregated outfit. That year the change in racial politics also picked up the pace in the Supreme Court.

In *Brown v. Board of Education*, the Supreme Court reversed the separate-but-equal doctrine of the 1896 *Plessy* ruling. A year later, in a separate ruling, the justices softened the order by allowing schools to be integrated over time with "all deliberate speed" to appease and lessen white resistance. It did not help. "Massive resistance" became a political battle cry, as segregationist politicians attacked the federal courts with charges of interference with "states' rights." They refused immediate or gradual integration of schools. With no enforcement mechanism in place to ensure that integration actually took place, a reluctant President Dwight D. Eisenhower had to send a thousand members of the 101st Airborne to Little Rock, Arkansas, in 1957. He knew he needed to protect the Supreme Court's standing as the nation's top judicial body and the power of its decisions by ensuring that just nine black students were able to attend Central High School.

Meanwhile, in Congress there was a new kind of civil war between white segregationist Democrats and Northern Democrats with growing black constituencies. A draft of the Civil Rights Act of 1957 recommended giving the Department of Justice the power to sue states that enforced local laws to keep black people out of public accommodations. But Southern segregationist Democrats, led by Senators Richard Russell of Georgia and James Eastland of Mississippi, hacked the bill to pieces—allowing only an ineffective version of the bill to pass through the Senate.

The Senate majority leader in the late 1950s was Lyndon Johnson, the future vice president under President Kennedy and later president after Kennedy's assassination. As majority leader, Johnson gave Northern Democrats enough of a victory to allow them to tell their constituents, especially the blacks, that new civil rights laws had been passed in the Senate. In fact those laws were empty vessels. Johnson worked with Russell and Eastland to strip out federal enforcement power to punish racist local practices in the South and elsewhere. Federal judges now had power over registrars who denied black voting rights. They could bring them to court—where, of course, they'd be tried by juries of all-white segregationists.

An attempt was made to strengthen the bill in 1960. And once again Southern Democrats blocked it. As in the earlier attempt, the Southern politicians made a deal to let a weak version of the bill pass into law. Author Clay Risen describes the 1960 bill as even more feckless than its predecessor. He called it "a weak echo of the 1957 act" that only gave courts the power to assign referees to oversee Southern courthouses where blacks were being denied voting rights.

Jacob Javits, the liberal Republican senator from New York, called the 1960 Act a "victory for the Old South." Senator Joseph Clark, a liberal Pennsylvania Democrat, proclaimed in a senate speech, "Surely in this battle on the senate floor the roles of Grant and Lee at Appomattox have been reversed." The implication here, of course, was that Southern segregationist Democrats were effectively trying to create a new battle front in the nearly one-hundred-year-old Civil War by blocking all attempts to make freed slaves—black people— into anything but a servant class.

During the early 1960s, the entire federal government was oblivious and unresponsive when black people complained about state and local governments, through the power of town sheriffs, enforcing segregation in restaurants, schools, jobs, and public transit. This was just the latest incarnation of the same defiant stand by segregationists against equal rights laws at the end of the Civil War.

By the late 1950s a new, younger generation of civil rights activists began pressuring Congress and the president for strong, federally mandated protection of their civil rights. These young people, black and white, conducted sit-ins, marched to protest, boycotted, and more. Their nonviolent tactics drew national attention, forcing the race issue on people who knew little about it in areas with few black residents in the West, in New England, and in small Midwestern towns. In particular, these young activists wanted the rest of the country to come face-to-face with the violence used to enforce the rules of segregation in the South. They saw themselves getting the political upper hand if the nation came to know the daily indignities experienced by black people, who were forced to sit in the back of the bus and denied the use of other public accommodations. To force the issue, these more militant activists risked arrest to walk down from the "colored" balcony at movie theaters and sit in the whites-only seating area. In all black and racially mixed groups they made a show of going into restaurants in the South where black people couldn't sit at the lunch counters.

The strategy worked. They got the nation's attention on a cold February day in 1960. Four black freshmen at North Carolina Agricultural and Technical State University—Joseph McNeil, Franklin McCain, Ezell Blair Jr., and David Richmond—staged a sit-in at a whites-only Woolworth's lunch counter in Greensboro. When they asked for coffee and were refused, they did not move and stayed there until the store closed for the day. The following day, February 2, thirty students came to sit in at the Woolworth's lunch counter, and by February 3 fifty students were participating.

The sit-in movement played big in newspapers across the nation. The protests spread across North Carolina. Beginning on February 9, Charles Jones, a twenty-two-year-old theological student at a Charlotte HBCU, Johnson C. Smith University, who had heard about the Greensboro sit-ins on the radio, led sit-ins at several Charlotte lunch counters. By February 11, over twenty students began a sit-in at a Woolworth's lunch counter in High Point, North Carolina, sixteen miles south of Greensboro. Within a week, protests spread to Winston-Salem, thirty minutes west of Greensboro. By the end of the month, sit-ins were being held all across the South, from Baltimore to Tallahassee, Richmond to Chattanooga. By the end of April, upwards of fifty thousand students had participated in the sit-ins.

The student-led sit-in movement captured the nation's attention that year. Eleanor Roosevelt called them "simply wonderful." When ABC's Edward Morgan asked President Eisenhower what he thought of the students' "Gandhi-like...resistance" during a press conference in late March, the president said that he was "deeply sympathetic with the efforts of any group to enjoy the rights, the rights of equality that they are guaranteed by the Constitution." During a lunch for African diplomats in 1960, John F. Kennedy, then a presidential hopeful, praised the student protests against segregation as a demonstration of the "American tradition to stand up for one's rights—even if the new way to stand up for one's rights is to sit down."

Presidential approval from a Republican and a Democrat energized the civil rights activists. So did polls showing increased public support outside the Southern states to end segregation in public accommodations everywhere.

Beginning in May 1961, and continuing into the summer, upwards of 450 black and white activists from CORE, SNCC, and the NAACP crisscrossed the South on a series of bus rides. Deliberately flaunting Southern custom that forced black people to the back of the bus, black Freedom Riders sat where they pleased. And black and white Freedom Riders sat next to each other. The Freedom Riders knew they'd be arrested. But that was the point—to deliberately break the law in order to expose the daily indignities that Southern black people were forced to endure. The plan worked. That May, news stories about Freedom Riders being attacked with pipes and chains made front-page news. So, too, did pictures of their Greyhound bus being firebombed in Anniston, Alabama. That summer three hundred Freedom Riders were arrested in Jackson, Mississippi, alone.

The murderous Jim Crow violence put pressure on politicians in Washington, most of all the new man in the White House, President Kennedy. The former Democratic senator from Massachusetts knew that he owed something to African American voters. Black voters had given strong support to President Eisenhower, but they had shifted to Kennedy in 1960, pushing him to a narrow victory over Eisenhower's vice president, Richard Nixon. The 1960 Democratic Party convention also responded to the turmoil down South by approving a platform calling for an "affirmative new atmosphere in which to deal with racial divisions" as well as "equal access for all Americans to all areas of community life." The DNC pledged that "the time has come to assure equal access for all Americans to all areas of community life, including voting booths, schoolrooms, jobs, housing, and public facilities." That November, Kennedy received 70 percent of the black vote.

The president also had geopolitical reasons to act. In the midst of the Cold War, Kennedy was acutely aware that the Soviet Union used the racist treatment of black people to argue that the United States was a sham democracy. Violent conflicts between angry white Southerners and nonviolent protestors also made Kennedy look weak in front of the Russians. And it wasn't just Russia. When African dignitaries visited the United States for meetings in New York and Washington, DC, the president's staff shamefully told them to fly and not drive from New York to Washington, DC, to avoid being shut out of whites-only restaurants in Maryland.

Despite all the embarrassment and protests, the president remained surprisingly ambivalent about jumping into the fight to help black citizens. The Democratic Party was divided between North and South. As author Todd Purdum notes in his book *An Idea Whose Time Has Come: Two Presidents, Two Parties, and the Battle for the Civil Rights Act of 1964*, the Democrats had big majorities in both the House and the Senate but "eighteen of those Senate Democrats were implacable segregationists, which meant that the president's party, by itself, could not muster a simple majority for civil rights legislation, much less the two-thirds vote that would be needed under the Senate's rules to cut off debate and force a vote on any bill."

Among these Southern Democrats were Senators Strom Thurmond of South Carolina and Richard Russell of Georgia, who drafted the 1956 Southern Manifesto, an attack on the Supreme Court's *Brown v. Board of Education*. This would become a defining document for Southern Democrats who would leave the party following the 1964 Civil Rights Act. The manifesto called *Brown* an "abuse of judicial power" that is "destroying the amicable relations between the white and negro races that have been created through 90 years of patient effort by the good people of both races." *Brown*, they argued, had replaced "heretofore friendship and understanding" with "hatred and suspicion." Black people, according to this view, were completely happy in their segregated lives. Thurmond had held a twenty-four-hour filibuster to block passage of the 1957 Civil Rights Act. And Russell had recently been compared to the general of the Confederate Army, Robert E. Lee, for gutting the 1960 Civil Rights Act of any meaningful reforms.

Also among President Kennedy's Democratic colleagues below the Mason Dixon Line was Senator James Eastland of Mississippi, who would call the disappearance of James Chaney, Andy Goodman, and Mickey Schwerner a "political stunt."

Following President Eisenhower's decision to send troops to Arkansas to enforce court-ordered school integration, Senator Herman Talmadge, a Georgia Democrat, called for Eisenhower's impeachment. Integration, he'd argued, led to the "mongrelization of the races."

President Kennedy knew there was no chance that these Southern Democrats, many of whom held important places in the Senate, would support a Civil Rights Act. And he didn't want to alienate them: he might need them for other legislative goals.

And so, for all of these reasons, when the first major civil rights event during his administration took place—the Freedom Rides in 1961—the president tried to hush the activists. In a public statement made in the lead-up to a June 1961 meeting in Vienna with Nikita Khrushchev, Attorney General Robert Kennedy told the Riders that continued protests would make President Kennedy look bad. "I think we should all keep in mind that the president is about to embark on a mission of great importance," he explained in patronizing tones. "Whatever we do in the United States at this time which brings or causes discredit on our country can be harmful to this mission." He claimed that a "cooling off period is needed."

Civil rights leaders responded angrily to the Kennedys' calls for moderation. James Farmer, national director of CORE, told reporters that "Negroes have been 'cooling off' for a hundred years" and would be "in a deep freeze if they cooled any further." When a media outlet asked Ralph Abernathy, of the Southern Christian Leadership Conference, if it mattered that the Freedom Rides might embarrass the nation, the future SCLC chairman flipped the question on its head: "Man, we've been embarrassed all our lives." Martin Luther King Jr., the head of the SCLC, told *Time* magazine simply: "Wait means 'Never.' "

Civil rights leaders had no trouble saying these things directly to the president's face. At a Peace Corps advisory council meeting, Harry Belafonte told President Kennedy he could show some heart by taking a public stand on the issue of racial bias and say "something a little more about the freedom riders." Eugene Rostow, the dean of Yale Law School who was also at the meeting, told the president that "there is a need now for moral leadership." After the meeting, President Kennedy, angry that he had been called out, told a top aide, Harris Wofford, who later became a US senator representing

Pennsylvania: "What in the world does [Rostow] think I should do? Doesn't he know I've done more for civil rights than any president in American history?"

The young president was in a trap, pressured by civil rights leaders and their Northern congressional allies while being pushed to the wall by fellow Democrats leading the charge for the Southern segregationist movement.

Things began to change by the fall of 1962 when pollster Lou Harris sent the president some numbers. During the riot by segregationists on the Ole Miss campus, support for Democrats jumped among African Americans, Jews, and Catholics. Taking a strong stand on civil rights was good politics.

On February 28, 1963, President Kennedy made his formal step toward civil rights legislation. He sent Congress a "Special Message... on Civil Rights." President Kennedy began by lamenting that when it came to black people, "the practices of the country do not always conform to the principles of the Constitution." He recommended several reforms. He asked for money to start a financial assistance program to help school districts integrate. Second, he recommended letting people register to vote if they had finished the sixth grade. That would do away with Southern literacy tests intended to keep black people from voting. He also recommended putting more money and power in the Civil Rights Commission, which had been established by the 1957 Civil Rights Act.

But the president didn't propose federal legislation to end racial segregation. Civil rights activists and major newspaper editorials dismissed Kennedy's proposals as dithering, a cop-out meant to appease the civil rights community without angering segregationist Democrats in the South. Dr. King was direct in assessing the president's lack of action in a March 31, 1963, article for the *Nation*. The president "wants the vote of both and is paralyzed by the conflicting needs of each," King wrote. "The time has come when the government must commit its immense resources squarely on the side of the quest for freedom."

That time came in late spring, and was the response to a series of protests in April and May 1963 led by Dr. King against segregation in Birmingham department stores. These boycotts, sit-ins, and marches presented the public and the president with a clear choice: support segregation or integration in a city that historian Manning Marable called "the citadel of white supremacy." The climax of the Birmingham campaign occurred in early May during the Children's Crusade, when literally thousands of black teens and children—some as young as six years old—marched through the streets of Birmingham singing and praying. On May 2, nearly a thousand children were arrested and taken to jail. When more children and teens came out the next day to march, they were attacked with police-trained German Shepherds, nightsticks, and fire hoses shooting water powerful enough to separate bricks from walls.

Images of the peaceful protest under assault by police in Birmingham circulated across the country. At a May 4 meeting with Americans for Democratic Action leadership, the president lashed out: "There's no federal law that we can pass to do anything about that picture in today's *Times*," he said, referring to a picture in the *New York Times* showing a protestor being attacked by a police dog. "Well, there isn't," he went on. "I mean what law can you pass to do anything about police power in the community of Birmingham?" he asked, concluding, "There is nothing we can do."

Within a month the president had changed his mind.

On June 11, 1963, Kennedy addressed the nation after using the Alabama National Guard to protect two black students, James Hood and Vivian Malone, seeking to enroll in the University of Alabama. President Kennedy began by reassuring the American people that both black students had entered the university despite the opposition of Governor George Wallace.

Yet the president wasn't here to talk to the American people about one isolated incident, whether it was Governor Wallace's refusal to allow two black people to attend a state university, the decision to unleash German Shepherds on peaceful protestors in Birmingham, or black students being refused service at a whites-only lunch counter in Greensboro.

Instead he spoke of the principle of equal rights. It was time for "every American, regardless of where he lives, [to] stop and examine his conscience." In the president's eyes "it ought to be possible for American students of any color to attend any public institution they select . . . to register to vote in a free election . . . to receive equal service in places of public accommodation . . . to register to vote in a free election." More broadly still, it ought to be possible "for every American to enjoy the privileges of being American without regard to his race or his color," or, invoking the Golden Rule, "to be treated as he would wish to be treated, as one would wish his children to be treated."

And yet "this is not the case." America, the president argued, was in the midst of a "moral crisis" that "cannot be left to increased demonstrations in the streets" and "token moves or talk." Thus, he continued, "it is time to act in the Congress." The legislature needed to "make a commitment it has not fully made in this century to the proposition that race has no place in American life or law." It was time, in short, for a new, powerful Civil Rights Act.

The president didn't go into the detail about the provisions of the law. But his top aides told reporters that President Kennedy had three goals. He wanted to give the federal government the power to enforce school integration, he wanted to protect voting rights, and he wanted a law to put an end to fights over segregated public accommodations by making them illegal.

"This," Kennedy concluded in his speech, "is a matter which concerns the country and what it stands for, and in meeting it I ask the support of all our citizens."

Minutes later, Dr. King telegrammed Kennedy, applauding him for "one of the most eloquent profound and unequivocal pleas for justice and freedom of all men ever made by any president." On June 19, the Kennedy administration sent H.R. 7152 to the House.

The key component of the Kennedy bill was the public accommodations provision. It was the "visceral, emotional heart of the bill," according to Todd Purdum; the "most significant new title," according to Clay Risen; the "most radical provision" of the civil rights bill, in the words of historian Hugh Davis Graham. The sit-ins, the Freedom Rides, all the way back to the Montgomery Bus Boycott nearly a decade earlier—these direct actions had all revolved around integrating public accommodations.

The Kennedy administration knew it would be significantly easier to get the bill passed through the House than the Senate. The House tilted liberal. And there was no filibuster. Congressional liberals were even able to expand the mandate against employment discrimination to make it universal, covering both the private and public sector.

After President Kennedy was shot and killed on November 22, 1963, President Lyndon Baines Johnson made the passage of the Civil Rights Act into an almost spiritual affair, a way to do justice to the dead president. On the twenty-seventh of November, he told a joint session of Congress: "No memorial oration or eulogy could more eloquently honor President Kennedy's memory than the earliest possible passage of the civil rights bill for which he fought so long." On February 10, 1964, the bill passed through the House, 290 to 130.

But sympathy for the assassinated president did not move Southern Democrats.

Richard Russell, the powerful Georgia senator, had long condemned the plan while the president was alive. He called it "a threatened crime against the whole philosophy of liberty," because it would force white people to associate with black people against their wishes.

Senator John Stennis of Mississippi had called it a "vicious proposal."

Lister Hill, a senator from Alabama, accused President Kennedy of putting "our most sacred rights...on the altar of political expediency."

Editorials in the South's leading papers denounced the bill as "another step in the direction toward a dictatorship in this country," as Mississippi's *Meridian Star* put it.

The Johnson administration knew there would be a Senate filibuster by the Southern segregationists. With the loss of those Democrats they'd need Republican support. The bill had to have sixty-seven votes, the super majority necessary to end the filibuster. Specifically, they'd need more than half of the thirty-three Republicans currently serving in the Senate.

Republicans, almost exclusively from the Northern and Western states outside the South, generally favored civil rights. But they opposed government telling white people that they had no choice but to follow orders and mix with black people. That was seen as an encroachment on individual liberties.

President Johnson identified one Republican as the senator able to convince fellow Republicans in the Senate to back the bill: the elderly Senator from that racist little town in Illinois, Everett Dirksen.

Dirksen had promised to support the civil rights bill when the late President Kennedy announced it the previous June. And yet, as a conservative, Dirksen was not completely on board with Title II, the public accommodations provision. He also took issue with Title VII, which banned employment discrimination. Dirksen wasn't sure whether it was the job of the Department of Justice to determine and punish the individuals and businesses that were being discriminatory. The central problem posed by the bill, as Dirksen wrote in his private notebook in capital letters, was whether: "congress [can] destroy FREEDOM OF ASSOCIATION in the case of privately owned and operated businesses." With a taste for the dramatic, during a February 1964 press conference, Dirksen said that he took his freedom the way he took his drinks: "Straight."

A diehard believer in the Senate as an institution, Dirksen also had some major qualms about breaking filibusters. Dirksen had once said they were "the only brake on hasty action."

And yet, tentatively, and with major reservations, Dirksen went to work.

It's hard to overestimate the spectacle of it all. On the one hand, the whole world watched as the Senate began to debate the most anticipated bill of the twentieth century. When the expected Southern filibuster began on March 30, 1963, Americans watched as senator after senator from the Southern segregationist bloc delivered racist tirades at the lectern.

At one point, Senator Russell Long of Louisiana argued: "The good Lord did as much segregating as anyone I know of when he put one race in one part of the world and another race in another part of the world." During a later speech, the senator debated whether "it not be fair to ask what kind of fix the colored folks would be in if they had not been brought to this country, but had been allowed to roam the jungles, with tigers chasing them."

Senator Jim Eastland of Mississippi said that he had "lived in the south my whole life" and had "not seen the first instance of economic discrimination."

Senator George Smathers, a Florida Democrat, claimed it was the Southerners who where the real victims of discrimination: "No southerner has been elected president of the United States for more than 100 years. Why? Because of discrimination."

And Senator Olin Johnston of South Carolina asked whether desegregation was the right move, given that there was more crime in the desegregated North than in the Jim Crow South.

And yet, as all of this absurdity was happening on the Senate floor, here was the sixty-eight-year-old Everett Dirksen, who hadn't really given much thought to civil rights during his career, suddenly working day in and day out to engineer revisions to the version of the civil rights bill that the House had passed that winter. His goal was to make it acceptable to small-government conservatives in the Midwest. He assigned a group of lawyers from the Judiciary Committee—nicknamed Dirksen's Bombers—to go through the bill line by line, looking for wiggle room, particularly in the portions that dealt with public accommodations. They looked for places where the bill's language could be broadened just enough to assure conservatives that the bill was not an encroachment on individual liberties.

Simultaneously, Dirksen needed to be sure that the changes he proposed were acceptable to Democrats, specifically Majority Leader Mike Mansfield and Majority Whip Hubert Humphrey. They were under pressure from President Lyndon Johnson to make a deal with Dirksen, but the Senate Democrats also faced pressure from NAACP lobbyist Clarence Mitchell and the powerful Washington union lawyer Joe Rauh Jr. not to allow Republicans to gut the bill and repeat the mistakes that had weakened the previous civil rights acts.

All the while, Dirksen maintained a dynamic mental map of his caucus: thirty-three Senate Republicans, seven of whom tilted liberal, five of whom were moderate, and twenty-one of whom, including himself, were conservative. A majority of them would be needed to successfully invoke cloture, a procedural rule designed to counter filibusters by forcing a vote.

And so Dirksen and his Bombers tossed out some amendments while insisting on others. A key instance of the kind of work Dirksen performed was the way he and Majority Leader Mansfield chose to define "discrimination." This was crucial, because if the Justice Department found instances of discrimination in public accommodations or employment, they'd be able to bring criminal charges against people and businesses. The issue, as author Charles Garrettson put it in a biography of Senator Humphrey, was "delineating when and to what degree the federal government in general, and the Attorney General specifically, would be authorized to intervene."

Dirksen and the Democrats' staff decided that the bill would use the phrase "pattern and practice of discrimination" to describe which businesses and employers the Justice Department would charge with breaking the law. Dirksen also called for language to prevent the Justice Department from instituting racial quota systems, even for businesses that were found to demonstrate a "pattern and practice of discrimination." If and when allegations of employment discrimination came up, Dirksen provided for a grace period when state and local governments—not the Justice Department—would have the chance to punish or otherwise deal with the employer who was breaking the law.

Dirksen, the Wizard of Ooze, knew that, in order to get Senate Republicans on board, he also needed them to believe that it wasn't being shoved down their throats by big-government Democrats. Meetings were held in Dirksen's office to reassure Republican senators that he was in charge. In fact, many of the changes that Dirksen made to the House bill weren't even that major. They were meant to assure Republicans that they controlled the final version of the bill.

By mid-May, Dirksen was feeling confident that he'd be able to get enough votes to invoke cloture. When President Johnson asked Senator Humphrey in a telephone conversation whether "Dirksen [can] get the votes for cloture," Humphrey responded: "Yes sir, he can get 25 votes. I had dinner with him last night and, Mr. President, we've got a much better bill than anybody ever dreamed possible."

On June 10, the day that had been set to attempt cloture, Dirksen lumbered to the front of the Senate to deliver the most important speech of his career. The senator was weak on his feet. As he spoke, an aide had to hand him some pills to swallow. Only a few weeks earlier he'd been bedridden with a cold. It wasn't anything serious. But for the last several months, this sixty-eight-year-old had been working nonstop. Now that all of this heavy lifting was done, Dirksen decided to skip the nitty-gritty details and frame the bill instead as a biblical battle between Good and Evil: "It is said that on the night he died, Victor Hugo wrote in his diary, substantially, this sentiment: 'Stronger than all the armies is an idea whose time has come.'"

The time had come. When Senator Lee Metcalf, a Montana Democrat, asked the room whether "the debate shall be brought to a close," seventy-one senators voted to invoke cloture, with only twenty-nine voting "nay." It was four more votes than President Johnson needed. Nine days later, the bill passed through the Senate with seventy-three votes.

In a brief White House speech on July 2, President Johnson urged the nation to "hasten that day, when our unmeasured strength, and our unbounded spirit, will be free to do the great works ordained to this nation by the just and wise God, who is the Father of us all." He then signed the Civil Rights Act into law. At the end of the ceremony, the president gave souvenirs to the people in attendance, He had used seventy-five pens to sign the law. He handed the first pen to Dirksen, the Republican Senator without whom the bill would not have become a law.

CHAPTER 4
BLACK VOICES

FOR ALL THE ATTENTION given to racial violence and protest marches, it is often forgotten that the 1964 Civil Rights Act grew out of a shift in American culture brought on by black writers, intellectuals, and ministers. These thought leaders inspired new thinking on race in popular movies, music, books, and magazines that put added pressure on a reluctant Congress that slowly worked to pass a federal law to protect the rights of black citizens.

The influence of these black intellectuals went beyond black America. White intellectuals and artists picked up on the power of art to express racial pain and injustice. That led to exchanges between black and white actors, musicians, and writers. Those energetic exchanges led to policy debates that caught the attention of top officials in the Kennedy and Johnson administrations.

In the Trump White House those conversations don't happen—the black voice is silenced. That is what happens when the president has no top black advisers and plays to his white political base with comments that degrade or dehumanize black people (and other people of color).

Unlike American presidents over the last 150 years, Trump has no black people outside the White House, no civil rights leader, no regular golf buddy, and no former business partner to help him see a black point of view.

Since 1863, when the former slave-turned-abolitionist Frederick Douglass went to the White House and told President Abraham Lincoln that black soldiers armed in the Union Army needed better pay and better treatment, white American presidents have generally learned to respect the leading African American voices of the day.

President Teddy Roosevelt dined with the black educator and civic leader Booker T. Washington. President Franklin Roosevelt had a Black Kitchen Cabinet of top black leaders of the period, including Mary McLeod Bethune. His wife, Eleanor, attended a rally for jobs for black Americans.

E. Frederic Morrow, the administrative officer for special projects in the Eisenhower White House, prodded the administration to show support for Emmett Till, the Montgomery Bus Boycott, and helped them to negotiate with black leaders like Roy Wilkins, and A. Philip Randolph. Presidents Kennedy and Johnson had Louie Martin Jr., a former newspaper publisher, in their inner circle. President Johnson relied on black lawyer Clifford Alexander. President George W. Bush appointed Colin Powell and Condoleezza Rice to be the first black secretaries of state. President Obama, in addition to being black himself, also nominated the nation's first black attorney general, Eric Holder, and the second, Loretta Lynch.

This pattern of white presidents embracing black advisors began in the late 1800s and early twentieth century. Often, the questionable power of the black vote acted to distort many of those conversations. Black people could neither elect nor oust a president with their limited access to the voting booth. The power of any white president was based exclusively on white voters.

Nevertheless, conversations between presidents and loading black voices were a constant feature of American history until now—until President Trump.

The best example of a black activist talking to a person at the highest level of political power is a little-known sit-down on May 24, 1963, between Attorney General Bobby Kennedy and the novelist James Baldwin.

Born in 1924 and raised in Harlem, Baldwin articulated searing critiques of white supremacy that made him a best-selling author and gave him rare status for any black person of his time among white intellectuals. As racial tensions turned to protests and riots in the spring of 1963, Bobby Kennedy asked Baldwin to assemble a group of black leaders for an off-the-record meeting in which they could tell the attorney general why black people were so angry.

The three-hour meeting was not a pleasant affair. Kennedy and his top aide, Burke Marshall, grew visibly uncomfortable as Baldwin's friends, all leading writers and activists, said the Kennedy administration was no better on race than the Southern segregationists. Robert Kennedy was insulted; he saw himself as a friend to the civil rights movement, but now he was hearing that he was still not doing enough. The meeting ended with Kennedy feeling these black voices, led by Baldwin, were being unrealistic. Baldwin was upset, too. He felt Bobby Kennedy, brother of the president, son of great wealth, was far too pleased with himself for not being an outright racist. Baldwin's group of artists demanded that Kennedy make the effort to understand why a black family living in fear of the KKK and bigoted Southern police might want the federal government to do more.

Despite his frustration with their strident demands, the conversation had an impact on Bobby Kennedy. By all accounts he became a significantly more vocal supporter of civil rights during the following years, specifically playing a leading role in encouraging his brother, John F. Kennedy, to back legislation that became the Civil Rights Act of 1964.

But more about Baldwin later. In 2018, President Donald Trump evidently doesn't care much what African American intellectuals, lawmakers, and policy experts have to say to him. When it comes to black voices, the Trump administration prefers silence. At best its members are interested in photo ops.

That much was made clear in the weeks and months after Trump's November 2016 election. Trump got 8 percent of the black vote and was widely criticized as being out of touch with blacks and Latinos, if not an outright racist. His staff wanted to repair the frayed ties to racial minorities by arranging a series of meetings with high-profile black athletes, musicians, and comedians at Trump Tower in Manhattan. On December 13, 2016, Trump took meetings with former Baltimore Ravens linebacker Ray Lewis, legendary Cleveland Browns running back Jim Brown, and rapper Kanye West. A month later, he met with black comedian Steve Harvey. And on the annual national holiday in January to honor civil rights icon Dr. Martin Luther King, the president-elect met with Dr. King's son, Martin Luther King III.

The expressed intent of these meet-and-greets was enormously vague, with Brown, Lewis, West, Harvey, and King III failing to mention any specific reforms or ideas that they discussed with the president-elect. They all limited themselves to generalized sound bites about poverty and crime in urban ghettos.

The fact is that Trump swept all segments of white voters. He won white people who had not gone to college. He won white college graduates. He won white men as well as white women, rich whites and poor whites. This astounding result came after eight years of the first black president, who won close to 90 percent of the black vote. The racial unease caused by the sharp contrast between the two presidents added to the urgent need for both sides to reach out to start a real conversation about race and politics. But the Trump transition team settled for photo taking.

Kanye West admitted this almost verbatim. When Trump and Kanye came down to the lobby of Trump Tower after their meeting, the musician told waiting reporters: "I'm just here to take a picture right now." The president-elect added that they had spoken about "life." West had been released from UCLA Medical Center for temporary psychosis a few days earlier. Other visitors offered the same lame, vague explanations. Jim Brown told CNN he and Trump had "talked about making America a better country. We talked about poor people. We talked about African American people. We talked about education, getting rid of violence, dealing with economic development realistically, and how to work together." In similar fashion, Ray Lewis said that he went "to explain to Trump what the problems are in urban neighborhoods."

Comedian Steve Harvey was more specific about what he had talked about with the president-elect during his Friday, January 13, meeting. He later explained to the *Hollywood Reporter* that he told Trump that he's "got keys to a lot of cities around this country,...I've got an ear to them really quick and find out what their real needs are." He suggested more money to the Department of Housing and Urban Development to "reopen [schools that have been closed down] as vision centers [for] STEM and computers and coding."

Yet by the following Monday, things were just as vague as they'd been in December. Following his conversation with Trump, Martin Luther King III—not a particularly noteworthy figure in the civil rights community and one whose only claim to fame is that his father was Dr. King—told reporters that the two had had a "very constructive meeting" about voting rights.

It didn't take long for black pundits to pick up on Trump's strategic deployment of African American celebrities. During a pointed debate on CNN, anchor Don Lemon asked Temple University professor Marc Lamont Hill what he thought about Trump's meetings with black headliners. Hill said, "I love Steve Harvey and I've got respect for Steve Harvey, and I think his intentions were...appropriate," and that Harvey was correct to seek out "a seat at the table." But Hill concluded that Harvey was "being used by folk like Donald Trump."

Getting a seat at the table is fine, Hill acknowledged. He was not jealous that Harvey got the invitation instead of him. But once Harvey agreed to the meeting, Hill said, he should have put "experts at the table...people who can challenge the president at the table." Hill noted that he doesn't "care if Steve Harvey's there. But if I'm Steve Harvey, I'm bringing Michelle Alexander," the legal scholar who has written powerfully on how "tough on crime" policies from the eighties and nineties have created a racial caste system—a New Jim Crow, as she calls it—in a seemingly colorblind country. "I'm bringing Cornel West," Hill continued. "I'm bringing Ahmadi Perry. I'm bringing Eddie Glaude. I'm bringing Michael Eric Dyson," all prolific black scholars who Hill meant to stand in for any number of black experts who would have been able to "challenge the president and inform the conversation." According to Hill, "to keep bringing up comedians, and actors, and athletes to represent black interests is demeaning, it's disrespectful, and it's condescending. Bring some people up there with some expertise, Donald Trump. Don't just bring up people to entertain!"

Bruce LeVell, an African American businessman and executive director of the National Diversity Coalition for Trump, also on CNN that night, accused Hill of making assumptions about an event he did not attend. Hill shot back: "Unless Steve Harvey turned into a policy analyst in the behind-the-scenes meeting, it doesn't matter whether I was there." To Hill, the African Americans visiting Trump Tower were "a bunch of mediocre negroes being dragged in front of TV as a photo op for Donald Trump's exploitative campaign against black people."

Marc Lamont Hill was immediately slammed by conservative talk radio and websites for denigrating the African Americans willing to talk to Trump when he called them "Negroes." Hill's use of the term suggested the black people meeting with Trump were acting as blacks of a time long ago when kowtowing was the only way for any black person to engage powerful white men. And, to be sure, it is wrong to imply that Steve Harvey, Jim Brown, Ray Lewis, and Kanye West are *just* comedians, athletes, and rappers. Each of these men has, to varying degrees, used their fame and money to give back to people of color living in tough neighborhoods. Harvey campaigned for Hillary Clinton, and actually took the meeting with Trump at the request of the outgoing Obama administration. The Obama team saw it as a small way for Trump's new White House to maintain ties with black culture leaders built and nurtured by the Obama White House.

But in retrospect, after more than a year of Trump's presidency, Hill's criticism was on target. There are still no black advisors with power inside the Trump White House. Blacks and Latinos with the best policy and conservative credentials got no job offers. Trump's *use* of Harvey, Brown, Lewis, and King III was an early example of the limited role Trump has for black people in his administration. His White House has become a model of the second-class, back-of-the-bus role that Trump's critics fear is all this president sees for black people in this country.

It is apparent that the most important function of Trump's black supporters is to push back against anyone who calls him a racist. Bruce LeVell—the man who sparred with Marc Lamont Hill on CNN—is an Atlanta jewelry company owner who endorsed Trump in 2015, telling an audience at a November 2015 rally in Macon, Georgia: "Donald Trump is not racist, guys." In April 2016 LeVell told the *Washington Post* that: "This man is no more racist than Mickey Mouse is on the Moon."

Whenever the president has made racially provocative statements, LeVell has been right there to defend him. When Trump was uniformly condemned for saying good people were among the white nationalists who rallied in Charlottesville, LeVell told CNN the following month that it was "disheartening to see this narrative being played out to put President Trump in this type of, you know, this category which is totally false."

According to LeVell, Trump meant to condemn "violence on all sides." Also in September, as the president was publicly feuding with mostly African American NFL players protesting police brutality by kneeling for the national anthem, LeVell told MSNBC that the players should "start your own league if you want to protest."

LeVell was never offered a job inside the Trump White House. But over and over again he played the role of a black man willing to attack the president's black critics.

BLACK VOICES

LeVell's role was played by several black people during the 2016 campaign. At times Trump has literally gone off script at his campaign rallies to call attention to the few African Americans in his overwhelmingly white audiences as evidence that he is not racist.

During a June 2016 campaign speech in Redding, California, Trump singled out a black man in the crowd and gushed: "Look at my African American over here. Look at him. Are you the greatest?" The black man in question, Gregory Cheadle, then a Republican candidate for California's First Congressional District, later told NPR, "I am not a Trump supporter," but went to the rally in Redding because "I have an open mind," and as he told CNN: "It was just a fun thing that happened."

But some of Trump's shout-outs to the lone black people at his events have turned out to be more politically sinister. During an October 5, 2016, speech in Sanford, Florida, a man carrying a "Blacks for Trump" sign was positioned by Trump's staff right up front near the lectern, where it could be seen in most television coverage of the event.

"I love those signs, 'Blacks for Trump,' oh ho ho," Trump gushed. "That seems to be the big surprise so far of this election. Blacks for Trump! Thank you, fellas."

As it turns out, the man with the 'Blacks for Trump' sign calls himself Michael the Black Man. He attended several Trump rallies, most famously seen right behind the president at an August 2017 speech in Phoenix, where he was wearing a T-shirt that read, "TRUMP & Republicans Are Not Racist." The shirt contains a URL address for his website—Gods2.com—which peddles various conspiracy theories. One of his provocative claims is that ISIS and Hillary Clinton are engaged in a "race war" to "KILL all BLACK WOMEN of America." He has also claimed that Cherokee Indians are secretly taking over the country.

Trump's white surrogates have also used cooperative black faces to deflect charges that they ran a racist campaign that led to a racist presidency. Following the blowback from Charlottesville, Trump's longtime lawyer, Michael Cohen, tweeted a pathetic collage of eight pictures featuring himself and various African Americans he described as his friends. The picture was captioned: "As the son of a holocaust survivor, I have no tolerance for #racism. Just because I support @POTUS @RealDonaldTrump doesn't make me a racist." Just like Trump, Cohen used black faces to escape criticism—in this case after Trump argued that both white nationalists *and* those who protested against them were responsible for the death of Heather Heyer, a white protestor who was run over and killed by a white supremacist.

Trump's use of black faces to defend himself from charges of racism led him to embrace people looking to make money from his political ascent. Beginning in the campaign, and following into the administration, Lynnette Hardaway and Rochelle Richardson, African American women from North Carolina—aka Diamond & Silk—made YouTube videos defending Donald Trump. Rather than debating policy or discussing what Trump might be able to do for African Americans, Diamond & Silk have cashed in on the spectacle of two black women defending a Republican candidate who received only 4 percent of black female voters. In the videos, which went viral, Diamond & Silk rap, drink what looks like Kool-Aid from wine glasses, and do take-downs of the NAACP, Eminem, Colin Kaepernick, Oprah Winfrey, Whoopi Goldberg, and Black Lives Matter activists—anyone who calls out Trump's racism. They speak in a loud, sassy, unapologetic, "tell it like it is" manner, playing to the stereotype of the "angry black woman" as silly, rude, and unfit for civil society. Trump has personally invited them onstage to speak at rallies around the nation. He has retweeted their videos. Records show that they were even directly paid by the campaign. They fit his role for black people perfectly. They not only excused his racist behavior but also entertained his overwhelmingly white fan base with a perverted, insulting rendition of African American culture, a kind of black minstrelsy that is as old as slavery itself.

And then there is Pastor Darrell C. Scott, a born-again Christian, founder of the New Spirit Revival Center, and cofounder—with Michael Cohen and Bruce LeVell—of the National Diversity Coalition for Trump. Pastor Scott delivered a keynote address in support of Trump at the Republican National Convention in summer 2016.

Again and again, though, Pastor Scott has proven to be an ineffective messenger. In November 2015, he volunteered to pull together a group of one hundred black ministers to meet with Trump and then endorse him. The ministers' names were even made public. Yet it turned out that Scott had signed up ministers who hadn't agreed to meet with Trump, let alone endorse him. "I never accepted Darrell's invitation to come," Detroit's Bishop Corletta Vaughn said in anger, "and I suddenly see my name on a flyer. There is no allegiance between the black church and the Trump campaign.... Don't use me to say the black female is behind you." The one-hundred-pastor endorsement never occurred, which Scott later explained to be the result of a "miscommunication that I take responsibility for."

It seems that Scott miscommunicated quite a bit during his short tenure with Trump. During a February 2017 listening session with black leaders in honor of Black History Month, the pastor reported that he had been in contact with Chicago gang leaders who were willing to cut deals with the Trump administration in order to lessen violence in the city. "I was recently contacted by some of the top gang thugs in Chicago for a sit-down," he said, who described the gang leaders as "guys straight from the streets—no politicians—straight street guys." He relayed that "they're going to commit that if they lower the body count, we'll come in and do some social programs."

Chicagoans were confused by Scott's promise to end gang violence in Chicago. "First of all, I've never heard of him before in my life," Michael Pfleger, a powerful Chicago Catholic priest and antidrug and gun control activist told CBS Chicago. "And second of all, if you've got this kind of relationship, where have you been?"

As it turned out, Scott had to go on a Chicago radio station later that afternoon and explain that he "misspoke." The truth is: "I only had three hours of sleep at the time. I meant to say former street thugs." In other words, the pastor hadn't been cutting deals with major gang leaders about how they could work with the administration to stop the violence. He'd simply been in contact with former, reformed gang members working on ways to stop the violence—a totally reasonable path to take, but not at all what he had promised in Trump's name earlier that day.

Despite these embarrassing episodes, President Trump never changed his strategy. He made no effort to get advice from African Americans who have devoted their life's work to dealing with the problems weighing on poor black people. At no point has he seemed interested in working with African Americans in law enforcement or public policy to hear the best available thinking on black-on-black crime. He has rejected efforts at community policing, in which police officers themselves are members of, and therefore understand and get along with, the communities they are assigned to protect. He made no effort to hear from African American gun control advocates who want to stop gang killings by limiting access to the stolen guns that, according to people dealing with the violence, are killing so many black people. He has ignored African American experts working on ways to reduce prison recidivism by reducing mandatory minimum sentences and making it easier for ex-cons to vote and re-enter the job market.

Trump's lack of interest in criminal justice reform is all the more difficult to watch because it comes at a moment when leading Senate and House Republicans have already signed onto proposals to lessen the racial imbalance in jails caused by mandatory sentencing rules. The harsh sentencing crushed poor blacks and became the subject of public debate under the theme of a cradle-to-prison pipeline for black men.

The lack of serious policy debate on topics of concern to black America has alienated the leaders of nearly every African American civil rights organization. Marc Morial, CEO of the National Urban League and former mayor of New Orleans, pointed to Trump "cutting civil rights offices at various departments." Morial had been critical of Trump's role as a leading supporter of the birther movement, suggesting President Obama was not an American because he falsely alleged Obama was born overseas. Derrick Johnson, president of the NAACP, was so disgusted with Trump he asked the president to stay away from the opening of the Mississippi Civil Rights Museum. Johnson told Roland Martin in a *TV One* interview that Trump would just use it as a "photo op.... He has done nothing to advance the cause of civil rights."

True, previous Republican administrations have had shaky and often downright antagonistic relationships with our nation's civil rights community. Many eyebrows were raised when then candidate Ronald Reagan appeared in August 1980 at the Neshoba County Fair in Mississippi—the same county where James Chaney, Andrew Goodman, and Michael Schwerner were lynched in 1964. Reagan intended to signal he was the white South's candidate by delivering a campaign speech on states' rights. President George W. Bush was widely criticized for his response to Hurricane Katrina, when, it was said, Bush didn't do nearly enough for the African American communities in New Orleans.

Yet these Republican presidents still saw political value in keeping open lines to black thinkers and leaders of historic civil rights organizations.

In August 1980, just after his appearance at the Neshoba State Fair, Reagan agreed to speak at an Urban League conference, pledging to "work together to solve the problems black America faces." In June 1981, only a few months after a black Alabaman named Michael Donald was beaten to death and hanged from a tree by Klansmen in Mobile, Reagan delivered a speech before an NAACP meeting in Denver. He condemned white racist "groups in the backwater of American life [who] still hold perverted notions of what America is about.... If I were speaking to them instead of to you, I would say to them, 'You are the ones who are out of step with our society. You are the ones who willfully violate the meaning of the dream that is America.'"

While campaigning for president in July 2000, George W. Bush addressed the NAACP, claiming that "discrimination is still a reality, even when it takes on different forms," an obvious break with prior conservatives' obliviousness to de facto discrimination: "Instead of Jim Crow there is racial redlining and profiling. Instead of 'separate but equal' there is 'separate but forgotten.'"

Bush's relationship with the NAACP did become enormously frayed when, in the fall of 2000, the group put out anti-Bush attack ads that used footage of the 1998 lynching of James Byrd, a black Texan who was dragged three miles by a pickup truck; Bush was the governor of Texas when the murder was committed. Byrd's daughter narrated the ad, claiming that when she heard Bush's refusal to support hate crime legislation during one of the presidential debates, it was like "my father [being] killed all over again." As a result, although he had addressed the group as a candidate, he didn't do so as president, and was on the verge of becoming the first president since Herbert Hoover not to speak to the organization. Yet Bush did eventually go to the NAACP in July 2006. Not only did he speak to the organization, but he addressed the tensions between the Republican Party and African American voters head-on, calling it "a tragedy that the party of Abraham Lincoln let go of its historic ties with the African-American community," and saying that "for too long my party wrote off the African American vote and many African Americans wrote off the Republican Party."

Yet during his campaign and early presidency, Donald Trump did not meet with either the NAACP or the Urban League. More damningly still, he has not met with or sought advice from black conservative experts and public intellectuals who've been not only willing but happy to assist previous Republican administrations. They too are disgusted by Trump.

Consider Thomas Sowell. A conservative to the bone, Sowell has called President Reagan "the most successful president of the United States." He has argued that the breakdown of the black family is *not* the result of slavery or Jim Crow but rather the "legacy of the welfare state." And in the September before the election, he told conservative radio host Ben Shapiro that a Hillary Clinton presidency would mean the permanent destruction of the First and Second Amendments. Yet Sowell has been enormously critical of Trump. In the same interview he told Shapiro that his "preference would be to leave the office vacant for four years and hope for better things." In a May 2016 article in the *National Review*, Sowell went so far as to argue that Trump, if elected, would spoil the image of the modern Republican Party, "an enduring affliction in future elections."

Similarly, Trump doesn't seem interested in seeking out the advice of black conservatives like Glenn Loury, a Brown University economist Ronald Reagan nominated as his undersecretary of education, or Walter E. Williams, an economist at George Mason University who worked on Reagan's transition team at the Department of Labor and later on as an informal advisor. He has no interest in Shelby Steele, a Reagan supporter and author of the important 1991 book, *The Content of Our Character*. There has been no successful Trump outreach to Robert Woodson, who helped create the Council for a Black Economic Agenda, which worked with the Reagan administration to redirect federal resources to local black communities and businesses. And there was no role for Armstrong Williams, the leading black owner of television stations in America and arguably the nation's top conservative black businessman.

The Trump administration has made no effort to seek advice from high-profile black Republicans, many of whom have publicly expressed their frustration with him. Following Charlottesville, Michael Steele, who chaired the Republican National Committee from 2009 to 2011, told a panel on MSNBC that the president had "pricked open" racial wounds "that we have been trying to heal since

Reconstruction." J. C. Watts, a black Republican who represented Oklahoma in Congress from 1995 to 2003, told MSNBC's Chuck Todd that Trump "doesn't understand the magnitude of what being a president is." Simone Perry, an African American who handles strategic partnership for Tea Party Patriots, told the *Washington Post* in April 2016: "We can no longer claim to be the party of freedom when we nominate a fascist, and we can't be the party of opportunity if we decide a racist can represent our values."

On the rare occasions Trump has sought out the advice from African American leaders—or, at the very least, the appearance of advice—he hasn't listened to them. A case in point was Trump's September 2017 meeting with Tim Scott (R-SC), the one black Republican in the US Senate.

Senator Scott, despite his party's fear of being labeled as the party of older, white America, is willing to break ranks and speak his mind on racial issues. In the summer of 2016, he delivered a powerful Senate floor speech detailing his own experience "driving while black," the scenario in which police officers are more likely to pull over black drivers because, it is assumed, they are doing something illegal. Scott noted that he'd been pulled over seven times that year. After Trump's mangled response to the white supremacist march in Charlottesville, Scott told *Vice News*, "I'm not going to defend the indefensible," that "what we want to see from our president is clarity and moral authority," and that Trump had "compromised" his "moral authority."

And yet, despite that condemnation, Scott met with Trump in September to discuss why so many Americans were perturbed by the president's reaction to Charlottesville. Following the meeting, he even gave Trump the benefit of the doubt, telling CBS that the president "has obviously reflected on what he's said, on his intentions and the perceptions of those comments," and that he was "very receptive to listening."

But Trump turned on the senator. On Air Force One the next day, Trump told reporters that it was Scott, not he, who had come around to his way of thinking during the meeting and agreed with his assessment that "especially in light of the advent of Antifa...you have some pretty bad dudes on the other side also," and *both* white nationalists and leftist protestors were to blame for what happened in Charlottesville. Trump totally misrepresented the black Republican's position. Scott did not like being used by Trump. In a follow-up statement, the senator's office sharply rebutted the president: "Antifa is bad...but white supremacists have been killing and tormenting black Americans for centuries. There is no realistic comparison. Period."

Indeed, the only African Americans President Trump seems to appoint as low-level advisors are people who see their role as limited to deflecting charges of racism aimed at the president. They also make a point not to challenge him on race.

President Trump's chosen black advisors seem to be celebrities and people with eyes full of dollar signs at the sight of the billionaire. Take Omarosa Manigault, for instance.

A graduate of Central State University with a Master's from Howard University, both HBCUs, and then an Al Gore and Bill Clinton staffer in the nineties, Omarosa became a minor celebrity as a cut-out-your-heart, mean-girl character on the first season of Trump's reality show, *The Apprentice*, in 2004. Omarosa was so popular as the villain that she also appeared on *All-Star Celebrity Apprentice*, as well as a short-lived Trump dating show called *The Ultimate Merger*.

Candidate Trump named her to be his campaign's director of African American outreach during the summer of 2016, and then, incredibly, as an assistant to the president and director of communications for the Office of Public Liaison in January 2017. Despite an absence of credentials and contacts, she was to serve as a liaison to the black community.

Yet Omarosa conducted herself in the White House in the same way she conducted herself on the *Apprentice*: a TV personality looking to stay in the news cycle. She had minimal ties to black leaders and thinkers and showed little interest in working to build relationships with influential black Americans. Earning $179,700 per year, Omarosa pocketed the highest level of pay for a senior White House staffer even though, as one headline in the *Daily Beast* put it succinctly: "No One Knows What Omarosa Is Doing in the White House—Even Omarosa." It's been reported that the administration simply created her position in order to ensure a black face could be seen near Trump in photographs. She raised many eyebrows when the *Daily Beast* reported that Omarosa held a personal bridal lunch and photo shoot in the White House in March 2017, in advance of her wedding that April.

But Omarosa did make news in the Trump White House. Last year she spread false rumors that April Ryan, a CNN analyst and White House correspondent for American Urban Radio Networks, was secretly paid by Hillary Clinton's campaign.

She made headlines again when CNN commentator Symone Sanders accused Omarosa of trying to intimidate people who disagreed with Trump. Sanders said during the National Association of Black Journalists Conference in August 2017, Omarosa "accosted me in the corner…in full display in the lobby of a hotel where everyone could see," and harangued her over comments that Sanders had made about Omarosa's role in the White House. During the same conference, Omarosa appeared on a panel to discuss police brutality but once more made headlines by getting into a loud confrontation with the moderator, Ed Gordon.

She had no better results with black conservatives. During an interview with the popular radio program *The Breakfast Club*, black CNN analyst Angela Rye reported that Omarosa felt threatened by more qualified black Republicans and made it harder for them to get positions in the administration. In another case *Politico* reported that Kay Coles James, who had worked for Presidents Reagan, George H. W. Bush, and George W. Bush, was blocked from joining the administration by Omarosa. She later became head of the conservative Heritage Foundation.

In December 2017, Omarosa was fired by General John Kelly, the White House chief of staff. But even then, she tried to stay in the news cycle, hinting that she'd be writing a revealing tell-all about racial comments and attitudes inside the Trump White House that made her uncomfortable. She told *Good Morning America*'s Michael Strahan that, as the only black woman senior staffer in the Trump White House, she saw things that "upset" her and not only "affected me deeply" but also "affected my community and my people." In full self-promotion mode Omarosa said that she had a "profound story that I know the world will want to hear."

The African American community, and African American women in particular, accused Omarosa of trying to cash in on her White House experience. Her departure from the White House was met with glee. "Bye, Felicia," said ABC's Robin Roberts, repeating a famous put-down for a mean girl getting her due by getting tossed. Yet this glee was accompanied by a dose of ambivalence. Despite her flaws, Omarosa was one of the *only* African Americans holding a position in Trump's senior staff or cabinet. The only African Americans left are Surgeon General Jerome Adams and Secretary of Housing and Urban Development Ben Carson. The HUD secretary ran against Trump for the GOP nomination and is an enormously accomplished doctor. But he has no experience working in housing and only seems to have been appointed because he is a rare African American who can successfully manage a relationship with Trump.

From Kanye West to Omarosa, Darrell Scott to Diamond & Silk, Jim Brown to Ray Lewis, the African Americans identified with President Trump are neither experienced at Washington politics nor wise about policies dealing with black America. The key characteristic of the black people he has embraced is that they are willing to defend him when he engages in racist behavior and comments. They do not challenge his portrayal of black Americans as a group of irresponsible people "living in hell," as he said during a 2016 presidential debate. They also tend to be upper-class or rich athletes and pop stars.

To Trump, the black middle class does not exist. The black policy expert does not exist. The black academic does not exist.

Black Americans under President Trump have no known, trusted presence in his inner circle, no one able to speak to him about how to handle race relations, about how to heal the racial wounds that he regularly aggravates. There is no Condoleezza Rice, an experienced foreign policy expert who is black, in his cabinet. There is no Colin Powell, the former secretary of state and chairman of the Joint Chiefs of Staff, regularly sitting with him. There is no Vernon Jordan, the former head of the Urban League and a respected lawyer, who was President Clinton's golfing partner.

It is not just the absence of smart black voices around Trump that creates a vacuum. He does not hire white people with appreciation for the history of the civil rights movement and an understanding of today's key racial issues. To the contrary, Trump hired people like Steve Bannon and Sebastian Gorka, people with ties to the "alt-right" universe of skinheads, neo-Nazis, and white supremacists.

The importance of having informed, well-connected, capable black and white voices speaking on civil rights near the president has been demonstrated across American history. For one example, when the notorious Bull Connor, the head of police in Birmingham, used mass arrests, attack dogs, and fire hoses against civil rights marchers, President Kennedy was able to have his Attorney General Bobby Kennedy and the assistant attorney general for civil rights, Burke Marshall, to negotiate a truce between the protest groups and the city's white leaders.

As singer-activist Harry Belafonte later wrote, "Without Bobby, the children may have stayed in jail a few days more. Violence might have erupted as angry parents filled the streets. Bull Connor might have declared martial law, and Birmingham might have gone up in flames, taking the delicate truce with it. Bobby deserved enormous credit, and I sensed, when I told him so, that he took quiet pride in having done not just what needed to be done, but what was the right thing, too."

Yet the concerned white attorney general also knew he needed to hear from black leaders. He told aides such conversations were important to his commitment to be fair to blacks in protecting their constitutional rights.

In Bobby Kennedy's eyes, the federal government was doing all it could to support black people marching for equal rights. It was the Kennedy administration that sent in the army to defend James Meredith's successful entry as the first black student at the University of Mississippi. It was the Kennedy administration that was proposing new civil rights legislation in February 1963. So why were so many black Americans so angry at him and his brother, President Kennedy?

All around the country, from Harlem to San Francisco, African Americans were becoming more militant in demanding immediate change on racial equality. Liberals like Kennedy could not understand why a man like Nation of Islam minister Malcolm X—who was not in the South fighting for civil rights—could gain so much black working-class support despite his criticism of leading civil rights activists. These were people who were putting their lives on the line in the South, including the revered Dr. Martin Luther King Jr., but Malcolm X dismissed them as "house Negroes" for fighting for integration. Then the attorney general got a letter from one of the leading black writers of the day, James Baldwin. It was a searing message that blamed the administration for the racial upheaval of the era, the kind of letter that would no doubt send someone like Donald Trump into a fit of anger and ill-considered tweets.

Yet unlike anyone with influence in the Trump administration, Robert Kennedy wanted to hear more from his own critics.

The attorney general's only personal knowledge of discrimination came from family stories about the bias faced by Irish immigrants to the United States in the late 1800s. He wanted to hear from Baldwin about the black experience with discrimination.

Baldwin was a child of poverty, did not know his biological father, and had left the country for years to escape the weight of racism against him as a black man. After World War I, Baldwin's mother,

Emma Jones, moved from Deal Island in southern Maryland for a better life up north in New York.

"A black boy born in New York's Harlem in 1924," as Baldwin recounted in a 1980 article for *Esquire*, "was born of southerners who had but lately been driven from the land." David Baldwin, a black man from Louisiana who married his single mother and whom James Baldwin considered to be his real father, was the child of a freed slave named Barbara. "He was of the first generation of freed men," Baldwin later wrote. "He, along with thousands of other Negroes, came north after 1919." David and Emma married in 1927 and had eight children together, giving James eight younger siblings. James's stepfather worked in a Long Island bottle factory by day and as a charismatic storefront preacher by night. That preaching included fiery stories of black people being lynched by whites and sad accounts of the damage done by slavery. James Baldwin's adopted father deeply resented white people, Baldwin would later note.

Like most of the African Americans living in Harlem—the northern section of Manhattan that, by 1920, held two-thirds of the borough's black population—the Baldwin family was poor. In a late essay entitled "Here be Dragons," Baldwin recounts literally racing a forty-year-old man to pick up a dime that someone had dropped at the subway station on 125th and Lenox: "Poverty is poverty and we were, if I may say so, among the truly needy." This combination of intense poverty, storefront religion, curiosity about one's unknown biological father, and the wounds of Southern slavery became the source material for Baldwin's breakthrough 1953 semiautobiographical novel, *Go Tell It on the Mountain.*

Despite the hard times, there was also joy. Harlem was the Mecca of the early twentieth century world of black artists and intellectuals. And Baldwin learned from these black voices, writing that "my education began, as does everyone's, with the people who towered over me, who were responsible for me, who were forming me. They were the people who loved me, in their fashion—whom I loved, in mine."

Baldwin had an innate desire to tell stories. He began as a speaker. In his teens he became a preacher like his stepfather, thrilling people from the pulpit of the Fireside Pentecostal Assembly. That led to writing. "I began plotting novels at about the time I learned to read," he recollected in the introduction to his 1955 collection of essays, *Notes of a Native Son*. He got support for his writing at school. Bill Porter, his African American ninth grade math teacher, took Baldwin to the New York Public Library's main branch one Saturday to do research for a paper entitled "Harlem—Then and Now." At a time when white policemen gave black kids a hard time for being anywhere outside of Harlem, Baldwin found a haven in the library, surrounded by white New York.

His good grades led him to be accepted into the celebrated De Witt Clinton High School in the Bronx, again outside of Harlem. Though the school was still mostly white, he got along well with the school's large number of left-wing Jewish students. He talked politics, testing out his ideas in poems, short stories, and plays, developing his "wiry, nervous, witty, argumentative" style, according to his biographer David Leeming. Baldwin as a high school student, Leeming wrote, already had "the verbal flamboyance that he had learned in part from his preaching, and which would mark his later work."

The next few years were difficult, yet transformative for Baldwin. He needed money, so he took a job laying railroad track in rural New Jersey. Unlike the cosmopolitan feel of Clinton High, southern Jersey was an openly racist area at the time. Baldwin was refused service at bars, diners, bowling alleys. People alternately ignored and insulted him. "I knew about Jim Crow, but I had never experienced it," he later wrote. Like his father, Baldwin developed an unmediated rage, a hatred of white people. At one point, Baldwin chucked a pitcher of water at a diner waitress who told him that "we don't serve negroes here."

It took some years for James Baldwin to translate this rage into art. Part of what did it was the death of his stepfather in late July 1943.

The funeral happened to coincide with the Harlem Riot of 1943, caused by a white cop shooting a black soldier. Driving with his family to the funeral through the wreckage of the rioting, Baldwin later wrote that he realized in that instant what mattered to him. "The dead man mattered, the new life mattered [his mother was pregnant again]; blackness and whiteness did not matter; to believe that they did was to acquiesce in one's own destruction."

But Baldwin's effort to make sense of racism remained strong, and was encouraged when he began working as a waiter at a restaurant on MacDougal Street called the Calypso, a haven for left-wing activists, artists, and writers. Here Baldwin was able to speak and socialize with literary giants like Jack Kerouac, Allen Ginsberg, and Henry Miller, and even some Harlem Renaissance icons like Claude McKay, Alain Locke, and the black Marxist historian C. L. R. James. He began writing reviews of other authors' books in the *Nation*, as well as essays in *Commentary*, even showing the already famous Richard Wright portions of the manuscript that would eventually become *Go Tell It on the Mountain*.

Despite the intellectually stimulating atmosphere of lower Manhattan, the young author—still in his early twenties—wanted out of the pressure that came with being black in the United States. In November 1948, at age twenty-four, he moved to Paris. Many major American authors either were living there or would pass through: his mentor Richard Wright, Truman Capote, Saul Bellow, Philip Roth, Chester Himes. Baldwin sat, spoke, and drank with them. But he also began writing and publishing the essays in literary magazines like *Commentary* and the *Partisan Review*. Baldwin was developing an audience. The editor of his 1950 essay in *Commentary* described Baldwin to readers as "the most promising young negro writer since Richard Wright." His reputation as a serious author of the day was secured with the publication of *Go Tell It on the Mountain* in 1953.

As Baldwin's literary career was gaining steam, so was the civil rights movement in the US. And "Baldwin was acutely aware of... his distance from it," explained Leeming. In a 1956 article for the

Partisan Review on famed white Southern author William Faulkner, Baldwin wrote that "Faulkner is so plaintive concerning this 'middle of the road' from which 'extremist' elements of both races are driving him that it does not seem unfair to ask just what he has been doing.... Where is the evidence of the struggle he has been carrying on there on behalf of the Negro?" Baldwin seemed to be writing about his own problem. As long as he stayed in Paris, he was just as guilty of not doing much to advance the front lines of the civil rights movement.

Baldwin made his first trip to the South in September and October 1957. His first stop was Charlotte, North Carolina, where he met Gus Roberts, one of the African American teenagers who was taunted by whites as he broke the color line at a previously all-white high school in Charlotte. He had his first ever conversation with Dr. Martin Luther King Jr. in Atlanta, which, along with another meeting with King during Baldwin's second tour of the South in the spring of 1960, became the source material for a 1961 *Harper's* essay called "The Dangerous Road Before Martin Luther King." Baldwin traveled to Montgomery, Alabama, and was so upset at having to use the "colored" entrance at a restaurant that when he got outside, he threw the food away, uneaten.

During his trips to the south, Baldwin's reporting centered on young people engaged in the student movement. In August 1960 he authored an article for *Mademoiselle* about the student movement, which concluded: "Americans keep wondering what has 'got into' the students. What has 'got into' them is their history in this country. They are not the first Negroes to face mobs; they are merely the first Negroes to frighten the mob more than the mob frightens them."

And yet—and this is crucial—even in an essay about the exploding black student movement Baldwin made it clear he was interested in talking to white people: "A population ignorant of its history and enslaved by a myth. And by this population I do not mean merely the unhappy people who make up the southern mobs. I have in mind nearly all Americans."

And that meant he wanted to talk to people like Attorney General Kennedy, people who condemned Southern racists without giving thought to their own role in the national story of continuing racial oppression.

"Northerners indulge in an extremely dangerous luxury," he warned in a 1960 article for *Esquire*. "They seem to feel that because they fought on the right side during the Civil War, and won, that they have earned the right merely to deplore what is going on in the south without taking any responsibility for it; and that they can ignore what is going on in northern cities because what is happening in Little Rock or Birmingham is worse."

To Baldwin, America's racial problem extended far above the Mason-Dixon line and resulted in hatred that would remain "no matter how many liberal speeches are made, no matter how many lofty editorials are written, no matter how many civil rights commissions are set up."

Baldwin's power as a writer reached full throttle in his landmark work *The Fire Next Time*. Excerpts were published in the *New Yorker* in November 1962, and the book came out in January. Widely considered Baldwin's magnum opus, the book allowed readers of all races inside the pain being felt by black people. It proved to be a primer for the troubles to come in the nine months after the book was published, as Americans lived through the assassination of Medgar Evers, and then the murder by bombing of the four black girls at the Sixteenth Street Baptist Church in Birmingham. Baldwin shared the pain to force a conversation about black rights with white people.

Split into two pieces of nonfiction, the first a short letter to his nephew "on the one hundredth anniversary of the Emancipation" and the second a much longer, sprawling essay on race, religion, and politics, *The Fire Next Time* was a banquet of insight into being a black American. For example, Baldwin described the unbelievable frustration felt by black World War II veterans who risked their lives for a nation that treated them worse than they were treated by Nazis in Europe. In the same book, he wrote about a dinner in Chicago he had been invited to by Elijah Muhammad, leader of the black group, the Nation of Islam, which saw white people as living devils.

The book was addressed to educated whites. That included the Kennedy administration and its white liberal allies. The president and the New England white liberals around him saw themselves as not racist and much better than the Southern governors keeping black children from going to school with white children. They counseled black activists to be patient. Their central advice to civil rights leaders was to refrain from confronting white segregationists with boycotts and marches that often led to violence and crowded jails. Their idea was that things would improve for black people if they just calmed down, remained patient, acknowledged all the progress that had already occurred, and trusted that more change would soon come.

These were false hopes, Baldwin argued. To the whites who "reference the triumphs of the N.A.A.C.P" as a barometer of how far African Americans had come, and how far they'd go if they just remained patient, Baldwin responded that "very few liberals have any notion of how long, how costly, and how heartbreaking a task it is to gather the evidence that one can carry into court." To the whites who spoke of the student sit-in movement as an example of how far blacks have come, Baldwin answered, "Not all Negroes are students and not all of them live in the south." He pointed out that too many white liberals were happy to applaud nonviolent protest in the South without understanding why blacks in the North considered nonviolence a cop-out. Baldwin argued: "The real reason that nonviolence is considered to be a virtue in negroes...is that white men do not want their lives, their self-image, or their property threatened." In a jab at what we now call "political correctness," Baldwin threw in "one wishes they [whites] would say so more often."

The Kennedy administration's repeated calls for a less militant, more pragmatic civil rights movement cut to the very core of black American frustration with well-intentioned white people. Baldwin charged that self-satisfied white civil rights advocates like the Kennedys falsely assumed that black people needed to be more like white people. "White Americans find it as difficult as white people elsewhere do to divest themselves of the notion that they are in possession of some intrinsic value that black people need, or want." This lie "makes the solution to the Negro problem depend on the speed with which Negroes accept and adopt white standards." And Baldwin said the error in such thinking is revealed in "Bobby Kennedy's assurance that a Negro can become president in forty years."

The November edition of the *New Yorker*, which excerpted most of the book, sold out. *The Fire Next Time* was on the *New York Times* best-seller list for forty-one weeks. Geoffrey Godsell, in his February 21, 1963, review for the *Christian Science Monitor*, wrote that the book was intended for "white liberals in New York, Chicago, or Boston" who "need no prompting to criticize things that have happened in Alabama or Mississippi" but who may not know "what is happening in their own backyards, in Harlem, the South Side, their own negro ghettoes." Godsell wagered that "perhaps no other negro writer is as successful as Mr. Baldwin in telling society just what it feels like to be a Negro in the United States."

Dan Wakefield, reviewing the book for the *New York Times* that April, wrote that Baldwin had meant to "disturb as well as to engage and inform" all readers no matter whether "we are white or black, northern or southern, conservative or liberal; if we are both American and literate, these letters are addressed to us."

In its February 2 review, a Long Island newspaper called *Newsday* noted that the book was "aimed at those who believe they are 'liberal' on Negro problems . . . and is calculated to shake them and shock them." It is "a mind-jolting book; highly-recommended for those sensitive enough to be touched by it and sturdy enough to take it."

It is unclear whether Bobby Kennedy read *The Fire Next Time*. But the book was a cultural sensation, and by the winter and spring of 1963, most well-educated Americans knew about Baldwin. During the months after *The Fire Next Time* was released, Baldwin's face appeared on the cover of *Time*. The writer was now the public intellectual face of the civil rights movement.

Baldwin was not one of the black people with pictures of President Kennedy and Dr. King prominently displayed at home. And he did not speak about the Kennedy administration in mythical terms as "Camelot." He saw the president and his brother as two white men reluctant to put themselves on the line to deal with the urgent need to protect blacks from racist whites. Baldwin first met the attorney general at the White House during an April 1962 dinner honoring Nobel Prize laureates. But even that meeting did not change his feelings. He was furious that the Kennedy administration hadn't responded more strongly to Birmingham. By May 1963 he sent Attorney General Kennedy the following telegram:

> Those who bear the greatest responsibility for the chaos in Birmingham are not in Birmingham. Among those responsible are J. Edgar Hoover, Senator Eastland, the power structure which has given Bull Connor license, and President Kennedy, who has not used the great prestige of his office as the moral forum which it can be. This crisis is neither regional nor racial. It is a matter of the national life or death. No truce can be binding until the American people and our representatives are able to accept the simple fact that the Negro is a man.

That cutting note would go straight to the trash can in the Trump administration. But in the Kennedy Administration, the attorney general was willing to listen to Baldwin and learn about why so many African Americans were angry not only at white segregationists but at him, the president, and other moderate white leaders around the country. He invited Baldwin to his home, an estate named Hickory Hill in McLean, Virginia, for breakfast with himself and the assistant attorney general for civil rights, Burke Marshall.

Eating poached eggs and drinking coffee, Bobby Kennedy and James Baldwin—born within a year and a half of each other—were the perfect odd couple. One of Baldwin's early biographers, Fern

Eckman, wrote in 1966 that the attorney general was "handsome, virile, clever, born to wealth and security and social position, by temperament enamored of sports and challenged by mountain peaks, a prime example of the cult of charisma, [the kind of man with political power and authority that] Baldwin instinctively distrusts."

Yet the attorney general's lack of pretense in asking Baldwin questions about the insistent anger among black people appealed to Baldwin's desire to be heard by the nation's top leaders.

"How important do you think the Black Muslims are?" Kennedy asked.

Baldwin didn't much care for Elijah Muhammad or the Nation of Islam more generally. And yet he bluntly told the attorney general: "The 'extremists' best articulate the Negro's pain and despair."

Kennedy pressed on in search of political compromise: "What do Negroes want?" "Which Negroes will other Negroes listen to?"

Baldwin was not a politician and not given to political solutions. Civil rights to Baldwin was a deeply felt, moral issue. And so he told Kennedy he needed to hear from black thinkers and artists who best gave voice to the pain and the dispossession felt by so many blacks. He told Kennedy he had to sit down with a writer like Loraine Hansberry, a singer like Harry Belafonte, and civil rights activists like the Freedom Riders. And so they struck a deal. If Baldwin assembled a group, the attorney general would meet with them and hear them out in New York the following day.

It took someone with Baldwin's network among African American artists, activists, and thinkers to get so many celebrated people to agree to come to the meeting in just one day's time.

Baldwin got singer Harry Belafonte and Lorraine Hansberry, author of the popular play *A Raisin in the Sun*, to agree to attend. Rip Torn, a white actor Baldwin wanted to star in his play *Blues for Mister Charlie*, was only asked whether he could attend the meeting around midnight, after performing in that night's rendition of Eugene O'Neil's play *Strange Interlude*. He, too, agreed to talk with the attorney general.

Baldwin also got singer Lena Horne to fly in from Palm Springs. She didn't know Baldwin well but respected his work immensely.

They got Edwin Berry, who headed the Urban League in Chicago; Clarence B. Jones, Dr. King's advisor and speechwriter and Baldwin's lawyer; famed black intellectual and psychologist Kenneth Clark; and Henry Morgenthau, who produced Dr. Clark's television show. He also got a yes from black twenty-five-year-old Jerome Smith, a Freedom Rider and CORE worker who "had probably spent more months in jail and been beaten more often than any other CORE member," one historian later reflected.

During a lunch interview with *New York Times* drama critic Lewis Funke on the day of the meeting, Baldwin let loose that "I'm going to a secret meeting with Bobby Kennedy this afternoon. Right from here, in fact." Funke's eyes went wide, and he told Baldwin, "That's a hell of a story," and asked, "Do you mind if I tell my paper? Because I will anyway." Baldwin responded: "Not at all."

With the media now alerted to what was happening, on the afternoon of Friday, May 24, 1963, the group assembled at Bobby Kennedy's apartment on 24 Central Park South—two blocks north and less than one avenue west of where Trump Tower now stands.

By nearly all accounts, the Baldwin-Kennedy meeting was disorganized and stressful. Some people had to sit on foot stools because of the lack of chairs. Though Baldwin had wanted to assemble as diverse a group as possible, he had no real strategy, no agenda for what to say to Kennedy. Some of them, particularly the whites, like actor Rip Torn, didn't know why Baldwin wanted them to come along.

But the real problem, at least according to Kennedy, was that Baldwin and his fellow artists and activists never acknowledged what his administration had done to help black people dealing with Bull Connor in Birmingham. Instead, for nearly three hours—the meeting was supposed to last only two—the black men and women James Baldwin had collected accused Kennedy, again and again, of failing to do enough for black people.

Jerome Smith, the black Freedom Rider, started the conversation with the following line: "It makes me nauseous to be here." By this, he meant that it was ridiculous that he should have to explain to the attorney general why it was the duty of the president to protect Freedom Riders and nonviolent protestors from racist segregationists who were out to lynch them.

Irritated, the attorney general shot back: "I'm not going to sit here and listen to that kind of talk."

Yet Smith didn't much care about the type of "talk" that Bobby Kennedy wanted to hear. He kept describing the abuse black rights workers endured in the South, how his wife and kids had been put in danger. When Baldwin asked Smith whether, given all of the pain he had endured from fellow countrymen, he could ever fight for the United States in the army, Smith said that he could not. Kennedy, clearly mad, exclaimed: "Oh, I can't believe that!"

David Baldwin, James's brother, chimed in: "By God, you'd better believe it!" Kennedy told David, "There is no need to use such language."

In reality it wasn't David Baldwin's impropriety that bothered Bobby Kennedy. Rather, it was the fact that after the American victory in World War II over Nazis and fascists, he was hearing a group of American citizens say they would not fight for the freedoms that exist in the United States. Kenneth Clark later noted that the attorney general "seemed genuinely unable to understand what Smith was trying to say." Burke Marshall later noted, "The thing the Attorney General really [disputed] was that no Negro would fight for the United States—and, by implication—no Negro would fight for the United States *ever*."

Things continued like this, with Baldwin's group shutting down Bobby Kennedy on every issue that was brought up. When the participants began discussing the federal government's unwillingness to investigate crimes against African Americans in segregated Southern towns, Baldwin addressed Kennedy directly: "Let me give you an example of what we're talking about, if I may intrude here. If I'm walking down Main Street in, let us say, Montgomery, Alabama, and three white men come up to me and beat me up and castrate me, the FBI might be assigned to the case. And the odds are that the FBI man who investigates the case will be one of those three who castrated me."

When Kennedy protested Baldwin's characterization of federal investigations as corrupt, Lena Horne, the black singer, chimed in: "But Mr. Attorney General—you've never been a Negro being questioned by the FBI in the Deep South...have you?"

Here, Burke Marshall tried to come to the defense of the federal government, saying that when FBI agents were deemed incompetent, the administration would send out "special men." This answer, was met with "almost hysterical laughter," Kenneth Clark later recalled.

At one point, Kennedy tried to counter their arguments about African American oppression, saying that his ancestors, as Irish immigrants, had been oppressed too. Yet they had, through their hard work, been able to make it. To this, Baldwin countered back: "You do not understand at all. Your grandfather came as an immigrant from Ireland and your brother is President of the United States. Generations before your family came as immigrants my ancestors came to this country in chains, as slaves. We are still required to supplicate and beg you for justice and decency."

In effect, the May 24, 1963, meeting at Kennedy's apartment was a microcosm of the argument that Baldwin had made in *The Fire Next Time*: that as long as white Northerners, liberals, and American presidents understood racism as an exclusively Southern problem caused by hooded Klansmen in Mississippi, as long as they believed that these issues could be resolved with a few soldiers here and some executive orders there, as long as white Americans did not fundamentally transform their own complicity in this system, America's racial problems could not be solved.

Kenneth Clark later reflected: "Suddenly I looked at the Attorney General and understood that he did not understand us and for just a minute I felt for him.... We were asking him to stop thinking about this as the special problem of a particular group of people and to begin to think about it as an American problem."

Whereas Marshall and Kennedy wanted to focus the conversation on Jim Crow states, Baldwin's people wanted to talk about a lot more. They also wanted to tell these powerful white men about the pain of being black and corralled in Northern city ghettos with bad schools and no jobs.

The meeting ended with Hansberry standing up, shaking Kennedy's hand, saying, "Good-bye, Mr. Attorney General," and leading the others out of the room.

Harry Belafonte tried to patch up some of the hurt feelings. He told Kennedy that, despite the criticism, "of course you have done more for civil rights than any other Attorney General." Kennedy shot back: "Why do you say this to me? Why didn't you say this to the others?"

Nor were things helped by Clarence Jones, Dr. King's lawyer, who told the attorney general: "I just want to say that Dr. King deeply appreciates the way you handled the Birmingham Affair." Kennedy accused Jones of "watch[ing] these people attack me over Birmingham for forty minutes and you didn't say a word. There's no point in your saying this to me now."

Kennedy later said he felt that the actors, activists, and writers were a bunch of whiners who knew nothing of politics. "They don't know what the laws are—they don't know what the facts are," Kennedy told his biographer, Arthur Schlesinger. "You can't talk to them the way you can talk to Martin Luther King or Roy Wilkins. They didn't want to talk that way." Kennedy concluded that "it was all emotion, hysteria." In the years following the meeting, the FBI opened a file on Baldwin. It is still unclear whether this decision was made at Kennedy's direction.

Baldwin, meanwhile, was shocked by how much the attorney general did not know. During a Channel 13 interview later that night with Kenneth Clark, Baldwin noted, "It was a great shock to me—I want to say this on the air—that the Attorney General did not know…that I would have trouble convincing my nephew to go to Cuba, for example, to liberate the Cubans in the name of a government which now says it is doing everything it can do but cannot liberate me [inside the United States]."

Bobby Kennedy and James Baldwin never resolved their differences. But the fact is that they did meet. They did talk. And they brought other people into a national conversation about race.

There was no moment where the attorney general telephoned Baldwin and told him he was right about everything. And Baldwin never apologized for demanding immediate action from the attorney general.

Baldwin's career continued on. In February 1965 he traveled to Britain to debate a leading American conservative, William F. Buckley, at the historic, all-white Cambridge Union on the question "Has the American Dream been achieved at the expense of the American Negro?" Baldwin won the debate. According to the *New York Times*, he was honored with a "two minute standing ovation from the nearly 1,000 Cambridge University students." The author continued to write through the decades. He passed away in 1987.

And yet Bobby Kennedy's brief, tense, uncomfortable encounter with James Baldwin did affect the attorney general, even if Kennedy never truly acknowledged it. Nick Katzenbach, Kennedy's Deputy Attorney General, later reflected that "after Baldwin, he was absolutely shocked." Schlesinger, in his 1978 biography of Robert Kennedy, noted that the attorney general "began, I believe, to grasp as from the inside the nature of black anguish. He resented the experience, but it pierced him all the same. His tormentors no sense, but in a way they made all sense."

Other historians have also suggested that the meeting with Baldwin convinced Bobby Kennedy to take on a much stronger civil rights position. It was, in part, on Bobby Kennedy's prodding that his brother, President John F. Kennedy, delivered civil rights legislation to Congress that summer that would eventually become the land-mark Civil Rights Act of 1964.

Baldwin biographer David Leeming writes that "in retrospect... it seems possible that the meeting was at least in part responsible for the Kennedy administration's apparent awakening...to the impor-tance of civil rights." Bobby Kennedy's meeting with Baldwin may very well prove the old saying right: that the best friends are the ones who tell you not what you want to hear but what you need to hear.

We will never know entirely how Bobby Kennedy felt about James Baldwin, or how big of a role the Baldwin meeting played in the Kennedy administration's subsequent actions on behalf of civil rights. The administration's decision to send Civil Rights legislation to Congress that summer was the result of many different historical and political factors. Yet what we know for certain is that Bobby Kennedy listened to James Baldwin. He didn't like what Baldwin had to say, but he heard him out.

Future US presidents would continue in this trend, developing special relationships with African American intellectual and political leaders. Even as the Republican Party solidified its status as the party of white Southerners and Midwesterners, their presidents made sure to seek the advice of prominent African American thinkers. Many participants in the December 1980 Black Alternatives Conference—a meeting of prominent black conservative thinkers that was held at the Fairmont Hotel in San Francisco and is now known as the Fairmont Conference—have played crucial roles in the modern con-servative movement: Thomas Sowell, Clarence Thomas, Walter E. Williams, and Clarence Pendleton. The event was sponsored by the Institute for Contemporary Studies, cofounded by top Reagan advi-sor Ed Meese. A few years later, President George H. W. Bush named Colin Powell chairman of the Joint Chiefs of Staff. President George W. Bush appointed two African American secretaries of state: Colin Powell and Condoleezza Rice.

Donald Trump, though, doesn't seem particularly interested in black conservatism. Just four years after the Republican National

Committee pledged to do more to woo black and Hispanic voters, Trump thought it was a better strategy to appeal to white discomfort with rising numbers of immigrants of color and black protests against police brutality. Instead of talking to leading black conservatives like Thomas Sowell and Colin Powell, he brought Omarosa to the White House.

Trump considers African Americans who criticize him unpatriotic, ungrateful, and, in the case of Barack Obama, *literally* un-American. This is a perspective that extends beyond the president. A 2012 American National Election Study found that less than 30 percent of whites feel that most African Americans are "very" or "extremely" patriotic, whereas more than half of white respondents felt that most whites were "very" or "extremely" patriotic.

Most insulting of all, he thinks that black voters are going to support him just because some of their best-known rappers, football players, and reality TV stars show up at Trump Tower. What is missing are leading black voices in American life, specifically those who speak in the tradition of cultural critics like James Baldwin, the writer who became celebrated for shouting and shaming the nation to take action against racism.

CHAPTER 5
EMPLOYMENT

THE WORDS THAT INSPIRED the title of this book came during a Trump campaign speech that many news reports falsely described as being addressed to African Americans. In really, it was a speech about them, not to them.

"No group in America has been more harmed by Hillary Clinton's policies than African Americans," Trump said at a 2016 campaign speech in Dimondale, Michigan. "If Hillary Clinton's goal was to inflict pain on the African-American community, she could not have done a better job. It is a disgrace."

Anyone watching Trump's speech could see that there were few black people in his audience. He was talking to a raucous rally full of older, suburban whites about those scary black people in the "inner city," so threatening to orderly suburban life. He was not calling for new efforts to help those trapped in bad neighborhoods. His point was to mock black people for stupidly ignoring their best interests by voting for Democrats instead of him.

"Look at how much African American communities are suffering from Democratic control," he told his white fans. "To [black people], I say the following: what do you have to lose by trying something new like Trump? What do you have to lose? I say it again: what do you have to lose? Look, you're living in poverty. Your schools are no good. You have no jobs. 58 percent of your youth is unemployed. What the hell do you have to lose?"

This fraudulent depiction of black life was a persistent campaign theme. Trump was telling whites that all blacks needed to do to fix their problems was to get in on "winning" by supporting him.

Later, after being criticized for saying that "fine people" marched with violent white supremacists in Charlottesville, the president was asked what he believes "needs to be done to overcome the racial divide." He repeated the same libel against black people, presenting them as a group of unemployed people waiting for help: "Jobs [are] going to have a big impact—I think if we continue to create jobs— over a million, substantially over a million—I think that's going to have a tremendous impact, a positive impact, on race relations."

It is true that a disproportionate percentage of black people remain in poverty. As President Obama reminded the nation in August 2013, the fiftieth anniversary of the March on Washington: "Yes, there have been examples of success within black America that would have been unimaginable a half century ago. But...black unemployment has remained almost twice as high as white unemployment.... The gap in wealth between races has not lessened; it's grown." Civil rights leaders said much the same thing when some economists celebrated rising black family income in the 1970s. Yes, many black people thrived when barriers of racial segregation started to come down and doors of opportunity opened. And yes, it is also true that poorly educated black people did not have the skills to take advantage of the new landscape. They were stuck and left behind. As the NAACP official John A. Morsell wrote in the *Crisis* in 1971, "here is where the misery is piled up, thick and toughly resistant—here is where the social dynamite is packed away."

President Obama and the NAACP called for the federal government to lift up those black people crushed by social and systemic problems—from a high number of single mothers to bad schools with high dropout rates. But Trump revels in vilifying them, offering stereotypes to stigmatize poor black people and stir up racial resentment in his white audiences. And he continues to caricature all black people as desperate for any job, even though that is far from the truth.

Even if Trump's distorted view of black workers is dismissed as mere political rhetoric from a racist man, there is danger here. His lies negatively influence public perception of black people. They also derail important discussions on the best economic and social policies to help the majority of black workers who are employed, who are in the middle class, and who are striving to stay there. Trump has yet to put on the table any ideas for helping the black middle class improve their financial stability. Where is his platform to create increased opportunities for job training and college education to promote black middle-class growth? Is he making health care more affordable for working-class families? Is he increasing access to capital necessary to start any business?

This is the heart of the financial challenge facing black America. Middle-class black families still lag far behind white families in achieving the financial stability that comes with savings, investments, and home ownership. "The typical black household . . . posses[ed] just 6 percent of the wealth owned by the typical white household," according to 2015 study by the Institute for Assets & Social Policy at Brandeis University. The median white household had $111,146 in wealth, the study found, while the median black household had only $7,113 in wealth. Also, 73 percent of white households owned their homes in 2011, while just 45 percent of black households were homeowners.

Closing the wealth gap requires honest assessments. Yet Trump does not even have his facts straight. For example, during the 2016 campaign he repeatedly said 58 percent of black youth are unemployed. The facts told a different story. Roughly 16 percent of African Americans between sixteen and twenty-four years old who wanted a job had no job. That is a far different magnitude of unemployment.

Solutions to that smaller but still significant level of youth unemployment are tied to improved outcomes for black students in schools and increased opportunities for youth job training. It is not a basis for speaking with contempt about black American youth as failures in the American economy.

Trump's twisted perspective does not allow him to respect the steady if slow economic advancement by black America from slavery to the American middle class. It is an inspiring story.

"The story of blacks in America is one of a people who refused to accept their dehumanization, fought for the Union, rose up from slavery, defied bombings, police dogs and water cannons to defeat segregation, demanded the country be true to what is said on paper and made America a better place for all its citizens," columnist Michael Gerson wrote in the *Washington Post*. "It is one of history's greatest stories of the human spirit, and Trump knows nothing of it."

No one person can take credit for the great story of black economic progress. But there is one man who deserves credit for setting in place the building blocks that created the black middle class of today: A. Philip Randolph.

The leader of the nation's first major union of black workers, Randolph came up with the idea for the 1963 march on Washington—the event that raised pressure on the White House and Congress to pass the 1964 Civil Rights Act.

When the marchers chanted "Pass the Bill," they were asking Congress to act on Randolph's demand for a civil rights law that punished employers who did not follow equal employment opportunity rules when they had jobs to fill.

In 2018, more than fifty years later, the Civil Rights Act's protections for black workers stand as the cornerstone of the largest black middle class in world history. Today 38 percent of black American households earn between $35,000 and $100,000 a year. Another 11 percent of black households take in between $100,000 and $200,000 annually. That means close to half of all black households are within or beyond the American middle class.

Randolph had a golden reputation as a fighter for black workers long before the March on Washington and the 1964 Civil Rights Act. In 1925 he became president of the Brotherhood of Sleeping Car Porters. That made him the first national black labor leader. The Pullman Company, a railroad car manufacturer, was the largest employer of African Americans at the time. Yet its employees were underpaid, never promoted, and too often treated with contempt by white travelers. Randolph unionized over half of the Pullman porters within a year of the union's formation. Under his leadership, the porters won overtime pay, a longer weekend, and roughly $2 million in pay raises—setting out a written framework for other industries to end exploitation of black workers.

Randolph's power reached into the White House. More than twenty years before he organized the historic March on Washington, he threatened a similar march if President Franklin D. Roosevelt did not ban employment discrimination in the defense industries. The president relented and ordered equal opportunity for those jobs in June 1941. Randolph then successfully pressured President Harry Truman in July 1948 to integrate the armed forces. And he later became the leading voice for black workers at the top of the AFL-CIO, further dismantling employment discrimination by demanding that black people be allowed entry in segregated labor unions. Those years of heavy lifting by Randolph successfully put in place the cornerstones that allowed the black middle class to be built over the next half century.

By 1963, when Randolph was seventy-four, he was still pushing to end bias against black workers. That is when he came up with the idea to repeat the call for a March on Washington. The threat of the march had been successful in opening some federal jobs to black people in 1941. Now he wanted a march to stand against job discrimination in the private sector. Randolph's lifetime of standing up for black workers made him a hero among younger, more militant civil rights activists. And he was revered by more moderate activists, like Dr. King and leaders in the NAACP, for breaking down segregation inside organized labor unions. Randolph used his stature to get rival civil rights leaders and rival union leaders to cooperate in planning and supporting the 1963 march.

After the march, Randolph's stature gave him access to congressional leaders and the White House. Randolph argued for the new law to go beyond making it illegal for employees to pass over, deny, advertise to or "otherwise...discriminate...limit, segregate or classify" employees and potential employees based on religion, sex, and national origin. He wanted the federal government to put its muscular law enforcement power into protecting equal job opportunities for all black workers. And he won when the bill allowed for the creation of the Equal Employment Opportunity Commission, a federal agency where workers could report employment discrimination. By 1972, the EEOC was given the right to bring civil suits against employers. And all employers with over one hundred employees were required to fill out forms indicating their employees' makeup by race and gender.

These powers within the Civil Rights Act of 1964, as prescribed by Randolph, resulted in the federal government bringing major lawsuits in the 1970s charging well-known corporations with hiring bias against black workers. Those companies included AT&T, United Auto Workers, Sears, General Electric, General Motors, Ford Motor Company, Goodyear Tire, and Uniroyal—all leading American employers and top brands. Seeing those companies called into court for hiring bias sent a sharp message to even the smallest companies about the urgent need to improve their minority hiring record. The alternative was to spend time and money defending themselves against federal charges of hiring discrimination.

"Fear is not too strong a word to use about the way companies feel about the EEOC now," noted one attorney at the US Chamber of Commerce. Writing in 1976, economist Richard Freeman noted that "federally required programs involving job quotas that favor minorities have made minority hiring an explicit goal of major corporations."

By 1979, half of the Fortune 500 companies that responded to a Heidrick & Struggles poll said they considered affirmative action when considering management adjustments. The poll also found that nearly half percent of Fortune 500 companies admitted that they had been threatened with loss of a government contract if they didn't comply with EEOC standards.

Reforms were made in federal contracting as well. A year after Congress passed the Civil Rights Act, President Johnson signed Executive Order 11246, which required private employers with over fifty employees and federal contracts worth more than $50,000 to prove their workforces included people of color and women. President Richard Nixon used that executive order to develop the Philadelphia Plan, which required construction companies in Eastern Pennsylvania to hire a preset percentage of black workers for their workforce unless they could show an absence of minorities capable of handling the jobs. Nixon's secretary of labor, George Schultz, wanted to increase the proportion of black people in Philadelphia's predominately white construction industry by 20 percent over four years.

The Republican Nixon administration also called for hiring more black people for government jobs. Issued on August 8, 1969, Nixon's Executive Order 11478 stated: "The head of each executive department and agency shall establish and maintain an affirmative program of equal employment opportunity for all civilian employees." That executive order yielded tremendous results. By the early 1970s, 57 percent of black male college graduates and 72 percent of black female college graduates took up government positions after college. By 1980, 27 percent of African Americans of working age worked for the public sector. Nixon's emphasis on affirmative action shaped federal government policies even after he resigned the presidency during the Watergate scandal. In 1977, Congress passed the Public Works Employment Act, which required that 10 percent of government public works funds be set aside for minority contractors.

Local and state politicians followed the federal government's lead. That was especially true as black migration from the South and white flight to the suburbs led to a wave of black mayors in major cities— more than two hundred by the late 1970s.

By 1978, black mayors led eight of the ten cities with the highest proportion of black workers in administrative positions. Black mayors also transformed the racial makeup of their police forces. Between 1967 and 1978, which coincides with Maynard Jackson's first four years as Atlanta's mayor, the percentage of positions held by black people in Atlanta's police force increased from 9 percent to 30 percent. Similarly, the percentage of black people in Detroit's police force increased from 5 percent to 30 percent under that city's first black mayor, Coleman Young.

Having the power of federal law enforcement on the side of equal job opportunities for black workers was Randolph's goal when he started black labor organizing in the 1920s. In the years since he pushed for passage of the Civil Rights Act, the results are stunning:

- In 2016, African Americans made up 9.1 percent of all Americans employed in management, professional, and related occupations.
- They made up 12.6 percent of Americans employed in sales and office jobs.
- 12.5 percent of preschool and kindergarten teachers are black, as are 10.3 percent of elementary and middle school teachers, and 15.9 percent of dietitians and nutritionists.

In public sector employment, African Americans are actually overrepresented. In 2014, African Americans made up 18.1 percent of the federal workforce. A 2011 study done by UC Berkeley's Center for Labor Research and Education found that, before the 2008 recession, an African American was 33 percent "more likely to be employed in the public sector compared to a non-black worker." In fact, 21 percent of US Postal Service workers are black. The same high proportion of black people can be found in the military. In 2015, African Americans made up 17 percent of active duty soldiers.

Clearly, most African Americans go to work every morning. Contrary to President Trump's harmful rhetoric, they are not lying around. They are not standing in the unemployment line.

And most of their jobs can't be categorized as small farmers, day laborers, nannies, and maids—the low-end jobs that define black employment in President Trump's distorted thinking.

The facts are clear on this point. In 1950, 24.6 percent of black men worked in farming, forestry, and fishing, all professions that require less schooling and more manual labor. In 2010, just 2.8 percent of black men worked in these industries, marking a drastic shift out of farm fields and into the cubicle. In 1960, some 37.5 percent of employed African American women worked as private nannies and housekeepers—a profession signified by the "mammy" figures in *Gone with the Wind* and Kathryn Stockett's book-turned-movie *The Help*. By 1989, they made up just 3.5 percent of employed black women. In 1960, 60 percent of employed black women worked as service workers (either cooks, janitors, hospital attendants, waitresses, nurses, or domestics). By 1989, the percentage of black women working in the service industry was more than cut in half, to 27.3 percent.

And despite Trump repeatedly telling black people that "you have no jobs," in December 2016 the African American unemployment rate was 7.4 percent, going all the way down to 6.8 percent at the start of 2018. African Americans made up 11.9 percent of employed US citizens over sixteen in 2016—just short of their total share of the United States population, which is 13.3 percent.

Even with a persistently high black poverty rate of 25 percent in 2018 and black unemployment rate at 6.8 percent—still about twice the white unemployment rate—the incredible reality of a thriving black middle class stands as the most consequential achievement of the civil rights movement.

To be sure, there is still much work to be done. The white median household income—$62,950 in 2015—is still almost twice that of the median African American household income, $36,898. And African Americans are not yet represented in the highest paid professions.

In 2016, black people made up just 4.4 percent of lawyers, 7.5 percent of physicians and surgeons, and 3.4 percent of business and financial chief executives. Closing these gaps will depend on continuing to build on policies, first enacted during the civil rights movement, to offer more working-class and middle-class black Americans the chance to enroll in top colleges, get credentialed for high-tech and high-paying jobs, lessen the pay gap, and open banks and businesses.

Across the board, from public sector to private sector jobs, the incredible rise of striving black workers is evident in US Census data. Between 1950 and 2010, the percent of African American men working in managerial and professional jobs—careers that paid a median salary of $67,681 in 2010—rose from 3.9 percent in 1950 to 16.5 percent in 2010, according to researchers at Indiana University. That is a 323 percent increase. The share of black women in those professions rose from 6.5 percent in 1950 to 24.8 percent in 2010—a 281 percent increase. By comparison, during that same time frame, the percent of white men working in managerial and professional jobs rose from 17.5 percent to 27.4 percent, which translates to just a 57 percent increase, and the share of white women in those professions rose from 16.5 percent in 1950 to 33.7 percent in 2010—a 104 percent increase.

Also between 1950 and 2010, the share of black men working in technical, sales, and administrative positions—with a $40,663 median income in 2010—rose from 4.4 percent to 21 percent, a 377 percent increase. The share of black women working in these professions rose from 6.4 percent to an astonishing 36.6 percent—a 471 percent increase—while the share of white women working in these positions shrank from 41.6 percent to 38.5 percent.

These numbers tell a story of recovering from slavery at a tremendous rate once the free market was open to their talents and with the help of antidiscriminatory policies created by American government and business.

But Donald Trump doesn't seem to care that much about carefully constructed government policies meant to ensure that more African Americans have a chance to compete on equal footing for better jobs. As a real estate magnate, Mr. Trump saw the equal employment clause of the Civil Rights Act as red tape—government interference in the form of annoying rules and regulations that didn't help his businesses make money.

Examples of this attitude abound in Trump's history as a businessman; some, like his removal of black employees from his casino when a racist gambler came to visit, are recounted elsewhere in this book. During an interview with Bryant Gumbel, also recounted in this book, Trump went so far as to say that well-educated African Americans were better off than their white peers, as part of a general critique of affirmative action. And so it comes as no surprise that President Trump has begun reversing and eliminating the very same programs that have helped so many African Americans get better jobs and better pay.

During the campaign, candidate Trump promised repeatedly to "drain the swamp." A catchphrase used previously by President Ronald Reagan and Pat Buchanan, "drain the swamp" means shrinking the size of government, streamlining federal agencies, and letting go of unnecessary employees. Tax dollars, they say, are being wasted on bureaucracy.

"Drain the swamp" means something entirely different to, let's say, a black woman whose steady job as a case worker at the Social Security Administration has allowed her to pay off her home mortgage and raise a family. "If you're black and work for the federal government," notes a November 2016 article by Charles Ellison in the *Root*, "you were among a small, but very anxious crowd of election night viewers who watched the results stream in with the intensity of a football fan who had just bet his house on a bad playoff game."

That is because African Americans, and black women in particular, are disproportionately represented in the federal workforce. As previously noted, in 2014, African Americans made up 18.1 percent of the federal workforce, though they made up only 13.2 percent of the total US population and 10.4 percent of the total civilian workforce. A May 2015 article in the *New York Times* by Patricia Cohen noted that "for millions of... black families, working for the government has long provided a dependable pathway to the middle class and a measure of security harder to find in the private sector, particularly for those without college degrees."

Thus far, Trump has followed through on his promise to shrink the federal government, instituting a "hiring freeze on all federal employees" for his first hundred days in office. "Historically there's been no doubt that even before the Civil Rights Movement, the black middle class has been built upon government employment," a labor history professor at the University of California at Santa Barbara told the *Washington Post* just after the freeze began. "The freeze will disproportionately hurt African Americans. There's no doubt about that." When the freeze was lifted in mid-April of Trump's first year, his director of the Office of Management and Budget, Mick Mulvaney, made it clear that the administration was just starting to slash the size of government. He noted that while the size of the government has "grown organically for the last 240 years," the Trump administration wanted to reengineer government employment "from scratch."

The same message came from the president's top political advisor, Steve Bannon. He called for the "deconstruction of the administrative state," beginning with not filling open positions and cutting jobs without concern for the government's disproportionately black workforce.

The Trump administration has also gone out of its way to eliminate a series of Obama-era regulations meant to continue the work of the civil rights movement's mandate against employment discrimination.

In August 2017, Neomi Rao, Trump's administrator for the Office of Information and Regulatory Affairs of the OMB, ordered an "immediate stay" on rules put in place by the Obama administration to document pay gaps in American private businesses across race, gender, and ethnicity. In a memo, Rao wrote that the Obama-era requirements "lack practical utility, are unnecessarily burdensome, and do not adequately address privacy and confidentiality issues." Rao called the rules "enormously burdensome."

In 2015, the pay gap remained a very real point of separation between the races. College-educated African American men earned merely eighty cents for every dollar earned by a college-educated white man, according to a July 2016 Pew report. Even worse, black college-educated women earned seventy cents for every dollar earned by a white man. "No one should be paid less simply because of her gender, race, or ethnicity," the chair of the EEOC, Jenny Yang, wrote in a memo to explain the request for data on wages.

Trump's daughter, Ivanka Trump, calls herself an advocate of female entrepreneurship. She has lauded German legislation that requires companies with over two hundred employees to record employees' salaries and went so far as to propose similar legislation in the United States. "I know that Chancellor [Angela] Merkel, just this past March . . . passed an equal pay legislation to promote transparency and try to finally narrow that gender pay gap," she said at a discussion with Merkel on female entrepreneurship in April 2017. "That's something we should all be looking at."

And yet Ivanka Trump defends the administration's backpedaling on Obama-era attempts to close the pay gap for women and people of color. "We don't believe it would actually help us gather information about wage and employment discrimination," she noted in a statement, after it came out that the Trump administration would no longer be collecting information on pay. "Ultimately, while I believe the intention was good and agree that pay transparency is important, the proposed policy would not yield the intended results." She did not bother to explain why a public record on wages would not be helpful.

Trump has also gone out of his way to roll back President Obama's attempts to regulate federal contractors. In July 2014, President Obama unveiled a Fair Pay and Safe Workplaces executive order, to ensure that federal contractors were following civil rights laws and labor laws that, again, were written to protect the most vulnerable workers, who are often people of color. Among other things, the executive order required potential federal contractors to reveal whether, during the previous three years, they'd violated provisions of the Civil Rights Act related to hiring, migrant workers, and the minimum wage. It also required agencies to give contractors a chance to disclose how they are fixing unlawful practices. Yet Republicans labeled the executive order a "blacklisting rule" that tarnished the reputation of federal contractors. In late March, Trump signed House Resolution 37, which nullified Obama's executive order.

During the Obama years, labor activists began the Fight for Fifteen, the move to raise the federal minimum wage to fifteen dollars per hour. It has been widely reported that a national minimum wage hike, even to just ten dollars per hour, would disproportionately help low-wage workers. In 2014, when members of Congress were considering the Minimum Wage Fairness Act, the Urban League noted that "African Americans are disproportionately represented among the 30 million Americans who will benefit from a higher minimum wage."

But President Trump has a different view of the minimum wage. The billionaire said during his campaign that American workers are already getting paid too much. During a November 2015 GOP primary debate, when asked whether he'd support a fifteen-dollar minimum wage, he said that the "taxes [are] too high, wages [are] too high." When asked to clarify his position on MSNBC's *Morning Joe*, Trump said that while it's "a tough position, politically," he believes that "we have to become competitive with the world. Our taxes are too high, our wages are too high. Everything is too high." His new labor secretary, Alexander Acosta, has yet to take a firm position on the minimum wage.

Trump has also rolled back Obama-era efforts to ensure that middle-class workers are properly compensated for overtime work. In March 2014, President Obama asked Labor Secretary Tom Perez to eliminate a loophole in the Fair Labor Standards Act: the so-called white-collar exemption, in which salaried workers making more than $455 per week ($23,660 per year) are not given overtime pay when they work more than forty hours a week. Organized labor had long pressed for a new law to "address the changing nature of the workplace" in an era when so many middle-class Americans hold salaried office jobs. Secretary Perez's Labor Department announced a new rule that, as of December 1, 2016, white collar workers making up to $913 per week ($47,476 per year) would be entitled to overtime pay. As with a minimum wage increase, this reform would have disproportionately helped African American salaried workers, most of whom make under $47,476 per year.

But before the new rule took effect, a Texas district judge agreed to strike it down at the request of twenty-one states led by Republicans. To his credit, Trump's labor secretary, Alexander Acosta, appealed the judge's decision. And he has indicated that he planned to increase the share of workers who'd be covered for overtime pay. But it would be a far more limited expansion of overtime pay than the one that former secretary Perez had proposed.

This isn't a surprise. During his campaign and early presidency, President Trump signaled his opposition to Obama-era overtime pay protections. During an August 2016 interview with *Circa*, Trump explained that "we have to address the issues of over-taxation and over-regulation and the lack of access to credit markets to get our small businesses thriving again. Rolling back the overtime regulation is just one example of the regulations that need to be addressed to do that." In October 2016, just before Election Day, candidate Trump announced that "labor issues like minimum wage, overtime rules, and union organizing all take their toll."

Along with his attempt to roll back Obama-era regulations that help lower-income workers, who are disproportionately blacks and Latinos, President Trump's 2018 and 2019 budget blueprints recommended eliminating several programs meant to assist minority-run businesses.

The biggest assault on the black middle class is the president's plan to cut the Minority Business Development Agency. The MBDA, created by President Nixon in 1969, helps minority-owned businesses to do market research and compete for start-up money. Efforts to eliminate the almost fifty-year-old agency were "deeply concerning," Ron Busby, the CEO of the U.S. Black Chambers Inc., told *Black Enterprise* magazine. This is especially true at a moment "when black entrepreneurs are leading as the fastest growing population of entrepreneurs in the U.S."

Trump's 2018 and 2019 budget proposals also recommended dropping the Community Development Financial Institutions (CDFI) fund, which helps fund private sector banks and other financial institutions that are set up to invest in small businesses in low-income communities. Since it was established under President Clinton in 1994, the Community Development and Regulatory Improvement Act has helped 191,000 small businesses get loans through the CDFI fund.

Trump's harsh budget blueprints also called for gutting the Community Development Block Grant program, a HUD program established in 1974 that brings business investment into low-income areas, often big-city neighborhoods with a majority of residents of color in need of jobs. Since its creation it has been popular with both War on Poverty liberals and free-market conservatives. Based on HUD data, the Urban Institute reports that "between 2005 and 2013, CDBG created or retained 330,546 jobs." The Trump administration wants it gone.

As each of these programs is broken apart, Trump is attacking the legacy of A. Philip Randolph.

It was Randolph who said that without jobs all the victories we associate with the civil rights movement—the desegregation of housing, schools, restaurants, hotels, and stores—"will mean little to those who cannot afford to use them."

Randolph had personal experience with being black and poor in America. Born on April 15, 1889, in Crescent City, Florida—though his family moved to Jacksonville when he was two years old—Randolph saw how his father James, an African Methodist Episcopal minister, earned so little money from preaching to local black sharecroppers that he also ran a meat market, sold wood, and repaired clothes for money.

The Randolph family's situation reflected African American economic life at the start of the twentieth century. About 80 percent of African Americans didn't own their homes in 1900. If you were a black farmer at the time, you were most likely a sharecropper, living a life of deprivation. At a time in American history when groups like the American Federation of Labor spearheaded a massive movement for workers' rights, black workers were barred from most labor unions.

From a very young age, A. Philip Randolph understood that without the money that came from a steady paycheck, no man, black or white, could remove the chains of poverty and racism. His grandfather had been a slave. His father feared being penniless and taught Randolph and his older brother to respect black people who found success despite enormous odds. He heard stories of Harriet Tubman, Frederick Douglass, and Nat Turner—all "Negro leaders who fought for liberty and justice right in the fires of slavery," Randolph later explained. A religious man, Randolph's father "never failed to emphasize" the "historic fact" that the great biblical figures of long ago—Jesus, Moses, and Peter, among others—were not white but "colored or swarthy." He told his sons about the great black kingdoms in ancient Egypt and Ethiopia, promising them that the Kingdom in Ethiopia would, one day, again "stretch forth her hand to God." Randolph heard stories of Richard Allen, who had founded the African Methodist Episcopal Church, and Toussaint-Louverture, who had led a successful black revolution in Haiti. At the dinner table the family discussed the merits of Booker T. Washington's call for more "up-by-the-bootstraps" black success apart from racial integration and W. E. B. Du Bois's focus on ending racial segregation.

After graduating as high school valedictorian from the Cookman Institute in 1907, Randolph worked in several jobs: at a lumber yard, a grocery store, and an insurance company—the only type of work for smart black men without money for college. In 1911, he and a childhood friend named Beaman Hearn decided it was time to get out of the South. They boarded a ship for New York City. At age twenty-two, Randolph lived with Hearn in a rented room in the fabled black mecca of Harlem.

With childhood dreams of becoming a stage actor, Randolph did some acting, performing in several productions of Shakespeare plays organized by the Methodist church. He even memorized the entirety of *Hamlet, Othello*, and the *Merchant of Venice*. As an actor Randolph developed his dignified British accent and booming tone of voice. But acting jobs that paid were few for black people. So Randolph switched routes. He immersed himself in City College night classes on politics and history while doing a number of menial jobs by day to pay his tuition.

Randolph was immediately swept up by the intellectual milieu of City College, particularly the conversations about socialism and workers' rights that were occurring at the time in New York. He later said he "began reading [Karl] Marx as children read *Alice in Wonderland*." That turned his attention to exploited workers in America's factories and the black workers who could not even get a job in those sweatshops. He saw how poorly the black cooks were treated while working as a waiter on a steamboat that traveled from New York City to Boston. He even tried to organize some of his fellow employees while working as a porter for Consolidated Gas, though black workers, living in fear of a quick firing, "had no ear for that kind of talk," he later explained.

But in 1917 a labor union called the Headwaiters and Sidewaiters Society of Greater New York provided him with a bigger platform for his message. They invited Randolph and his friend Chandler Owen, a black socialist Columbia law student, to edit their newspaper, the *Hotel Messenger*. In less than eight months, however, the union fired Randolph and Owen for writing about how senior head waiters regularly stole money from lower-level busboys and staff. With Owen, Randolph responded by opening his own newspaper in November 1917, the *Messenger*, "devoted to the problem of the exploitation of the black worker in particular and the exploitation of workers in general." And the new paper was political: it criticized US participation in World War I. The paper was an immediate financial success; within months it had a readership of twenty thousand.

Randolph quickly learned what could happen to a black intellectual who wrote about Marx and promoted rights for black workers. He and Owen were arrested in Cleveland while delivering a series of speeches denouncing US participation in the war. When they were released, the judge told them to "get out of town." In 1918 the US postmaster general classified them as radicals and made them pay extra to mail out copies of the *Messenger*. In 1919 the Department of Justice identified Randolph's newspaper as "by long odds the most able and the most dangerous of all the Negro publications" in a report to the US Senate on black radicalism. The attorney general agreed, calling Randolph and Owen "the most dangerous Negroes in the United States."

Randolph's radical reputation helped him in one way: in 1925 the black porters on Pullman trains decided he was perfect for the dangerous job of organizing a union for them. At the time, the Pullman Car Company, which built, ran, and staffed sleeping cars on nearly every train in the United States, was the largest employer of African Americans in the country.

Pullman was also, according to author Larry Tye, "the most antiunion company in the nation." And the lives of black Pullman porters—most of whom were college-educated but unable to find any other job—symbolized all that was wrong about the state of black workers at the time. Laboring "in an environment akin to sharecropping," according to historian Rhonda Jones, black porters worked twenty-one-hour shifts, earning a measly eighteen cents per hour—much of which was deducted to pay for the price of their uniforms and food. Black porters were not allowed to become train conductors. Pullman porters had no forum to fight for workers' rights. Though white railroad workers were heavily unionized by the turn of the century, "in few industries...was the exclusion of black labor from unions more complete than in railroads," according to historian Beth Tompkins Bates.

And the Pullman Company wanted to keep it that way, going out of its way to appear as if it were contributing to the black community even as it exploited its black workforce. In Chicago's South Side, home to four thousand black Pullman porters, George Pullman and his daughter Florence financed Provident Hospital, the first black-operated hospital in the country. Pullman also donated to the YMCA and the Urban League in Chicago and was a major advertiser in black newspapers like the *Chicago Defender*. They also offered money to black church leaders.

When A. Philip Randolph officially founded the Brotherhood of Sleeping Car Porters (BSCP) during a 1925 meeting at Harlem's Imperial Lodge of Elks, union members were forbidden from discussing the union in public. Part of the reason for selecting Randolph to lead the union was that he was not a Pullman employee; he couldn't be pressured or fired. A complicated system was set up to ensure that secrecy was maintained. Porters paid union dues on street corners, in pool halls, and in barbershops. If they saw Randolph walking down the street, they immediately crossed the street. They had a secret password—"solidarity"—and a secret hand signal—a clenched left fist facing down.

When he spoke to members of the nascent union, Randolph made it clear that the Brotherhood of Sleeping Car Porters was fighting for workers' rights to advance black people's civil rights. He told the audience that first day in Harlem "what this is about is making you master of your economic fate." The BSCP developed slogans like "Fight or be slaves." The porters and their wives were attracted to Randolph's dignified yet strident manner, which, they believed, would allow him to stand up to the Pullman Company leaders.

Excitement about the porters' union spread across the nation. The *Amsterdam News*, a black paper in New York, called Randolph's first meeting with the porters "the greatest labor mass meeting ever held of, for and by Negro working men." An article in the *New York Age*, another black newspaper, went so far as to suggest that Randolph had "become [the black porters'] Moses," the man to lead them "out of his industrial wilderness" with a union that could improve working conditions. The *Age* called the porters' bid to unionize "really and truly a laudable effort."

Randolph's initial demand to Pullman was that the company more than double porters' salaries. He also wanted time-and-a-half pay if they worked more than 240 hours in a month. With this message, the BSCP unionized over half of the Pullman porters within a year of its founding.

Pullman executives fought back. Several black ministers advised congregants not to join Randolph's union. The company paid to place flattering stories about its record of hiring black people in selected black newspapers. Porters who were found to be union members were fired.

The Pullman Company also got violent. Ashley Totten, a Pullman porter and immigrant from St. Croix—the man who initially approached Randolph about speaking to the porters while he was walking to his *Messenger* office in 1925—was attacked and had his skull fractured by a police officer who used to work for Pullman. The company also spied on union meetings, even raiding members' homes and intimidating their wives.

The union-busting tactics worked.

Union membership shrank from 4,632 in 1928, to 2,368 in 1929, and all the way down to a total of 772 members in 1932.

Pressure also increased on Randolph. Roy Wilkins, later the head of the NAACP, told the story of how George Pullman, the owner of the railroad, offered Randolph $10,000 to stop organizing the union. When Randolph refused, Pullman called once more to offer $20,000. When Randolph did not respond, Pullman sent a blank check. Randolph said no thanks.

And Randolph fought back with innovative approaches to organizing. He created the Women's Economic Councils (WECs), comprised mostly of porters' wives and relatives. The WECs raised money and cheered on the importance of black workers standing together in a union. Like Randolph, these women didn't have to worry about getting fired from Pullman because they'd never been hired. And even though they had yet to secure a deal from the Pullman Company, the Brotherhood took care of its own: organizing soup kitchens and rent parties for fired porters.

With the election of labor-friendly President Franklin D. Roosevelt in 1932 came renewed interest in the only black union. Membership in the Brotherhood climbed from 658 in 1933 to 2,627 in 1934. Also in 1934, an amendment to the 1928 Railway Labor Act forced companies to negotiate with the union that a majority of their employees supported—and not, as Pullman had done in the past, company-controlled unions that kept workers in line. In 1935, the BSCP became the first black union given a charter by the American Federation of Labor.

Within two years the Pullman Company offered Randolph a deal. Under the terms of the contract, Pullman was required to pay overtime to anyone working more than 240 hours per month. Minimum salaries would rise from $77.50 to $89.50. Porters would be compensated for time spent prepping for trips. And they were given three hours of sleep during every twelve-hour shift and four hours of sleep if the shifts were longer than that. The significance of this contract—the first ever contract between a black union and a white company—was not lost on the NAACP, whose magazine, the *Crisis*, proclaimed: "As important as is this lucrative contract as a labor victory to the Pullman porters, it is even more important to the Negro race as a whole, from the point of view of the Negro's up-hill climb for respect, recognition and influence, and economic advancement."

Randolph's success was all over the news, in both white and black newspapers. He was now the best-known black leader in the country, wrote William Harris, author of a book on the Brotherhood titled *Keeping the Faith*.

That high profile put Randolph at the center of arguments among black leaders over whether the United States should enter World War II. On street corners, in churches and bars, African Americans across the country saw hypocrisy in the call to condemn Hitler and Nazism. Where were the calls to condemn racial tyranny inside the United States?

"We are as much political refugees from the South as any of the Jews in Germany," Pauli Murray, a black lawyer and activist, wrote to President Roosevelt in 1938. Randolph agreed, writing in a 1941 edition of his monthly magazine, the *Black Worker*: "Let us tear the mask of hypocrisy from America's democracy." Randolph expanded on the concept of the "Double V"—a call by black newspapers for victory over Nazi oppression abroad as well as racial oppression at home. Writing in the *Chicago Defender*, Randolph put it simply: "Negroes are fighting on two fronts.... They are trying to stop Hitler over there, and they are determined to stop Hitlerism over here."

A key battle in the fight for equal treatment during World War II was the demand for jobs in the military and the newly booming defense industry. The motive was best illustrated on the cover of the July 1940 edition of the *Crisis*. It displayed a seemingly patriotic tableau of two fighter jets flying above the clouds. The bottom half of the page showed a hangar with several planes under construction by American workers, people making middle-class wages to bring their families out of the Great Depression. Yet this happy and patriotic image was stamped "FOR WHITES ONLY." The caption read:

"WARPLANES—Negro Americans may not build them, repair them, or fly them, but they must help pay for them."

The pictures told the sad truth about the African American workforce on the eve of the United States' entrance into World War II. In the summer of 1940 white unemployment, after starting at a Depression-level high of 17.7 percent, dropped to 13 percent within half a year. That impact came with President Roosevelt's order to US factories to build airplanes, ships, and guns. But black people could not get jobs in those factories. Once again, racial segregation was being used to leave them behind. The African American unemployment rate, at 22 percent, barely moved at all. African Americans made up 0.2 percent of the 107,000 Americans employed by the aircraft industry. They made up 0.5 percent of 29,215 workers employed in ten New York wartime manufacturing plants. In April 1941, people of color made up a mere 2.5 percent of workers in the twenty war productions plants across the country.

Things were equally bad in the military. When Japanese warplanes attacked Pearl Harbor on December 8, 1941, there were 5,000 blacks among the 230,000 people in the army. And the army was completely segregated by race, with only four black units. In 1939, just five black men served as army officers, and three of the five were only there to serve as chaplains. Neither the US Air Force (then called the Air Corps) nor the marines accepted black recruits. Each of the four thousand African Americans serving in the navy served as mess men—effectively servants to the white navy men.

African Americans knew that they were being given a raw deal. Walter White, the head of the NAACP, wrote an article in the December 14, 1940, *Saturday Evening Post* entitled " 'It's Our Country, Too': The Negro Demands the Right to Be Allowed to Fight for It." At a time when "Negroes constitute a great reservoir of trained and skilled workers," White wrote, and "thousands of them are trained workers and, therefore, assets in the nation's defense construction program, the evidence seems to indicate that here," as with the army and the navy, "the policy seems to be to get along without Negroes."

White's article was accompanied by a picture of a sad black man wearing a suit and top hat, staring blankly at a sign that read, "AT-TENTION! Enlist in the United States Army—Make It Your Career or Learn a Trade." Every black person who saw the advertising knew the jobs in the army were for white men only.

In September 1940, Randolph, along with leaders of the NAACP and the Urban League, met with President Roosevelt. The Selective Training and Service Act, passed that month, required all American men between twenty-one and thirty-six to register for a draft number. If their number was picked, they'd be required to do a year of training. The black leaders told the president that young black men needed to be treated as American citizens—not second-class citizens—if they were subject to the draft. That meant, they said, the military had to be desegregated.

President Roosevelt was receptive to the black leaders, who left the meeting convinced the president was on their side. He promised to get back to them after consulting with military officials.

Within days, Randolph realized the president had sandbagged him. First, the military announced it was "not the policy to intermingle colored and white enlisted personnel in the same regimental organizations." Integration, they explained, would "produce situations destructive to morale and detrimental to the preparation for national defense." In other words, the military would remain segregated. The meeting with the president had been a failure.

African Americans were furious. "If Negroes in the army cannot intermingle with whites," asked an article in the *New York Age*, "will that same policy hold true in the event of duty on the field of war? Is the War Department going to refuse to send Negro soldiers into battle because they will be fighting alongside of or with white soldiers?"

Randolph was also hurt by the black public perception that he had failed in his meeting with the president. "Never again would he meet with a president and walk away without something to show for it," wrote historian David Lucander. Randolph was beginning to realize that if he wanted to integrate the military, he needed to put political pressure on the president and force him to ignore the old-school generals.

Randolph's new attitude led him to an idea as he traveled on a Pullman train in late 1940.

"We got to do something about [getting more] jobs around here," because "we're not getting anywhere," the frustrated Randolph told his colleagues as the train sped south from New York.

He then proposed bringing "ten thousand Negroes" to "march down Pennsylvania Avenue, and protest. What do you think about it?" Then and there, as the train sped over the Potomac River, the March on Washington Movement began.

The southern Brotherhood members with whom Randolph shared his plans were somewhat stunned. These were the early forties. *Brown v. Board of Education* wouldn't be ruled on for nearly fifteen years. Black Southerners who stepped out of line were lynched. The prospect of ten thousand African Americans marching on Washington was, quite frankly, threatening to white politicians and alarming to black workers. Benjamin McLaurin, who worked as an organizer for the Brotherhood, later explained that the concept of a March on Washington "scared some of them to death...including myself."

But in January 1941, Randolph announced his plans to go ahead with the march. Other black leaders, including Lester Granger, the new head of the National Urban League, Walter White of the NAACP, and black scholar Rayford Logan, supported Randolph's call to march. Front-page headlines in the black press brought more attention to the proposed protest in Washington during the winter and spring of 1941. In a late January article on the march printed in the *Philadelphia Tribune* and the *Pittsburgh Courier*, Randolph took a decidedly militant tone, arguing that "power and pressure do not reside in the few, the intelligentsia." Rather, power "lie[s] in and flow[s] from the masses." It was time to demand—"in no uncertain terms"—a fair share of jobs in the military and defense industry, he wrote. He said it was time to take the "gloves off."

Randolph got the best response to the proposed march from black residents of Northern cities with fast-growing populations of black people who had migrated from the South. For example, members of the Brotherhood spread through Harlem's "streets, shops, bars, and beauty parlors" to tell the black working class about the march, wrote Jervis Anderson in his Randolph biography. Both the NAACP and the Urban League announced they would give Randolph money to support the march. "Negroes were so aroused about being turned away from defense plants where they applied for jobs that there was no doubt about their responding to the call for the march," Randolph explained. By the spring of 1941, Randolph publicly increased his estimates of the potential crowd size to one hundred thousand. "In this period of power politics," he wrote in the *Black Worker*, undoubtedly referring to the world wars and Hitler's aggressive expansion into Europe, "nothing counts but pressure, more pressure, and still more pressure."

Planning the march was about more than logistics. There was the serious possibility of local whites attacking unfamiliar black faces, sparking an all-out race war. Randolph decided that black World War I veterans would serve as special "deputies" for the march. They would dismiss anyone who was drunk or carrying a provocative sign.

Still, the size of the proposed march and the possibility of race riots created pressure on the White House and Congress. In a June 12, 1941, letter to an NAACP organizer in Queens, Walter White wrote that he had word from "at least three sources in Washington" that "this proposed march is disturbing the administration more than anything that has happened among Negroes in recent months." The administration did its best to stop Randolph.

In a June 10 letter to Randolph, Eleanor Roosevelt struck what she believed would be a reasonable tone, telling him that she had discussed the march with her husband and she believed going through with the march would be "a very grave mistake." What if an "incident" occurred? She said that would make Congress even less likely to agree to desegregate the military.

The administration began making shows of support for black workers. They sent a letter to defense contractors urging them to "examine their employment and training policies at once and determine whether or not these policies make ample provision for the full utilization of available and competent Negro workers." President Roosevelt endorsed the letter to defense contractors, adding that it was unacceptable to turn away "much needed workers" because of their "race, religion, or national origin."

And then, on the advice of Stephen Early, President Roosevelt's press secretary, Randolph and White were invited to a meeting on June 13 at New York City Hall with First Lady Eleanor Roosevelt and Mayor Fiorello La Guardia. The mayor was popular with black New Yorkers, and so was Mrs. Roosevelt. But the meeting went badly after the first lady told Randolph that his march would end in violence. Randolph held fast and told her "sorry, but the march will not be called off unless the President issued an official order banning discrimination in the defense industry."

Mayor La Guardia tried to salvage the meeting by proposing that Randolph return to the White House to talk with President Roosevelt. But Randolph worried that he would be played as he had been played the previous September. He refused to cancel the march, he told Roosevelt via telegraph. "The hearts of Negroes are greatly disturbed."

The president agreed to a personal meeting with Randolph and White. Other attendees were Secretary of War Henry Stimson, Secretary of the Navy Frank Knox, and Mayor La Guardia.

There is no complete transcript of the forty-five-minute meeting that ensued. Varied accounts all tell us that President Roosevelt went into the meeting still hoping to get Randolph to call off the march. But even the greetings did not go well.

"Hello Phil, which class were you in at Harvard?" asked the president, obviously trying to schmooze the black labor leader before asking him to cancel the march. But Randolph, unlike Roosevelt, hadn't gone to Harvard. "I was sure you did," Roosevelt continued after Randolph corrected his error. "Anyway, you and I share a kinship in our great interest in human and social justice."

Roosevelt's good-natured small talk did not defuse Randolph's sense of urgency. "Mr. President, time is running out," Randolph said, interrupting. "What we want to talk with you about is the problem of jobs for Negroes in defense industries. Our people are being turned away at factory gates because they are colored. They can't live with this thing."

He finished by asking the president a simple question: "Now, what are you going to do about it?"

At first Roosevelt tried to compromise, saying that he planned to speak with defense contractors directly and tell them to begin hiring black workers. But Randolph considered that idea too weak. How would Roosevelt's rules be enforced? It would not do. "We want you to do more than that," Randolph pleaded. "We want something concrete, something tangible, definite, positive, and affirmative"—an executive order forbidding employment discrimination in the defense industries.

Roosevelt resisted the idea. An executive order, the president said, would create a bad precedent, a slippery slope where anyone would be able to come in and ask for an executive order because it had been granted to Randolph. Anyway, he couldn't promise anything until Randolph called off the march. But Randolph refused to make that deal.

"How many people do you plan to bring?" the president finally asked Randolph.

"One hundred thousand, Mr. President."

Hoping to expose Randolph's crowd estimate as a bluff, Roosevelt asked Walter White the same question. White gave him the same response as Randolph had.

In his 1948 autobiography, *A Man Called White*, White described how the president sized him up, "look[ing] me full in the eye for a long time in an obvious effort to find out if I were bluffing or exaggerating. Eventually he appeared to believe that I meant what I said." It was at this point that Fiorello La Guardia recommended that Randolph and White work with Roosevelt staffers and draft an executive order on which both sides could agree. They agreed that if that was accomplished, Randolph would cancel the march.

Things happened very quickly at this point. The next day, Wayne Coy at the federal Office of Emergency Management called in Joe Rauh Jr., a young, thirty-year-old lawyer working in the administration's lend-lease program. Coy told him to "get your ass over here" because "we got a problem." Rauh dropped everything, came to the White House, and spent the next eighteen hours drafting what would come to be called Executive Order 8802—Prohibition of Discrimination in the Defense Industry.

But when Randolph saw the proposed draft of the order, he rejected it as too weak because it lacked any enforcement mechanisms. When news got to Rauh that Randolph hadn't liked the early draft, Rauh exploded: "Who is this guy Randolph?" "What the hell has *he* got over the President of the United States?" Nevertheless, he went on to draft a new executive order with strong, clear penalties. This time Randolph approved.

Unveiled by President Roosevelt on June 25, 1941, Executive Order 8802 declared that "there shall be no discrimination in the employment of workers in defense industries or government because of race, creed, color, or national origin." It declared it the "duty of employers and of labor organizations, to provide for the full and equitable participation of all workers in defense industries." In order to enforce this mandate, the order created a five-member Fair Employment Practices Commission (the FEPC) to ensure that Roosevelt's mandate was followed: to "receive and investigate complaints of discrimination" and then "take appropriate steps to redress grievances which it finds to be valid." An article in the *Chicago Defender* called the order "one of the most significant pronouncements that has been made in the interests of the Negro for more than a century."

It took time for wartime manufacturers of military supplies to begin hiring black laborers. But by the end of the war in 1945, roughly 2 million African Americans were at work in defense-related industries. The change was particularly drastic on the West Coast, home of the major World War II shipyards. By 1944, Cal Ship, a shipbuilding manufacturer in Los Angeles, was employing 7,000 black laborers. Kaiser Company shipyards, located in the San Francisco Bay Area, employed 18,000 black workers. By 1944, over 7,700 African Americans were employed at shipyards in Portland, Oregon. That year, over 7,000 black laborers were working at aircraft companies in Los Angeles. During the war, the average yearly black income rose from $457 to $1,976.

For all the good achieved, Executive Order 8802 did not desegregate the military, which Secretary of War Henry Stimson and Secretary of the Navy Frank Knox vehemently opposed. Historian Andrew E. Kersten suggests that White and Randolph "agreed to set aside this request" in negotiations over the march to avoid being accused of trying to "overplay their cards."

But Randolph kept raising the issue after winning his fight to get black workers into the military factories. In the fall of 1947 Randolph threatened a major African American boycott of the peacetime draft that President Truman was planning on instituting in the summer of 1948. Truman, it turned out, was a willing listener. He wanted the black vote in the presidential election that fall. On July 26, 1948, he signed Executive Order 9981, which desegregated the US military.

In the first half of the twentieth century the jobs available to black laborers had changed dramatically. During the war, over five hundred thousand black workers had joined unions: not segregated unions like the Brotherhood but major, integrated unions that were part of the AFL-CIO. Randolph had even become a vice president of the labor council. And yet, according to labor historian William P. Jones, both the AFL and the CIO "had supported the civil rights movement since the 1940s but had argued that they lacked the authority to discipline local affiliated unions that excluded or discriminated against black workers"—which is what Randolph wanted.

At the July 1959 NAACP convention in New York City, Randolph and sixty black labor advocates drafted a resolution calling for the AFL-CIO to ban any local union that did not allow African Americans to join. George Meany, the cigar-chomping, long-term president of the AFL-CIO, did not like the demand: "Who the hell appointed you as guardian of all the Negroes in America?" Meany shouted at Randolph during the AFL-CIO's convention the following year.

In response to Meany's resistance, Randolph created the Negro American Labor Council (NALC) to fight for black workers' rights to join trade unions. The new group's fast registration of more than four thousand members in twenty-three cities was threatening to the leadership of the AFL-CIO. The AFL-CIO executive committee voted to censor Randolph for his "incredible assertions, false and gratuitous statements, and unfair and untrue allegations," and tried to throw him out of the AFL-CIO. The new union fired back. During an emergency NALC meeting, a female NALC member and laundry worker organizer named Odell Clark proposed the idea for a mass rally of black workers to pressure the AFL-CIO. Suddenly, other members suggested revising Randolph's 1941 tactic with President Roosevelt. "Let's March on Washington," shouted L. Joseph Overton, a NALC vice president.

Among the demands for this march was a "massive federal program to train and place all unemployed workers—Negro and white—on meaningful and dignified jobs at decent wages." They also called for a minimum wage capable of giving everyone "a decent standard of living," recommending two dollars per hour, which would be over thirteen dollars today. And they proposed toughening the Fair Employment Practices Act, which outlawed discrimination by government, employers, employment agencies, contractors, and trade unions.

Nobody at that meeting could have imagined that their proposal of a new March on Washington would attract a quarter million people and forever become a celebrated moment in American history. But one sign of its coming success could be seen in the large furies of racial anger blowing across the nation. The moment Birmingham, Alabama, police used sharp-toothed dogs and powerful blasts from fire hoses to take down black schoolchildren marching for the right to shop in the city's stores, protest leaders saw passion for the march grow coast to coast. Randolph gave the event a new name: the March for Jobs and Freedom. (Note that jobs remained the top issue.)

Suddenly, religious leaders, civil rights leaders, union leaders, Hollywood actors, and singers signed up. New York trade union leaders held a benefit concert at the Apollo Theater featuring Stevie Wonder and Thelonious Monk. The new attention brought an endorsement from Walter Reuther, head of the United Auto Workers with its thousands of black members, and that attracted sixteen other international unions. The Industrial Union Department of the AFL-CIO, also run by Reuther, financed buses and trains to fit five thousand people and paid for the $19,000 sound system that was used during the march.

Randolph, as the head of the big march, appointed Bayard Rustin—who'd worked closely with him during the 1941 March on Washington Movement—as deputy director in charge of organizing everything from bus routes to portable toilets.

And in his opening remarks at the march, in the heat of late August 1963, Randolph made it clear that all that we usually associate with the civil rights movement—namely equal rights, public accommodations open to all races, and black voting rights—were meaningless until black people could get better jobs and better support for their families. "We know that we have no future in a society in which six million black and white people are unemployed and millions more live in poverty," he declared. "Yes, we want all public accommodations open to all citizens," he noted. "But," he continued, "those accommodations will mean little to those who cannot afford to use them."

Randolph's words to the big crowd took on singular power when he spoke of the importance of the tremendous turnout: "Let the nation and the world know the meaning of our numbers," he said. "We are not a mob. We are the advanced guard of a massive moral revolution for jobs and freedom. . . . The March on Washington is not the climax of our struggle but a new beginning, not only for the Negro but for all Americans who thirst for freedom and a better life."

Speaker after speaker made a point of hammering home the call to end hiring discrimination against blacks.

At the beginning of his famous "I Have a Dream" speech, Martin Luther King Jr. spoke of job discrimination when he said it had been a century since the signing of the Emancipation Proclamation—ending slavery—but black Americans were still "not free." The "chains of discrimination," in hiring and in other parts of American life, he said, still crippled black people. To be black was to live "on a lonely island of poverty in the midst of a vast ocean of material prosperity," King said. His poetic words rolled across the biggest civil rights march the nation had ever seen. "One hundred years later, the Negro is still languished in the corners of American society and finds himself an exile in his own land." And the heart of that "exile" was the lack of opportunity for black families to move up the ladder of economic opportunity because of white employers' refusal to hire black workers.

Randolph concluded the march with a pledge. He instructed the marchers to "affirm [their] complete personal commitment to the struggle for jobs and freedom for Americans. . . . I pledge that I will not relax until victory is won."

The Kennedy White House, it turned out, was watching, listening, and ready to pressure Congress. Randolph and the others were invited into the White House immediately after the march. The president promised to begin serious work on a new civil rights bill.

A few months later, President Kennedy was assassinated. The public pressure for the bill did not go away, and less than a year later, on July 2, 1964, President Johnson signed the great Civil Rights Act, Title VII of which forbade employment discrimination on the basis of race, religion, sex, and national origin.

When the bill was signed, Randolph was invited to the White House and given one of the pens Johnson used to sign it. Even after that celebration, Randolph continued to push for black workers' rights, releasing A "Freedom Budget" for All Americans in 1966. The pamphlet—endorsed by more than two hundred scholars and activists—called for full employment for those able to work and guaranteed income for those unable to work. The goals laid out in Randolph's "Freedom Budget" became central to Dr. King's proposal of a 1968 Poor People's Campaign.

While Randolph's demands in his "Freedom Budget" were never put into action, by the time he died in 1979 his legacy was secure. Because the Civil Rights Act banned discrimination in hiring, African Americans began making tremendous gains in both the public and the private employment. The black middle class had taken root. Randolph's dream of good jobs for qualified black workers was becoming a reality.

Yet it was also true that tensions caused by decades of poverty and racial isolation led to riots from East to West, with smoke rising from Los Angeles to Buffalo.

Now, in President Trump's America, the conversation about race is less about economic opportunity and more about police shooting black men and the "constant carnage" of black-on-black shootings, as President Trump described it in his inaugural address. But all of us would do well to remember a simple lesson taught to us by A. Philip Randolph: that jobs and a thriving black middle class are essential to fulfilling the nation's founding promise of all Americans being treated as equals.

EMPLOYMENT

Trump's deconstruction of civil rights hinges on undermining government policies that produced the rise of the black middle class while he attacks the black poor as undeserving. It is a picture of black people without progress that appeals to the worst racists and tears at the nation's racial fabric.

CHAPTER 6

HOUSING

ONALD J. TRUMP IS very much Fred Trump's son. "My legacy has its roots in my father's legacy," he proclaimed as he began running for president.

Trump is right on several fronts. Father and son both made millions doing residential building construction in New York City. And like his father, the son was a landlord who had no problem exploiting racial fears to increase the value of his properties. He made money by turning away black people from his apartments as a way of attracting white tenants. And that meant that when the 1968 Fair Housing Act was passed, both Trumps resented government efforts to force them to integrate their apartment buildings and risk declining property values.

Frederick Christ Trump, the president's daddy, was so famous for enforcing segregation in his buildings that the legendary folk singer Woody Guthrie wrote a song about Trump's racially exclusionary practices: "I suppose / Old Man Trump knows / Just how much / Racial Hate / he stirred up / In the bloodpot of human hearts / When he drawed / that color line / Here at his / eighteen hundred family project." Guthrie, while renting a place at a Trump housing development in Brighton Beach, wrote a second song about Trump-style racism that included these lines: "Beach Haven looks like heaven / Where no black ones come to roam! / No, no, no! / Old Man Trump! / Old Beach Haven Ain't my home."

The folksinger found Trump's racism so troubling he began fanta-sizing about replacing the whites-only Beach Haven property with a building that allowed people to rent who had "a face of every bright color laffing and joshing in these old darkly weeperish empty shad-owed windows." In one notebook entry Guthrie imagined yelling out greetings to a "Negro girl yonder that walks along against this headwind," wishing that he could say that he "welcome[s] you here to live. I welcome you and your man both here to Beach Haven to love in any way you please."

Guthrie could have lashed out at the federal government as well. Trump's buildings in Brooklyn were built thanks to Federal Hous-ing Administration grants given to developers to spur construction of affordable housing to World War II veterans. At that point, the government never objected to Trump's racist refusal to rent to black people.

The combined power of the federal government's silence on racial segregation in housing and Trump's hard line against renting to black people led Guthrie to realize he was also complicit in harming black people as someone paying rent to live in a Trump apartment.

In a letter from Beach Haven to a friend, Guthrie wrote that, worse than "ninety and nine clauses in his damnable old tenant's contract" was the fact that "I'm dwelling in the deadly center of a Jim Crow town where no Negroid families yet are allowed to move in and to live free-like."

Even before imposing racist rules to keep black renters out of his apartments, the elder Trump (1905–1999) was known to disapprove of the rush of immigrants moving into New York City and taking part in civic life, including white Catholics. In 1927, at age twenty-one, Fred was arrested at a Klan rally near his home in Jamaica, Queens. The rally was organized to protest the alleged overrepresentation of Roman Catholics in the New York Police Department. To call some-one a Roman Catholic in those days was code for "foreigner" with little intellect who took orders from the pope. The newcomers dealt with anger from "native-born" Protestant Americans, such as Trump, who saw them as cheap laborers, taking away their jobs and changing New York's culture.

A Klan flier for the rally justified taking action against the recent arrivals as a necessary "stand in defense of the fundamental principles of your country." A follow-up article on the rally in the *New York Times* noted that "1,000 Klansmen and 100 policemen staged a free-for-all battle in Jamaica." Police commissioner Joseph A. Warren told the press that "the Klan not only wore gowns, but had hoods over their faces almost completely hiding their identity." According to the *Times*, "Fred Trump of 175-24 Devonshire Road, Jamaica, was discharged."

So it should come as little surprise that when Fred Trump hit it big in residential construction after World War II, building houses and apartment complexes in Brooklyn and Queens, he didn't think twice before excluding black people. At the time, the city had a growing population of African Americans, many of whom had traveled north in the Great Migration of the 1930s and 1940s. They were fleeing the Jim Crow South to seek a better life in cosmopolitan New York City.

In June 1946, Donald Trump began life in a neighborhood with few Catholics and no black residents. That area of the borough of Queens is known as Jamaica Estates. It was then reserved for upper-class white Protestants. The segregated surroundings sent a message that young Trump took to heart: a good, safe, wealthy neighborhood was an all-white neighborhood. The corollary of that message for the future real estate magnate was that racial segregation pushed up property values.

By the middle of the 1960s, the civil rights movement turned its attention to the segregated real estate landscape created by developers like the Trumps. Just before he was assassinated in 1968, Dr. Martin Luther King was leading a march against rigid housing segregation in Chicago. He railed against the poor-quality housing in black ghettos.

After King's death, Congress passed the Fair Housing Act—technically Title VIII of the Civil Rights Act of 1968—which made it *illegal* to refuse to sell or rent a housing unit to someone based on his or her "race, color, religion, sex, familial status, or national origin." The Fair Housing Act and its subsequent amendments gave the federal government a mechanism to investigate developers who, like Fred Trump, refused to let black people rent from him.

Yet Fred Trump and his son Donald, who was raised to take over the family business, never believed that these regulations should apply to them. In 1973, Donald, who was now in charge of the Trump brand, and his father were sued by the Department of Justice for blocking people of color from renting in their buildings. Employees had been instructed to tell would-be black renters that there were no openings. And if black people insisted on applying for an apartment, the Trump staff was told to mark their applications with the letter *C* for "colored."

A doorman at a Trump building in Brooklyn told investigators he had been instructed by the Trumps that "if a black person came to 2650 Ocean Parkway and inquired about an apartment for rent... I should tell [the black person] that the rent was twice as much as it really was."

Instead of admitting they were in violation of the new law, the Trumps became defiant. They hired the notoriously combative lawyer Roy Cohn to accuse the federal government of defamation and countersue for $100 million. The *New York Times* later wrote that the younger Trump "turned the lawsuit into a protracted battle, complete with angry denials, character assassination, charges that the government was trying to force him to rent to 'welfare recipients.'" The countersuit went nowhere, and under terms of a settlement the case was dismissed "with prejudice." The Trumps were "enjoined from" refusing to sell or rent to "any person on account of race, color, religion, sex or national origin." They were banned from "discriminating against any person in terms, conditions, or privileges of sale or rental of a dwelling... [as well as] making printing or publishing... any notice, statement or advertisement with respect to the sale or rental of a dwelling that indicates any preference, limitation or discrimination based on race, color religion, sex or national origin."

The settlement specifically mentioned the newly passed civil rights law, and demanded that the Trumps stop "coercing, threatening or interfering with…any person in the exercise or enjoyment of the right to equal housing opportunity protected by the Fair Housing Act of 1968." The Trumps also had to advertise their rentals in black newspapers and inform major civil rights groups, such as the Urban League, when an apartment opened up.

Shortchanging tenants living in apartment buildings they own is a generational trend in the Trump family. Jared Kushner, the president's son-in-law and a real estate developer like Trump, has also skirted around rules meant to protect working-class tenants from greedy developers. When applying for construction permits to build in New York, Kushner allegedly failed to report at least three hundred apartment units that were under rent-stabilization rules, according to a March 2018 Associated Press story. Kushner was trying to avoid the difficulty of getting construction permits to upgrade buildings where tenants were living in rent-stabilized units. The local government had passed the laws to protect tenants from being forced out when developers created apartments for high-income tenants. But Kushner was willing to break the law to avoid losing the chance to develop buildings that catered to the upper class.

Kushner's effort to get around the law is in keeping with the president's behavior when he started building luxurious hotels, casinos, and golf courses in the 1980s. Again he perpetrated belief that the presence of any black person drove down property values. His perspective was on display in 1989, when he publicly worried that black criminals made it less attractive for wealthy whites to live in his Manhattan properties. He funded an $85,000 ad campaign advocating for the death penalty for the four black teens and one Hispanic teen—the Central Park Five—who were charged with raping and nearly killing a white woman. It was later found out that these five young men had nothing to do with the attack. But Trump, with no evidence other than the color of their skin, continues to claim to this day that the boys were responsible.

On the 2016 campaign trail, especially while he was trying to court black voters, Trump frequently spoke about African Americans' low-quality, inner-city housing conditions. At an October 2016 rally in Toledo he told his audience to "take a look at what's going on...where you have inner cities and you have so many things, so many problems...the violence, the death, the lack of education." At his inauguration he spoke of "mothers and children trapped in poverty in our inner cities."

And yet in all this lament over poor living conditions in black ghettos, Trump does not talk about how much he could have done *for* black communities if he and his father had not promoted segregated housing and encouraged white renters to resist living alongside black people.

Now, as president, Trump has made his racist attitudes a matter of government policy by attacking federal aid for low-income housing as well as federal grants for construction of housing for working-class people. His 2018 budget proposal recommended cutting the Department of Housing and Urban Development's budget by $6.2 billion—or 13 percent. His 2019 budget went even deeper. It would have cut 18.3 percent of the funding HUD received in 2017. These budget cuts will likely be felt most dramatically by African Americans and Latinos, who are a high percentage of public housing residents as well as a high percentage of Americans who rely on government vouchers to subsidize their housing.

Today, roughly 45.3 percent of the families that rely on public housing in New York are black, and 44.7 percent are Hispanic—which means that a shocking 90 percent of New York's housing projects are occupied by either black or Hispanic families. In New York City, public housing is so intimately connected to African American culture that just the sight of a housing project—a series of high-rise, boxlike buildings often covered with reddish bricks and surrounding a courtyard of some sort—indicate that you're in a predominately black neighborhood.

These astonishing demographics are present in other cities across the United States. In Philadelphia, 91 percent of households in public housing are African American. African Americans make up *99* percent of public housing residents in Detroit, and *98* percent in both DC and New Orleans. Overall, African Americans compose roughly half of residents living in public housing and half of renters who use Section 8 vouchers, though they make up roughly 13 percent of the nation's population.

This, makes poor African Americans disproportionately vulnerable to the huge cuts to HUD that President Trump proposed in his 2018 budget. That is because HUD funds more than three thousand local Public Housing Authorities across the country. That money helps to build public housing developments and subsidize housing vouchers.

Even before Trump was elected president in November 2016, public housing authorities across the country were in trouble. NYCHA estimated it needed an additional $17 billion to repair existing housing developments, 75 percent of which are more than four decades old, and all of which suffer from everything from broken elevators to moldy ceilings to busted light bulbs. That is why Trump's budget cuts will rob NYCHA of upwards of $200 million. When the budget was released, the group's chair, Shola Olatoye, denounced Trump's HUD budget cut as an "assault on public...and affordable housing as we know it." Similar scenarios are playing out around the country. Rich Monocchio, the head of the Cook County Housing Authority—covering much of the Chicago suburbs—called the budget proposal a "doomsday scenario" because it takes away at least $8 million dollars from his budget, preventing the housing authority from providing homes for eight hundred families.

The budget proposal prompted critics to argue that real people were suffering as a result of the cuts. Their lives were quite literally at stake because of Trump's refusal to provide money to repair broken-down public housing units. The *New York Amsterdam News* wrote about one mother who was worried that a cracked ceiling, caused by leaky pipes, would fall on her five-year-old son. The paper also reported on an elderly woman who "uses a garden hose her son has attached to the bathroom sink" to fill her tub because the bath water doesn't run. And it described a seventy-six-year-old who had to walk up twelve flights of stairs because her building's elevator wasn't working. "I thought I was going to die on the 10th floor," she said. "I got there tired and scared."

In the nation's capital, the Washington, DC Housing Authority (DCHA) provides housing units to more than twenty thousand city residents. The DCHA estimates that it needs an additional one billion dollars to repair crumbling public housing facilities. But with Trump's HUD cuts, the amount of money given to the DCHA would likely shrink by roughly $10 million, blocking the city from both paying for repairs and paying off old debt. "Clearly any continued cuts to the public housing program would be extraordinarily challenging as evidence by our current funding," said a DCHA spokesperson following the release of Trump's budget proposal.

In Chicago, a city whose high crime and poverty rates are frequently referred to by President Trump, the public housing operating fund is expected to lose over $20 million in the new budget, and the housing choice voucher fund is predicted to lose another $40 million, according to the website Affordable Housing Online.

Trump's policies have an additional agenda. In New York, for example, Trump's requested budget cuts have sped up the financially struggling NYCHA's plans to sell public housing land to private developers. Only one quarter of the 13,500 new apartments to be built by private developers on that land would be reserved for public housing residents. According to a March 14, 2017, article by Emma Whitford in the *Gothamist*, "Residents have predicted that an influx of wealthier residents (half of the 1,000 apartments will be market rate) will drive affordable amenities out of their neighborhoods, and possibly drive NYCHA tenants out altogether." In other words, Trump's budget cuts fulfill his long-held desire to drive poor residents out of the city and open more land in central cities, the highest priced, most desirable locations, to private developers.

The same type of policy shift is at work in Trump's proposed elimination of the HOME Investment Partnership Program (HOME). Founded in 1990, HOME is the biggest federal block grant program set up exclusively to help with lower-income housing. Unlike Community Development grants, only a fourth of which are used for lower-income housing, more than half of HOME funds in 2012 were used to develop housing for lower-income tenants. Another quarter of the remaining HOME funds have been used to help out lower-income homebuyers with down payments and closing costs. In order to receive HOME money, participating states and local governments are required to match one-fourth of the federal dollars. Between 1992 and 2012, 32 percent of the people qualifying for HOME grants have been African American, meaning that HOME money disproportionately assists black people.

Beginning in 2012, a charity called Southern United Neighborhoods used HOME money to fix homes in New Orleans' Lower Ninth Ward, a largely African American neighborhood that was nearly destroyed by Hurricane Katrina. In 2013, a Greenville, Mississippi, group used $1 million in HOME money to rebuild an eight-unit apartment strip. The program has been lauded for the decision-making power that it gives state and local governments. But Trump's budget justified its elimination by claiming that, even without federal aid, "state and local governments are better positioned to serve their communities based on local needs and priorities."

President Trump also plans to eliminate Choice Neighborhoods, an Obama-era HUD program founded in 2010 to offer an incentive for local governments, nonprofits, and businesses to revitalize poor neighborhoods. The idea is that federal support to build housing for middle-income people will inspire private sector investment in those neighborhoods. The intended result is to create a better quality of life in urban areas.

In 2011, for example, Choice Neighborhoods awarded $30.5 million to a coalition of nonprofits and local leaders in Woodlawn, located in the heart of Chicago's overwhelmingly poor and black South Side. With the money, a nonprofit developer called Preservation of Affordable Housing Inc. replaced a decaying Section 8 housing complex near the University of Chicago with a new six-building, affordable housing complex. Another $30.5 million grant went to New Orleans to help two poor and black neighborhoods, Iberville and Treme, where the public housing stock was devastated by Hurricane Katrina. With money from Choice Neighborhoods, the 821 previously boarded up public housing units are being replaced by over two thousand mixed-income units.

The administration's proposal to eliminate the Community Development Block Grant program—discussed in the previous chapter— would also take an enormous toll on housing available to low-income and working-class blacks. In 2013, nearly 95,000 housing units were repaired with CDBG money, and between 2004 and 2013, CDBG money has been used to rehabilitate 1.3 million housing units. In Baltimore CDBG funds enabled HUD-certified counselors to provide help to 832 homeowners whose home had been foreclosed, allowing them to keep their home or protecting them from the damaging financial consequences of having a home foreclosed.

Fortunately, Trump's budget cuts were rejected by Congress. They rebuked him by giving $4 billion more to the Department of Housing and Urban Development. According to the National Low Income Housing Coalition, the spending bill sent a "clear message" to the president: that these kinds of irresponsible funding cuts would not be tolerated. Several other housing programs slated to be cut were also restored.

Beyond budget cuts, Trump has gone out of his way to eliminate Obama-era efforts to reverse the history of residential segregation in American cities. The Fair Housing Act of 1968 was enormously successful in barring outright housing discrimination. But it did little to untangle the consequences of past housing segregation. Under President Obama, HUD announced plans to take "significant actions to overcome historic patterns of segregation, achieve truly balanced and integrated living patterns, promote fair housing choice, and foster inclusive communities that are free from discrimination."

In 2015, Obama's Secretary of HUD, Julian Castro, announced that districts around the country that receive HUD money would be required to submit reports that "identify and evaluate fair housing issues." The goal was to use federal policies to spur local housing integration. But conservative white critics described the Obama efforts to decrease residential segregation as another failed socialist experiment. They drew comparisons to the failures of school busing to achieve public school integration in the 1970s. Unsurprisingly, then, in January 2018 President Trump ordered the Department of Housing and Urban Development to slow down the work to "affirmatively further" the nation's commitment to fair housing, extending all assessment submissions until October 2020. The department effectively suspended the program and asked the public "to comment on those rules that might be excessively burdensome or unclear." Sherrilyn Ifyll, president of the NAACP's Legal Defense and Educational Fund, called Trump's move "yet another attack by this administration on communities of color across the country." Diane Yentel, President and CEO of the National Low Income Housing Coalition, called it a "misguided...step in the wrong direction."

Lower-income housing initiatives are being undermined by Trump in other ways, too. Currently, businesses that invest in affordable housing get the added benefit of a Lower-Income Housing Tax Credit (LIHTC) to offset their taxes. The LIHTC is, according to HUD's website, "the most important resource for creating affordable housing in the United States."

Trump's success in lowering the corporate tax rate from 35 percent to 21 percent without revising the LIHTC made the program less attractive to investors. Again, the Trump administration has made it more likely that developers looking for neighborhoods for new residential construction will cut into black neighborhoods with projects for upper-middle-class, mostly white people while pushing out the less affluent, mostly black people.

Affordable housing developments felt the effects of Trump's tax cuts before they even passed through Congress. A new housing development with space for moderate- to low-income residents in Boston was delayed for half a year because investors provided $700,000 less than projected, according to Elaine S. Povich, writing for the Pew Charitable Trust. She quoted the head of the nonprofit group in charge of the development as saying, "Investors paused and said, 'Wait a minute, if I'm getting a stream of tax deductions at a tax rate of 35 percent now, and I'm pretty confident that the rate is going to be lower, I'm going to hold off here and figure out what's going on." The accounting firm Novogradac and Company recently estimated that Trump's newly reduced corporate tax rate will result in 235,000 fewer affordable housing units built over the next decade. The loss of those new residential apartments intended to attract people across racial lines with high and low incomes also means no change in the stubbornly high rates of residential racial segregation.

According to a March 2016 article in the *Chicago Sun Times*, reporting on a study done by the Chicago Urban League, "a century after the start of the Great Migration...a quarter of Chicago's 77 communities remain as racially and socioeconomically segregated as ever." Another neighborhood in Chicago's South Side, Washington Park, is over 95 percent black. Woodlawn, also on the South Side, is 85 percent black.

That harsh housing segregation is also on view today in Philadelphia. At first, the city's population looks like a paragon of diversity: 44 percent of the city is African American, 35 percent of the city is white, and 13.6 percent of the population is Hispanic. But it takes only a quick look to see that African Americans are concentrated in seventy-eight of the city's four hundred census tracts. Whites make up 90 percent of the population in thirty-four of the census tracts. Similarly, in Detroit more than half of the city's 962,000 African American inhabitants live in majority-black neighborhoods.

The racial makeup of a neighborhood comes with life-changing consequences in modern America. It is a major factor in determining income, education opportunities, and access to health care. Researchers at the University of Minnesota have found that Detroit contains fifty-five "racially concentrated areas of affluence," which they have defined as census tracts in which more than 90 percent of the population is white. In those white neighborhoods the median income is more than four times the federal poverty level. On the other hand, Detroit contains 147 "racially concentrated areas of poverty," which is defined as census tracts where over half of the residents are black or nonwhite and over four in ten residents live in poverty.

In Chicago and cities across the United States, the public schools with the highest percentage of students going to college and the lowest drop-out rates are found in those "racially concentrated areas of affluence," where the population is almost all white. When budget deficits forced the Chicago Board of Education to shut down forty-nine elementary schools in 2013, almost 90 percent of the students affected were in black neighborhoods, according to a report in the *American Prospect*, though black students were 40 percent of the school district population. In Philadelphia, 88 percent of the students affected by the twenty-three budget-related school closings in 2013 were African American.

The same dynamic applies to crime rates, public parks, movie theaters, and even supermarkets. Just 8 percent of African Americans—compared to 31 percent of white Americans—live in a census tract that also includes a supermarket. Less access to fresh meat and produce means that African Americans have to rely on fast food chains and corner stores.

Trump's apathy to the housing needs of African Americans matched with that of the Senate, which passed a bill in March 2018 that rolled back requirements for banks to report data on who is approved for mortgage loans. Previously, those financial institutions had been found to discriminate against people of color in making the loans. The Senate bill "once again place[s] low-income and borrowers of color at risk of falling prey to the same unscrupulous lending practices that helped cause the Great Recession," wrote the president of the National Urban League, Morc Morial, in a letter to the Senate.

Trump's view of the federal role in housing is reflected in his choice of Dr. Ben Carson to be his secretary of housing and urban development. The only black person in Trump's cabinet, Carson is a brilliant and world-renowned neurosurgeon. But Carson has zero experience in housing.

Growing up without a father in federally subsidized housing, Carson certainly knows on a personal level what it *feels* like to be a poor black man in America. As Senator Marco Rubio said during his confirmation hearing, Carson knows what is possible in America not "because he watched some documentary on PBS" but "because he has lived it." Yet Trump hired Carson because he has consistently opposed welfare programs and urged people to get out of public housing. In a 2014 book entitled *One Nation: What We Can All Do to Save America's Future*, Carson wrote that government programs intended to help the poor are often "cruel because [they] tend in many cases to create dependency and rob people of their God-given dignity." He said many government welfare programs take away "the incentive to engage in self-improvement activities." In a 2015 book entitled *A More Perfect Union*, Ben and his wife, Candy Carson, compared welfare recipients to mooching relatives who "continually want to borrow money from us, and if we allow it, the requests are never ending and the money is almost never repaid."

During a late October 2017 hearing with the Financial Services Committee, Secretary Carson had a tense exchange with Congressman Al Green (D-TX). Carson said he didn't want to talk about how Trump's cuts to the HUD budget hurt public housing and Section 8 vouchers. But Green insisted and repeatedly asked Carson about potential damage from cuts to "public housing, housing vouchers... and other aid to low income persons." Carson said the cuts would equally affect many HUD programs, but Green asked once again,

"How much from public housing, Mr. Carson?" Finally, Carson responded by admitting that public housing was going to lose "if you combine all the programs, two to three billion [dollars]."

The conversation intensified. "How much from housing vouchers, Mr. Carson?" Carson, getting frustrated, told Green that he would not tolerate being given a pop quiz. Green responded: "It is not a quiz, Mr. Carson. I have the time to ask you questions about things that you should have some knowledge of." And he continued: "Again, how much from housing vouchers?" But Carson refused to tell Green how much money would be taken from the Community Development Block Grant program. When Carson began to say, "I want to talk about...," Green cut him off: "Mr. Carson, you do not get to talk about what you want to [talk about] today. You get to talk about what *I* want you to talk about. You get to answer the questions that I pose, Mr. Carson." Green then told Carson, "Poor people are not poor because they choose to be," and poverty is not, as Carson had suggested during a May 2017 interview with Armstrong Williams, a "state of mind." Green clearly held the opinion that Carson's emphasis on encouraging the poor to be self-reliant had nothing to do with solving the problem of poverty.

Given President Trump's distaste for the Fair Housing Act and for the idea of fighting residential segregation, his presidency has taken the country back in time. After all, it was the real estate tactics of men like Fred Trump that inspired the creation of HUD and the Fair Housing Act in the first place.

When Woody Guthrie commented on the lack of black faces at Fred Trump's apartments in Brooklyn, there were similarly high levels of residential segregation around the country. The segregated housing policies practiced by Fred Trump fit with the way many major developers made money and many major politicians won elections: they kept whites and blacks in separate neighborhoods.

Before the twentieth century, according to historians Richard R. W. Brooks and Carol Rose, residential segregation in Northern cities was mostly informal. As early as 1793, a Salem, Massachusetts, minister complained that the idea of building even one "Negro hut" drove down the prices of other properties. Several years later, white New Haven residents even drew up a petition arguing that the recent movement of black people into their city lowered property values by upwards of 50 percent. In 1847, residents of south Boston bragged that there was "not a single colored family" in their midst. A few African Americans did live among whites in poor neighborhoods like Five Points in Lower Manhattan. Yet the reality of housing integration before the Civil War was that so few African Americans lived in cities that the issue of residential integration was not a big problem.

Things changed drastically in the decades following the Civil War, when formerly enslaved African Americans moved from the rural South to nearby Southern cities like Atlanta, Nashville, Raleigh, and Washington, DC. At the start of the twentieth century the migration extended north to cities like New York, Chicago, and Detroit. Between 1910 and 1940, the number of African Americans in New York City rose from 142,100 to 661,100; in Philadelphia from 119,200 to 347,800; in Chicago from 58,100 to 346,800; and Detroit from 9,000 to 168,600.

Realtors placed "whites only" signs on buildings that they planned to lease or sell. Developers made home buyers sign racially restrictive housing covenants that blocked them from selling their home to all people of color. A 1944 deed to a house in Richmond, Virginia, forbade the house from being sold to "anyone not of the Caucasian race." In Chappaqua, New York, one homeowner signed a covenant reading that "no persons of any race other than the Caucasian race shall use or occupy any buildings or lot." A 1921 covenant signed by thirty white residents in DC (Northwest) in 1921 ruled that "no part of the land now owned by the parties hereto... shall ever be used or occupied by, or sold, conveyed, leased, rented, or given to, Negroes, or any person or persons of the Negro race or blood." One study found that more than half of three hundred private developments built between 1935 and 1947 in Nassau County, Westchester County, and Queens, New York—where Trump grew up—had racially restrictive housing covenants.

The growth of racial covenants was not an accident. In 1924, a powerful trade association among real estate brokers called the National Association of Real Estate Boards (NAREB), now the National Association of Realtors, included an amendment to its code of ethics which stated that "a realtor should never be instrumental in introducing into a neighborhood... members of any race or nationality... whose presence will clearly be detrimental to property values in that neighborhood." A realtor could get kicked out of the NAREB for violating the rules of segregation, and that meant losing their business connections and network.

White developers and residents were not just shunning poor African Americans. In the 1920s W. E. B. Du Bois, the famed sociologist who was the first black person to earn a doctorate at Harvard, tried to buy a house in Forest Hills, an upper-middle-class development in Queens. The house was "designed for the class of white-collar workers to which I belonged," Du Bois explained in his 1940 memoir, *Dusk of Dawn*. But he was "finally and definitively refused, simply and solely because of my dark skin."

The government also played a powerful role in keeping black people out of white neighborhoods. Established in 1934, the Federal Housing Administration (FHA), which insured home mortgages, refused to insure mortgages in neighborhoods it deemed risky and circled on maps in red ink. The practice of "redlining" was punishing to black people, who were kept inside those redlined areas and prevented from entering white neighborhoods through restrictive covenants and racist real estate practices. Without access to neighborhoods with rising property values, black people did not have the chance to increase their family wealth. Furthermore, the FHA blocked would-be black home owners from buying property in white neighborhoods. In its *Underwriting Manual*, published in 1936, the FHA urged "valuators...not [to] hesitate to make a reject rating" if the loan would mean the mixing of "inharmonious racial groups."

The federal government didn't just block the integration of African Americans into formerly white neighborhoods. At points, the federal government actually encouraged and helped create segregated neighborhoods. Nowhere was this more apparent than in the creation of public housing during the New Deal. Funded by the Public Works Administration, a 1933 initiative was set up to provide homes for low-income Americans and construction jobs for unemployed workers who could build them. These housing projects were most often segregated by race. Of the forty-seven housing projects established through the PWA, seventeen were for African Americans, twenty-four were for whites, and just six were mixed-race.

Harold Ickes, President Roosevelt's secretary of the interior, believed that the racial composition of the housing projects should reflect the existing racial mix in the neighborhood. In reality, though, the PWA rarely took a neighborhood's racial composition into account when deciding who should live in a given housing project. The housing was either all-white or all-black, and most went to white families only.

Techwood Homes, built in an Atlanta neighborhood where one-third of the 1,600 families were black, was advertised for whites only. In DeSoto-Carr, a working-class St. Louis neighborhood with equal shares of black and white residents, an all-black housing project was built. It was the same story in Cleveland, Detroit, and New York City—whose first housing project, the Harlem River Houses, was for African Americans, and whose second project, the Williamsburg Houses in Brooklyn, was built for whites only.

Americans tend to think of residential segregation in Northern cities as a result of individual choices and not something encouraged by the government. But Richard Rothstein's 2017 book, *The Color of Law: A Forgotten History of How Our Government Segregated*

America, tells a different story. He writes: "We say [cities] are '*de facto* segregated*,*' that they result from private practices, not from law or government policy. *De facto* segregation, we tell ourselves, has various causes. When African Americans moved into a neighborhood… a few racially prejudiced families leave, and then as the number of black families grew, the neighborhood deteriorated, and 'white flight' followed." To the contrary, Rothstein presents an historical record which shows that current patterns of residential segregation resulted from "public policy that explicitly segregated every metropolitan area in the United States."

It was in this environment that Fred Trump was able to get away with renting only to whites in his Brooklyn apartment buildings in the early 1950s. His success led him to be lionized as the "Henry Ford of the home-building industry" by the *Brooklyn Eagle*. He built segregated homes and apartment complexes all over Brooklyn.

Fred's son, Donald, grew up in a segregated neighborhood in Queens. As Trump once said in an interview, "Different parts of Queens were rough; this [area] was an oasis." According to Fred Quint, the future president's next-door neighbor, "racially speaking," Donald Trump "grew up in white America."

And yet, at the very same time that young Trump was being taught that a good neighborhood was a white neighborhood, there were major changes taking place in Washington, DC. A very formal, Harvard-educated black man began working to transform government policies that had allowed father Trump to build segregated housing.

That man is the little-known Robert Clifton Weaver.

In virtually every way imaginable, Weaver was the opposite of Donald Trump.

Where Trump is boisterous and Twitter-savvy and loves to be in the headlines, Weaver was reserved and sometimes overlooked because of his lack of charisma. Even as he spent his career fighting for black housing rights, no one ever called him a civil rights leader. Where Trump sees government regulation as an annoyance,

Weaver pushed integration into federal housing regulation for thirty years before President Lyndon Johnson named him the first cabinet secretary of the Department of Housing and Urban Development. When the president signed the 1968 Fair Housing Act, Weaver was the head of HUD. That law, designed as an extension of the 1964 Civil Rights Act, was the first attempt by Congress to have the nation break away from racial segregation in housing.

Born in 1907, Weaver was raised in a black family whose history was defined by an explosive mix of race, property, and money. The family story begins with Weaver's great-grandfather. He was born a slave in North Carolina. When he was able to buy his freedom in the 1840s—from money he earned as a prized carpenter—he proudly took the name Freeman. Richard Freeman moved his wife and six kids to Washington, DC, where, over the next few generations, they became part of Washington's black elite, the so-called Black 400, of higher income and successful black families. Freeman's son was part of the first class at Harvard University's dentistry school, becoming the first professionally trained African American dentist in the country. The Freeman family owned property in Washington, DC, as well as a vacation home at Highland Beach on Maryland's Chesapeake Bay. It was purchased after the family was denied entry into a white resort. The family property was eventually passed down to Weaver.

Weaver's family and the Black 400 were mostly light-skinned black people who had been freed before the Civil War. Weaver's mother, Florence Freeman, went to a high school for children of the black elite at a time when very few black women, light or dark skinned, went to high school. But her family's connections and money put her in the school, where she learned Latin. She married another light-skinned member of the city's black elite, Mortimer Grover Weaver, the father of the future HUD secretary.

Weaver was born into a family pushing to integrate schools, white neighborhoods, and professional work from medicine to the law. As an adult he told an interviewer that his mother's number one lesson dealt with achieving racial integration by winning acceptance from white America. "The way to offset color prejudice is to be awfully good at whatever you do," he recalled. At a time when black leaders demanded racial equality, Weaver's parents had a different approach. "No militancy, no call to arms" from his folks, Weaver said. Their emphasis was on getting whites to make "merely an affirmation of [black people's] right to enjoy the integrity and self-respect that are the birthright of every American." Since his family saw excellence as the way to demonstrate that they were equal to whites, Weaver was held to a high standard in school. "If you did not do well, you felt that you had let your parents down—and they let you know it," Weaver said.

As a teen, Weaver attended Washington's Dunbar High School, the first black high school in the country to send large numbers of black students to Ivy League colleges and universities. Dunbar's pipeline to elite white schools was powered by the sad fact that African Americans who earned degrees from top schools did not get teaching jobs at most white colleges. Their best job option was to teach at black high schools. In DC, that top school was Dunbar. The famed psychologist Kenneth Clark called Dunbar "a white school in a segregated system... excellence at Dunbar represented the few—the percentage of Washington's black community that was middle class and upwardly mobile." And Weaver excelled at Dunbar. He was in the honors society and leader of the school's speech and debate team. In 1925, he graduated sixth in his class of over 250 students. He won a DC oratorical competition as a senior and, most incredibly, the young black man won admission to Harvard.

Yet before he entered his freshman year at Harvard University in 1925, the Harvard president, Lawrence Lowell, announced that black students would not be allowed in freshmen dorms. Weaver was hurt. Opposition to Lowell's decision came not only from incoming black students, but also from whites. The decision to segregate freshman dorms "was one which affected me rather personally," Weaver later explained. Instead, he lived with his brother, Mortimer, who was then getting a master's degree at Harvard.

Weaver started out in the engineering program but his success in economics courses led him to switch majors. Meanwhile, he made connections with several future civil rights leaders who were on campus. His sophomore year roommate, Louis Redding, became one of the NAACP's lead lawyers on the group of cases ending legal school segregation, *Brown v. Board of Education*. And he lived next door to William Hastie, who went on to become the nation's first black federal judge. Another college friend was Ralph Bunche, who would later win a Nobel Peace Prize as a diplomat and serve as undersecretary general of the United Nations.

After college Weaver enrolled in Harvard's PhD program in economics, earning top marks. In a recommendation letter, Professor Arthur Cole called Weaver's exam performance "the best in the entire group...a pleasant, well-appearing sort of fellow so agreeable, in fact, that one forgets at once that he has some Negro blood in him." Another professor noted that Weaver was "universally admired by students and associates" and "it would be a pity to allow racial prejudice to handicap him." After leaving school to teach economics and sociology for a short while at North Carolina A&T, a historically black college, he returned to Harvard to write his dissertation, becoming, in 1933, the first African American to get a doctorate in economics from Harvard and the second African American to get a doctorate in economics in the country.

President Roosevelt's New Deal brought the young economist into the world of national politics. Weaver and Harvard classmate John P. Davis saw the New Deal as a chance to push the federal government to back racial integration. By the summer of 1933, President Roosevelt was in the midst of creating the National Recovery Administration (NRA), a government agency to set labor standards for industry. But to Weaver and Davis's dismay, the NRA treated African American workers as inferior to whites. For instance, the NRA decided that blue-collar jobs in the textile industry—an industry relatively open to black laborers—would not be included in the administration's discussions about raising the minimum wage.

Weaver and Davis, fresh out of school and still unknown among government officials, formed the Negro Industrial League to testify before the NRA. They called for equal rights for black workers. Though they won minimum wage protections for Southern lumber workers, Weaver and Davis had few other victories. But their early work testifying for the NRA put them on the radar of both civil rights leaders and white Washington insiders. "They seemed to be the only Negroes in Washington who had any intelligent idea of what was going on down there," the NAACP activist Roy Wilkins told the group's leader, Walter White, in an August 1933 letter.

With help from civil rights leaders, Weaver got a job in the Roosevelt administration in the fall of 1933, when he was appointed assistant advisor on the Economic Status of Negroes, a position in the Department of the Interior. A year later, in October 1934, he was promoted to special advisor on the Economic Status of Negroes.

It was at this point that Weaver turned his longstanding fight for racial equality into a singular focus on ending housing segregation. The housing component of the New Deal attracted Weaver because it was just that: *new*. Given that it was such an original program, it would provide Weaver with the chance to secure equal rights for black people from its beginning. When Ickes, the Secretary of the Interior, asked Weaver if he knew enough about the housing industry to handle the job, Weaver admitted he knew "very little." Undeterred, Ickes responded: "You'll do fine. None of those sons of bitches know anything about it either."

Weaver initially planned to start his housing integration efforts with public housing. But first Weaver was able to open jobs to African Americans on Public Works Administration construction sites. He even succeeded in setting new rules for labor unions to get approval for contracts on federal construction projects if they hired a fair percentage of black workers. The appropriate share of black workers would be determined by the share of black workers in a given occupation according to the 1930 census. In 1935 and

1936, Weaver reviewed each PWA project proposal to determine the share of black workers that needed to be employed. He traveled across the country to negotiate with employers who refused to hire black workers. And he made sure that black architects were hired to work on construction sites. When Weaver began working at the US Housing Authority, which took over the work of the PWA in 1937, he was able to ensure that African Americans got 11.6 percent of the jobs.

At the same time, Weaver continued pushing for public housing integration. At one point he warned that it was "a dangerous precedent [that was] encouraging families of other races to believe that they have a prior claim, by virtue of race, to sole occupancy of a given neighborhood." Weaver predicted, correctly, that "the existence of such a label will create resistance to the introduction of Negro families [into public housing and private residential buildings] at a later date."

Yet he also knew, "if you went too far out [with demands for integrated public housing]...you were apt to lose your followership." In New York, for example, Weaver explained that "the desire to produce [more] housing also overwhelmed concerns about racial separation." And so Weaver directed most of his energy to ensuring that African Americans were given separate but affordable housing. While negotiating plans to build a housing project in a black Atlanta neighborhood, he told a colleague that needy black people in the neighborhood should be given preference for the new apartments: "The division should not be 50/50," with whites, he said. Weaver wanted to ease the shortage in the black neighborhoods since white neighborhoods refused to accept black residents. "That is the point which we can fight on," Weaver argued. It was a convoluted position for an integrationist, but Weaver saw leverage for future negotiations with local housing leaders in holding the line against giving whites half of the new apartments in new federally subsidized housing projects in the black section of town.

In 1944 he was appointed to lead Chicago's Committee on Race Relations, which had been formed in response to earlier race riots in Detroit as a means of preventing similar violence in Chicago. With his Washington connections and Harvard education, Weaver had unique status among both blacks and whites in Chicago. After less than a year of dealing with racial tensions, he became director of community services at the city's American Council on Race Relations. The new job allowed him to once again turn his attention to residential segregation and racially restrictive housing covenants, long a problem in Chicago. In the summer of 1944 he wrote that white excuses for keeping black people trapped in run-down ghettoes was weak because where black residents integrated white neighborhoods, "the Negro is proving to be a good tenant and a good neighbor." Weaver also tried new approaches to the argument over housing segregation. At one point he proposed replacing bans on black residents with other types of restrictions—like only selling houses in a designated area to single-family households or people in certain kinds of occupations. He was looking for any idea to give whites a sense of exclusivity without relying on "restrictions on account of race, creed, and color."

The idea did not work. Weaver then joined in the NAACP's effort to make it illegal to use racial covenants to prevent blacks from buying houses. In July 1945, while Weaver was working at the American Council on Race Relations, Thurgood Marshall, the NAACP counsel, organized a meeting in Weaver's office of over thirty lawyers and activists. Their goal was to end racial covenants. In a follow-up memo, Weaver wrote: "In the whole network of devises and practices for exclusion, the race restrictive housing covenants have gained currency as a respectable and legitimate device. This is a fiction that must be disputed by sociological and legal attacks."

In fact, it was Weaver who became the architect of the NAACP's "sociological attack" on racially restrictive housing covenants. Marshall presented federal courts with briefs based on research done by Weaver. Marshall argued that racially discriminatory housing covenants produced "enormous overcrowding" in black neighborhoods around the nation. Corralling black people in neighborhoods with poor housing, they contended, led to high rates of "disease, death, crime, immortality, juvenile delinquency, racial tensions and economic exploitation."

The NAACP's challenge to racial covenants on houses grew out of two cases. In the summer of 1945 a black family, Ethel and J. D. Shelley and their children, bought a home in a white St. Louis neighborhood. But alarmed white neighbors pointed out that the property bought by the Shelley family was under a restrictive covenant that precluded its sale to people of the "Negro or Mongolian race." The Shelley family found themselves locked in a court battle with little chance of winning and asked the NAACP for help. Also that year, a black Detroit couple, Orsel and Minnie McGhee, was told that a new house they bought could only be occupied by whites because of a restrictive covenant. In Washington, DC, at around the same time, a white real estate broker and Italian immigrant named Raphael Urciolo was being sued by a white real estate attorney for selling property with racially restrictive housing covenants to black residents. Each of these cases reached the Supreme Court in June 1947.

NAACP lawyers argued that no court could enforce restrictive covenants because that clause in housing contracts was in violation of the Constitution's equal rights protections. It was the first use of federal law against racially restrictive housing covenants. The NAACP's top legal minds, Thurgood Marshall and his mentor Charles Hamilton Houston, understood that housing covenants had become accepted across the nation and they needed a new argument to win over the Supreme Court. In addition to citing constitutional protections, they also wanted to show the high court that covenants were bad for society. That is why they turned to Weaver, with his long history in housing, to go beyond the law in making the case that restrictive covenants produced racial conflict.

The two restrictive covenant cases to reach the Supreme Court—*Shelley v. Kraemer* (the St. Louis case) and *Hurd v. Hodges* (the DC cases)—received sensational press coverage. It is hard to exaggerate how much controversy surrounded the case, given that so much property around the country had racially restrictive housing covenants. Three Supreme Court justices—Stanley Reed, Wiley Rutledge, and Robert Jackson—had to recuse themselves because they lived on property with covenants. An alliance of liberal groups, including the ACLU, the American Jewish Committee, and big labor's Council of Industrial Organizations, along with the US Justice Department, all sided with the black families.

The NAACP won both cases. The Supreme Court ruled that the covenants could not be enforced in court because they were unconstitutional. The NAACP proclaimed that the ruling broke the paralyzing grip of racism on the real estate industry and gave "thousands of prospective [black, Jewish and other minority] homebuyers throughout the United States new courage and hope in the American form of government." The top black newspaper in Chicago, the *Chicago Defender*, predicted that the ruling meant the beginning of "a new era of racial relationships in Chicago and the nation."

Weaver's success in Chicago led him to become New York State rent commissioner from 1955 through 1959. In 1960 the celebrated fighter for housing integration became chair of the New York City Housing and Redevelopment Board. By now Weaver was well known nationally.

After John F. Kennedy won the 1960 race for the White House—with strong backing from black voters—he put Weaver in charge of all federal housing programs, including public housing and federally insured housing mortgages, as head of the federal Housing and Home Finance Agency. But the sad truth is that the Kennedy Administration was using Weaver as a buffer against demands from civil rights groups that the president take immediate action on a campaign pledge to issue an executive order desegregating all federally subsidized housing, most of all public housing projects.

During the 1960 campaign Kennedy criticized the incumbent Republican, President Eisenhower, for failing to do just that: "I renew my call on the President to issue the order...if he does not do it, a new Democratic administration will." Closer to Election Day, Kennedy turned up the pressure on his opponent, Republican Richard Nixon, by reminding black voters that President Eisenhower "could sign an Executive Order ending housing segregation tomorrow," and "one stroke of the pen would have worked wonders for millions of Negroes who want their children to grow up in decency."

But when Kennedy won the 1960 election, he got cold feet. He decided a ban on segregation in federal housing projects was too much of a political risk, especially in the South, which was then a stronghold for Democrats. The president came under pressure from black groups to keep his campaign promise. Now Weaver's job was to explain the president's hesitancy to the black community while looking for a legislative compromise to keep the president out of political trouble.

Weaver did his job. The compromise that was devised called for federal agencies to take a stand against racial segregation in housing. But other top administration officials negotiated limits on the government's power to enforce the new law. Top Kennedy aides wanted the effort to be mostly symbolic. They won. The new order, signed by the president in November 1962, did not apply to public housing that had already been built. And it was left up to nervous bureaucrats at each government agency to decide if states were practicing racial discrimination in their use of federal subsidies for public housing and to back increased availability of home mortgages. President Kennedy knew the order was weak and feared that if Weaver resigned, he could come under attack in the black press and suffer damaged relationships with civil rights leaders.

Weaver was upset, but he bit his tongue and stayed on the Kennedy team. He later said he "recognized...two choices. I either went along with that, or else I resigned. And I wasn't ready to resign. So I went along with it." As Weaver saw it, he had spent the last three decades fighting for fair housing for African Americans. And he was now the highest-ranking African American in the US government, practically a cabinet secretary with an enormous amount of influence on housing and other issues. And he believed that he could wield his unprecedented power as a black federal official most effectively by continuing in government instead of quitting and becoming an open critic of the president. He had no interest in falling on his sword to become a martyr for the civil rights community. It did not fit his personality or the lifetime of work he had put into ending racial bias in the housing industry.

And there was one more consideration: President Kennedy was already advocating for the creation of a new cabinet department with the potential to deeply affect the housing options for African Americans: the Department of Housing and Urban Development.

During his campaign, and then in a March 1961 message to Congress, Kennedy called for "the establishment in the Executive Branch... a new, Cabinet-rank, Department of Housing and Urban Affairs" to address the fact that "urban and suburban areas now contain the overwhelming majority of our population, and a preponderance of our industrial, commercial, and educational resources."

Kennedy also saw political advantage in trumpeting the new housing agency to counter criticism of failure to sign a more powerful executive order banning housing discrimination. But he spoke about the proposal for a housing department in general terms, highlighting the increasing need for the federal government to address the unique problems facing fast-growing American cities in the post–World War II era. Senator Joseph Clark of Pennsylvania, a Kennedy ally and former mayor of Philadelphia, wrote a *New York Times* column arguing that a department designed to pay attention to urban affairs, including housing, would give "the city dweller the same status and recognition that the farmer has enjoyed for more than a century."

Weaver campaigned for the president to open the doors of a powerful housing agency. It was vindication for his decision to stay in the administration after the loud complaints about the president's tepid executive order. And the odds favored Weaver as the president's choice to head the new department. During a 1961 speech before the US Conference of Mayors, Weaver argued for creating of the new department on the grounds that the agency he currently headed, the Housing and Home Finance Agency, was a "bureaucratic monstrosity." Weaver, with obvious approval from the White House, told the mayors that money was being wasted and opportunities lost as a result of "overlapping areas of responsibility and areas where nobody seems to have any responsibility." He kept beating the drums for congressional approval of the new agency during a later speech before the National Association of Mutual Savings Banks. Weaver told the mortgage lenders "we need an efficient, consolidated structure that will place these vital, expanding [housing] programs...under the direct surveillance of the President."

In Congress, the Democrats' push for the new cabinet agency met a wall of opposition from Republicans. The conservatives feared federal interference in state and local housing programs. When the president announced that Weaver would head the new department, even liberal Republicans like Congressman John Lindsay of New York accused Kennedy of making it seem their opposition to a new department was due to racism. Lindsay said that he respected Weaver, and that "the President's injection of the civil rights thing into it is a terrible shame." That dissent found support among segregationist Southern Democrats opposed to the prospect of Weaver, a black man, becoming a cabinet secretary with more power to push for racial integration. A February 1962 piece in the *Washington Star* called it "deplorable that the fact of Mr. Weaver's race is alienating southern Democrats' votes," but "even more deplorable, however, that the fact of his race is being used in an attempt to coerce Members of Congress into voting for a government reorganization plan in which, on its merit, they do not believe."

Public support for the new housing agency was still growing a year later, when President Kennedy was assassinated. His vice president,

Lyndon Johnson, used the president's death as part of a strategy to rally support for the president's legislative agenda, including the creation of the housing department.

President Johnson signed the Housing and Urban Development Act on August 10, 1965. The Department of Housing and Urban Development was officially established that September.

Johnson, a Texan who knew the power of the Southern wing of his party, had several reasons to be hesitant about putting Weaver at the helm of the new department. Obviously, the so-called Dixiecrats, or Southern Democrats in Congress, wanted to be sure that a black man was not about to dictate racial policy to them. Less obviously, there was also reluctance among liberals. Weaver's moderate and pragmatic demeanor—which had allowed him to stay in government for over three decades—made him seem weak at a time when civil rights activists in the South had to defy being jailed and several Northern cities saw rioting in black neighborhoods. During a conversation with Roy Wilkins, who headed the NAACP, President Johnson explained, "You know, I love Bob Weaver and I admire him, but Bob Weaver is not a dynamic fellow that we're going to need and I don't know whether we really want to insist on putting a Negro at the head of urban affairs when we get it."

But Weaver's reputation as a Harvard-educated black man willing to make political deals carried the day in the Johnson White House and on Capitol Hill. On January 13, 1966, President Johnson announced that Weaver would be his nominee. The argument over Weaver's appointment had been going on for so long that there was little new to debate when he came before Congress for confirmation hearings. With surprising speed—given the intensity of earlier arguments over Weaver's race and low-key character—he was confirmed and sworn in as the first secretary of HUD because racial moderates in Congress saw political value in being able to point to the first African American cabinet member in the history of the United States.

But racial tensions continued to grow across the nation during Weaver's first days in office. In the South, civil rights activists continued to force daily confrontations with white segregationists to test the power of the new Voting Rights Act, signed in August 1965. On the West Coast, bloody riots broke out in Watts, a poor black neighborhood in Los Angeles, just a week after President Johnson signed the act. And in Chicago, Dr. Martin Luther King Jr. started the Chicago Freedom Movement, a drive coordinated with the city's biggest black churches and political groups, to improve the economic situation of black Chicagoans, with a focus on ending the strict racial segregation that sealed much of the city's black population in run-down housing projects and neighborhoods full of despair.

King's decision to move the focal point of his civil rights activity from the South to a Northern city and to make Chicago's segregated housing his prime target stirred racial bitterness. White Northerners who supported King's fight for equal rights to vote or go into Southern hotels and restaurants now found their lives disrupted by his movement.

King moved his family into one of the city's black slums to attract television cameras. He led a raucous march to city hall to place a list of demands on its doors. That was just the start. And it coincided with the focus on segregated housing in Washington, as Weaver took control of the federal government's new housing department.

During the summer of 1966, King led protest-picnics at parks in all-white Chicago neighborhoods, hosted night vigils at real estate offices, and arranged for demonstrations outside the doors of real estate brokers. King was in the papers daily. He called out the city's real estate board, brokers, banks, and savings institutions for enforcing the lines dividing black and white neighborhoods. King demanded that the city's real estate power brokers make public statements vowing not to discriminate based on race as they gave out loans and showed properties. He wanted more low-cost housing and a larger police presence in public housing. And he pushed for more building inspection in low-income neighborhoods.

Frightened by the prospect of black families moving in next door, working-class white Chicagoans in some neighborhoods responded with violence. White counterprotestors flying Confederate flags and swastikas threw bricks, bottles, and cherry bombs at black demonstrators. They slashed the tires on cars carrying the marchers and smashed their windshields.

The conflict became national news when King, leading eight hundred protestors from Marquette Park to a real estate office, was hit in the head with a rock. He toppled to the ground. Later in the same march, someone threw a knife at King, missing him and hitting one of King's white allies. He later said he "had never seen as much hate and hostility on the part of so many people."

The threats of violence against King grew even louder when he announced plans for a major march in the all-white Chicago suburb of Cicero for Labor Day. "Cicero in the north symbolizes the same kind of hard-core resistance to change as Selma in the south," King told reporters. "And I think it will in fact eventually be the Selma of the north in the sense that we've got to have a confrontation in that community."

Only a few months beforehand, in May 1966, a black seventeen-year-old applying for a job in Cicero had been beaten to death by a group of white teens. Chicago's mayor, Richard Daley, a white Democrat, asked King to cancel the march in exchange for moderate reforms, such as a promise from city bankers' associations not to consider race when determining who could take out a mortgage. Daley also offered to have the Chicago Real Estate Board end its opposition to a state fair housing law.

King welcomed the proposal but still planned to march. Daley won a court injunction. King was angry over the court order but did not march. He traveled to Memphis, Tennessee, to support striking garbage workers and was shot to death on a hotel balcony. More riots broke out across the nation.

By this point, President Johnson and Weaver had already called for a Fair Housing Act, as an extension of the 1964 Civil Rights Act. It would be a law that, unlike President Kennedy's earlier executive order, covered both public and private residential housing. "Once more this year I am asking the Congress to join in an attack on the discrimination that still afflicts this land," Johnson wrote in a message to Congress asking for passage of a Fair Housing Act. He wanted the legislation to "prohibit discrimination, on either racial or religious grounds, by owners, brokers and lending corporations." His proposal also gave the attorney general and private citizens the right to file lawsuits when there was proof of racial bias against home buyers and renters.

Testifying on behalf of the bill before Congress that May, Secretary Weaver noted that housing was "the one commodity in the American market that is not freshly available on equal terms to everyone who can afford to buy." At a November 1966 speech before the National Association of Real Estate Boards, he argued that fair housing was "required if we are to revitalize our cities."

The problem of residential housing segregation in American cities was put vividly on display the following summer—dubbed the Long Hot Summer of 1967—as race riots erupted in segregated black residential areas of cities like Detroit, Cincinnati, and Buffalo. In all, 159 riots across America resulted in more than eighty deaths.

Weaver, who had spent three decades working to end housing segregation, identified the long-term residential separation of the races by neighborhoods as a central cause of the race riots. In July 1967 testimony before the Senate Subcommittee on Housing and Urban Affairs, Weaver made headlines when he said that rioting in Newark was due to the damaging effects of housing segregation. "While we condemn disorder and violence in urban America, we must also understand why they occur," he said, before pointing to "decades of neglect, discrimination, and deprivation" in black ghettoes.

The Long Hot Summer of 1967 led President Johnson to ask the governor of Illinois, Otto Kerner, to lead a commission to recommend policies to end the violence. The Kerner group also linked the summer of rioting to housing segregation, recommending "a national, comprehensive, and enforceable open occupancy law," as well as billions of dollars in new investment in housing available to people across color lines.

The report warned in words that have been heavily quoted ever since that "our nation is moving toward two societies, one black, one white—separate and unequal."

Though the Kerner Commission's report angered Johnson—he thought it gave his administration too little credit—at this point the president had already proposed another Fair Housing Bill, which finally did pass through Congress as Title VIII of the Civil Rights Act of 1968. It was signed by the president on April 11, 1968, just one week after King's assassination.

Under the Fair Housing Act of 1968, it became illegal to "refuse to sell or rent...or otherwise make unavailable or deny, a dwelling to any person because of race, color, religion, sex, familial status, or national origin." It was deemed illegal to change the "terms, conditions, or privileges" when renting or selling to someone from a protected class. And it was made unlawful to "make, print, or publish... any notice, statement, or advertisement...that indicates any preference, limitation, or discrimination based on race, color, religion, sex, handicap, familial status, or national origin." Racially restrictive housing covenants, made unenforceable by the Supreme Court in 1948, were now officially illegal. Under the law, "aggrieved persons" could bring a civil suit against a potential lawbreaker in US district court. They could also inform HUD, which would then investigate the claim and create what the law called a "conciliation agreement" between the aggrieved person and the lawbreaker. If the lawbreaker failed to cooperate, the secretary of HUD was to bring the case to the attorney general. And, of course, the Fair Housing Act ordered "all executive departments and agencies [to] administer their programs and activities...in a manner affirmatively to further" the overall goal of fair housing.

President Johnson decided not to seek reelection in 1968, and Weaver resigned from HUD as the president left office. He took a job as president of Baruch College, part of the City University of New York system. He later served as a professor of urban affairs at Hunter College.

The housing agency he built in Washington continued to play a central role in race relations. Its mission statement still calls for "inclusive and sustainable communities free from discrimination." In 1977, during confirmation hearings for Patricia Roberts Harris to serve as President Carter's HUD secretary—and the first African American woman to serve in the cabinet—racial bias in housing remained the central issue. Harris was asked if her career as a partner at a prestigious law firm, her time overseas as ambassador to Luxembourg, and her wealth prevented her from understanding the housing troubles facing America's poor and minorities. Harris responded in defiant, personal tones. She testified that despite her success, she was "a black woman who even eight years ago could not buy a house in parts of [Washington, DC]."

Since Weaver christened the department as the first black cabinet secretary, presidents of both parties have put more blacks and Latinos at its helm than any other cabinet-level agency. Five HUD secretaries have been black, and three have been Latino.

Since Weaver's trailblazing work to create HUD, there has been a decline in segregation in most of the nation's housing markets. Yet American cities remain heavily segregated by neighborhood. As mentioned earlier, public housing residents in major cities such as Philadelphia and Detroit are nearly all black and in cities such as New York and Los Angeles nearly all black and Latino. Even private home ownership remains divided by race. The 2010 census found 45 percent of blacks and 48 percent of Hispanics owned a house. By comparison, 71 percent of whites had their own house. A 2012 report from the Manhattan Institute found increasing racial integration in American neighborhoods. Much of the improvement was due to more Asians and Hispanics living in mixed neighborhoods with blacks. Residential segregation between blacks and whites also declined somewhat, but it remained relatively high. The study concluded "there is every reason to relish the fact that there is more freedom in housing today than 50 years ago and to applaud those who fought to create the change."

But the improved rate of housing integration has come against the backdrop of the long history of highly segregated residential housing in America. "While recent modest declines in black segregation levels are welcome, the 2010 census shows that the average black resident still lives in a neighborhood that is 45 percent black and 36 percent white," the chief demographer at the Brooking Institution, William Frey, told the *New York Times*. "At the same time, the average white lives in a neighborhood that is 78 percent white and 7 percent black. Black segregation levels are even higher for children, signaling the continued separation of black and white families across communities with different levels of resources available for schools and other services important to nurturing the next generation."

This lack of progress has many causes. Some will argue that, by 1968, patterns of segregation were already impossible to break down. Secretary Patricia Roberts Harris pointed to the lack of power HUD was given to punish the people making money by keeping the lines of neighborhood segregation in place. Harris complained that the Fair Housing Act merely allowed HUD to "ask the discovered lawbreaker whether he wants to discuss the matter." HUD has also been criticized for not referring nearly enough cases to the Justice Department, even when lawbreakers were being uncooperative.

And politics played a role. As suburban areas drew whites from cities, many politicians turned away from aggressively pursuing enforcement of the Fair Housing Act. They felt no need, as cities were becoming predominantly minority. Economics also was a factor. Despite the growth of the black middle class, African Americans generally have less money in the bank and are not able to buy property in more expensive city neighborhoods that remain mostly white. These trends are exacerbated by the efforts of greedy real estate developers, who concluded that, despite the Fair Housing Act, it was worth the risk to discriminate against African Americans in order to protect their investments by using racial segregation to maintain high property values. In 1973, Donald Trump, who had taken over his father's real estate company, was accused by the Justice Department of still refusing to rent apartments to African American tenants, thus violating the five-year-old Fair Housing Act.

Yet the discrimination continued. Even after the initial consent decree between Trump and the Justice Department expired, the government was still reviewing charges of housing discrimination against Trump. "We believe that an underlying pattern of discrimination continues to exist in the Trump Management organization," a government lawyer wrote to Trump's lawyer in 1978. "While more black families were now renting in Trump-owned buildings...many had been confined to a small number of complexes," the *New York Times* later reported. "And tenants in some of these buildings had complained about the conditions, from falling plaster to rusty light fixtures to bloodstained floors."

When Hillary Clinton brought up the lawsuit and the consent decree at the first presidential debate, Trump denied the facts: "Now as far as the lawsuit, yes when I was very young. We settled the suit with zero—with no admission of guilt. It was very easy to do." Using his lavish financial resources to make social problems disappear is a textbook example of Trump's privilege. His response illustrates his ignorance of the history of Robert Weaver's long fight to break down residential segregation. President Trump views the burden of being black in America as less important than his biased view that whites are being unfairly asked to deal with the history of racial discrimination against black people. As a housing developer he was more interested in making money than in confronting the experience of black people being racially isolated in bad neighborhoods, stereotyped, and subject to discrimination by schools, employers, and police. In his inaugural presidential address he spoke to the nation about scary black neighborhoods full of "crime and gangs and drugs," without offering compassion or solutions for the people in those neighborhoods. Instead he promised his white supporters to keep the chaos at a distance, saying, "This American carnage stops right here and stops right now."

As president, Trump's personal history of resenting efforts to achieve racial equality has opened the door to undoing the racial progress made over the past fifty years. A president without any understanding of the basics of black American history saps the force from Martin Luther King's famous suggestion that the arc of history bends toward justice. How can history have an arc if the nation's top leader keeps pushing it back in time?

Any honest review of Donald Trump's life, career, and early presidency must conclude that he is ignorant and resentful toward African American history. Despite working in real estate, he opposes equal housing for black people. Despite bragging about his expensive education, he shows no concern for the education of black people. His promise to "Make America Great Again" evoke a time when black people were excluded from restaurants, hotels, and public facilities. And, of course, his campaign pitch to black people, commemorated in the title of this book, illustrated just how little he cared about them or had to offer. It was merely an assertion that they had nothing and couldn't do any worse.

Of course, even the litany of racist behavior described in these pages cannot fully capture Trump's lack of respect for people of color. It is outside the scope of this book to deal with the administration's tragic lack of response to the hurricane in Puerto Rico and with Trump's desire to turn away immigrants of color from what he infamously called "shithole countries." These pages have not dealt with his planned deportation of the Dreamers, young people whose parents illegally brought them to the country. Yet those stories all reinforce the picture of a president who has no concern, or indeed even patience, for people who aren't white.

In truth, much of America's progress toward equality was made possible by a historic civil rights movement. People, mostly outside the government and mostly black, won hard fights to end segregationist laws and pass the Civil Rights Act, the Voting Rights Act, and the Fair Housing Act, which are now essential parts of America's history.

So many victories were powered by the smarts and the personal sacrifice of people like Robert Weaver, A. Philip Randolph, James Meredith, Everett Dirksen, Robert Moses, and James Baldwin.

That's why the answer to "What the hell do you have to lose?" is simple: a lot. Far more, it appears, than he will ever know.

Acknowledgments

Writing this book took me back to my first book—*Eyes on the Prize: America's Civil Rights Years, 1954–1965*. It was published exactly thirty years ago in collaboration with a celebrated PBS documentary of the same name.

The man behind that project was Henry Hampton. He saw something in my work as a *Washington Post* reporter and asked me to write the book. Now I feel as if he had been passing me a baton. Henry gave me time to interview leaders of the civil rights movement. He pushed me to go into archives, to visit the places where civil rights history was made, and to tell the story honestly.

That fit with high expectations set by my mentor and editor at the *Post*, Herbert Denton. Herb was a demanding teacher. On every story—from obituaries to articles on schools, politics, and civil rights—he pushed me to do more reporting, to cover all sides and to write with passion. His goal was always to give voice to people never heard from in big newspapers.

I begin these acknowledgments with their names because their years of tutelage equipped me to answer President Trump's insulting question to black people: "What the hell do you have to lose?"

A very heartfelt thank-you to Joshua Bucheister. His ability as researcher, his care for the written word, and his drive proved all-important to telling this story with accuracy.

Thank you to my home team: Delise, Antonio, Rae, Raffi, Erika, Morgan, and Patrick. With newcomers Elias, Pepper, and Wesley, we are joyfully watching a new generation climbing to greater heights. My sister, Elena Jenny, and my brother, Roger Williams, have always been role models for their baby brother. Bill Lightfoot, Gabe Mehretaab, Barrett Nnoka and Armstrong Williams are my buddies.

Peter Osnos, the founder of PublicAffairs, has been a friend since his days as a top editor at the *Post*. He later published my biography of Supreme Court justice Thurgood Marshall. A caring man and journalist, Peter lived through America's tumultuous times on race. He believed in this book from the start. I am so grateful for his vision and confidence.

Thank you to Benjamin Adams, the executive editor of PublicAffairs, for his belief in this book and his work to make it a success. Clive Priddle, publisher, and Jaime Leifer, vice president, associate publisher, and director of publicity, helped this book take flight. Collin Tracy skillfully guided the copyediting.

Thank you to Eric Lupfer, my agent at Fletcher & Company, literary management. His confidence in the urgent need to tell this story proved critical to finding a publisher and getting this book into print.

Thank you to Joe Sangiorgio for his tremendous help with research for my column and television work.

A big salute to my Fox cohosts on *The Five*: Kimberly Guilfoyle, Greg Gutfeld, Dana Perino, and Jesse Watters. That show is the best. The production team is so wonderful: Megan Albano, Deb Cote, Emily Cyr, Queenette Karikari, Sean O'Rourke, Mina Pertesis, and Susan Wertheim.

Special thanks to my brother-in-law, Dr. Arthur (Scooter) West, and his wife, Leathia. That also goes for their children, Chip and Marissa, and son-in-law, Nick Nasrallah.

The team at Fox includes such good people, beginning with our leader, Rupert Murdoch. That Fox family includes executives who have spurred me to do important journalism: Jack Abernethy, Shari

Berg, Porter Berry, Bryan Boughton, Dianne Brandi, John Finley, Brian Jones, Jessica Loker, Bill Sammon, Suzanne Scott, and Jay Wallace.

My inner circle of Fox hosts is always there with a good word, pushing to new heights: David Asman, Bret Baier, Shannon Bream, Harris Faulkner, Sean Hannity, Bill Hemmer, Ed Henry, Brit Hume, Brian Kilmeade, Lisa Kennedy, Howard Kurtz, Martha MacCallum, Charles Payne, Geraldo Rivera, Shepard Smith, Leland Vittert, and Chris Wallace.

Jimmy Finkelstein, publisher of the *Hill*, is passionate about the news. So is his wife, Pamela Gross Finkelstein. Niall Stanage, the editor of my *Hill* column, and Bob Cusack, the *Hill*'s top editor, are top-rank journalists.

Thank you to my personal friends!

My church family, the wonderful people at Trinity Episcopal Church, is led by Father John Harmon.

Thanks to my cousins: Calito, Gracie, Haroldo (his wife, Lulu; children, Omar and Nadia; daughter-in-law, Andrea; and son-in-law, Jorge), Javier, Ligia, and her terrific son, Jonathan Mason. I am grateful to Ricardo, Rilda, Rogelio, Armonia, Donna, and Ruby-Linda.

Thanks to Oakwood Friends School and Haverford College.

I also have a family of friends: Arthur Aidala; Susan Alexander; Jodi Allen; Ronnie Allen; Jim Arrington; David Axelrod; Fred Barnes; Bishop Nathan Baxter; Fritz Bech; Lucille Blair and Liam Blair-Ford; Catherine Cook-Holmes; Chris and Lynne Cowan; Spencer Crew; Eric and Tina Easter; John Eshun; Karen Finney; Michael and Ulrika Francis; David Garrow; Cheryl Gibert; Paul Gigot; Spiro Gioldasis; Ken Gormley; Don Graham; Warren Graves; Gina Wishnick Grossman; Cherie Grzech; my neighbors Scot, Karen (Vossler), and Gavin Hagerthey; Bill and Gail Herald (my fellow grandparents); Michael Hicks; Jim and Ann Hudson; Dante James; Rhonda Jenkins; Colby King; Lars Larson; Marsha Levick; Bob Ley; Bill and Cynthiana Lightfoot; Charisse Lillie; James Loadholt; Lynne Jordal-Martin; Lori Martin; Cam MacQueen; Nancie McPhail; Susan

Mangold; Thurgood Marshall Jr.; Michael Meyers; Courtland Milloy; Rob Monaco; Sarah Mullins; Vincent and Lisa Napolean; Ruben Navarette; Jerralynn Ness; Arthel Neville; Dr. Michael Newman; Kojo Nnamdi; Judy Nnoka; Ali Noorani; Franco Nuschese; Cathleen O'Brien; Jeremy Peters; Bret Perkins; Amb. Edward Perkins; Joe Piscopo; Jennifer Pond; Joe Quinlan; Diane Rehm; Jason Riley; Ed Rogers; Bob Schwartz; Senator Tim Scott; Steve Scully; Steve Selden; Scott Simon; Brent Smith; Dr. Sian Spurney; Bret Stephens; Richard and Michelle Strauss; Jessica Tarlov; Chris Teal; Paul and Mendy Thaler; Julie Talarico; Justice Clarence Thomas and Ginny Thomas; Diane Thomson; Robert Traynham; Sterling Tucker; Fay Vincent; George Will; Bob Wilson; Chris Wilson; Philip Winder; Jason Wrenn; Ryan Yeisley; David Zinn; Barry Zubrow.

Thank you to my Fox family: Addisu Bekele, Dana Blanton, Jason Chaffetz, Megan Clarke, Andrew Conti, Kevin Corke, Allison Deblois, Don Grannum, Jennifer Griffin, Jaclyn Giuliano, Lacey Halpern, Mary Katherine Ham, Marie Harf, Stephen Hayes, John Huber, Tony Jarrett, Ashley Koerber, Charles Krauthammer, Mary Kreinbihl, Mara Liasson, Stacia Lynds, Lori Martin, Gwen Marder, Dagen McDowell, Angela McGlowan, Connell McShane, Chris Mills, Ron Mitchell, Arnon Mishkin, Jennifer Montalvo, Andrew Napolitano, Iraida O'Callaghan, Jazzmin Patterson, Patricia Pert, Lauren Cowan Pick, Katy Ricalde, Craig Rivera, Cristina Robbins, Doug Rohrbeck, Ed Rollins, Karl Rove, Lauren Schneider, Anita Siegfriedt, Amy Sohnen, Chris Stirewalt, Gillian Turner, Caroline Whiteman, Eboni Williams, Gerri Willis, Jezzamine Wolk, Jack Wright, and Eldad Yaron.

Thank you.

Bibliography

Introduction

Abdul-Jabbar, Kareem. "What It Means to Be Black During a Trump Administration: On Hopelessness—and the Way to Escape It." *Washington Post*, November 10, 2016. https://www.washingtonpost.com/?utm_term=.d33fa4d 8cb86.

"AP Poll: U.S. Majority Have Prejudice Against Blacks." *USA Today*, October 27, 2012. https://www.usatoday.com/story/news/politics/2012/10/27/poll -black-prejudice-america/1662067.

Blanton, Dana. "Fox News Poll: Voters' Mood Sours, 56 Percent Say Trump Tearing Country Apart." Fox News, August 30, 2017. http://www.foxnews .com/politics/2017/08/30/fox-news-poll-voters-mood-sours-56-percent-say -trump-tearing-country-apart.html.

Coates, Ta-Nehisi. "The First White President: The Foundation of Donald Trump's Presidency Is the Negation of Barack Obama's Legacy." *Atlantic*, October 2017. https://www.theatlantic.com/magazine/archive/2017/10/the-first -white-president-ta-nehisi-coates/537909.

———. "How the Obama Administration Talks to Black America: 'Convenient Race-Talk' from a President Who Ought to Know Better." *Atlantic*, May 20, 2013. https://www.theatlantic.com/politics/archive/2013/05/how-the-obama- administration-talks-to-black-america/276015.

Confessore, Nicholas. "For Whites Sensing Decline, Donald Trump Unleashes Words of Resistance." *New York Times*, July 13, 2016. https://www.nytimes .com/2016/07/14/us/politics/donald-trump-white-identity.html.

Cooper, Alexia, and Erica L. Smith. "Homicide Trends in the United States, 1980-2008, Annual Rates for 2009 and 2010." U.S. Department of Justice, Office of Justice Programs, Bureau of Justice Statistics, November 2011.

Flitter, Emily, and Chris Kahn. "Exclusive: Trump Supporters More Likely to View Blacks Negatively." Reuters, June 28, 2016. https://www.reuters.com /article/us-usa-election-race/exclusive-trump-supporters-more-likely-to-view -blacks-negatively-reuters-ipsos-poll-idUSKCN0ZE2SW.

Friedman, Noah. "Trump 'Places Like Afghanistan Are Safer Than Some of Our Inner Cities.'" *Business Insider*, September 21, 2016. https://www.businessinsider .com.au/donald-trump-afghanistan-american-city-refugee-crisis-2016-9.

Graham, Bryan Armen. "Donald Trump Blasts NFL Anthem Protesters: 'Get That Son of a Bitch Off the Field.'" *Guardian* (London), September 23, 2017. https://www.theguardian.com/sport/2017/sep/22/donald-trump-nfl-national -anthem-protests.

Greene, Leonard. "Donald Trump, Black People Have Everything to Lose If They Vote for You." *New York Daily News*, August 26, 2016. http://www.nydailynews .com/news/politics/greene-black-people-lose-vote-trump-article-1.2766133.

Haberman, Maggie. "Donald Trump Blames Earpiece for Declining to Disavow David Duke." *New York Times*, February 29, 2016. https://www .nytimes.com/politics/first-draft/2016/02/29/donald-trump-blames-earpiece -for-declining-to-disavow-david-duke.

Ingraham, Christopher. "On Twitter, Trump Accuses Blacks of Racism Three Times as Often as Whites." *Washington Post*, August 14, 2017.

Jensen, Tom. "GOP Quickly Unifies Around Trump; Clinton Still Has Modest Lead." *Public Policy Polling*, May 10, 2016. https://www.publicpolicypolling .com/wp-content/uploads/2017/09/PPP_Release_National_51016.pdf.

Keneally, Meghan. "Donald Trump Says African Americans Worst Off 'Ever, Ever, Ever' in Latest Push for Black Voters." ABC News, September 21, 2016.

King Jr., Martin Luther. "Letter from a Birmingham Jail," April 16, 1963. In *The Portable Sixties Reader*, edited by Ann Charters. New York: Penguin Books, 2003.

Lopez, German. "How Trump Both Stokes and Obscures His Supporters' Racial Resentment." *Vox*, August 31, 2017. https://www.vox.com/policy-and -politics/2017/8/31/16226488/trump-identity-politics-racism.

Malloy, Tim, and Rubenstein Pat Smith. "By Huge Margin, Americans Say Clinton Is More Qualified, Quinnipiac University National Poll Finds;

Except for Honesty, She Tops Trump on Key Qualities." Quinnipiac University Poll, September 15, 2016. https://poll.qu.edu/national/release-detail?Release ID=2379.

Master, Cyra. "Black GOP Senator Condemns Trump for Failing to Denounce GOP." *Hill*, February 28, 2016. http://thehill.com/blogs/ballot-box/presi dential-races/271111-black-gop-senator-condemns-trump-for-failing-to -denounce.

Milbank, Dana. "Donald Trump's New Loose Cannon." *Washington Post*, August 24, 2016. https://www.washingtonpost.com/?utm_term=.152fea255e20.

Neal, Samantha. "Views of Racism as a Major Problem Increases Sharply, Especially Among Democrats." Pew Research Center, August 29, 2017. http:// www.pewresearch.org/fact-tank/2017/08/29/views-of-racism-as-a-major -problem-increase-sharply-especially-among-democrats.

"New Poll: Some Americans Express Troubling Racial Attitudes as Majority Oppose White Supremacists." Sabato's Crystal Ball, University of Virginia Center for Politics. http://www.centerforpolitics.org/crystalball/articles/new -poll-some-americans-express-troubling-racial-attitudes-even-as-majority -oppose-white-supremacists.

Obama, Barack. "Remarks by the President at Congressional Black Caucus Foundation 46th Annual Phoenix Awards Dinner." Speech, Washington, DC, September 18, 2016. https://obamawhitehouse.archives.gov/the-press -office/2016/09/18/remarks-president-congressional-black-caucus-found ation-46th-annual.

———. "Remarks by the President at Morehouse College Commencement Ceremony." Speech, Morehouse College, Atlanta, Georgia, May 19, 2013.

Pew Research Center. "As Election Nears, Voters Divided over Democracy and Respect." October 2016. http://www.people-press.org/2016/10/27 /as-election-nears-voters-divided-over-democracy-and-respect/.

"Poverty Rate by Race/Ethnicity: Timeframe 2016." Kaiser Family Foundation.

Reilly, Katie. "Read Hillary Clinton's 'Basket of Deplorables' Remarks About Donald Trump Supporters." *Time*, September 10, 2016. http://time .com/4486502/hillary-clinton-basket-of-deplorables-transcript.

Robinson, Eugene. "Trump 'Pivots' 360 Degrees, Back into the Mud." *Washington Post*, August 22, 2016. https://www.washingtonpost.com/opinions /trump-pivots-360-degrees-back-into-the-mud/2016/08/22/1b426786-689b -11e6-99bf-f0cf3a6449a6_story.html.

Rubin, Jennifer. "Republicans and Evangelicals Think They're Victims and Remain Unmoved by Real Discrimination." *Washington Post*, September 15, 2017.

Simmons, Ann M., and Jaweed Kaleem. "A Founder of Black Lives Matter Answers a Question on Many Minds: Where Did It Go?" *Los Angeles Times*, August 25, 2017. http://www.latimes.com/nation/la-na-patrisse-cullors-black-lives-matter-2017-htmlstory.html.

Sommers, Samuel, and Michael Norton. "White People Think Racism Is Getting Worse. Against White People." *Washington Post*, July 21, 2016.

"Table 43A Arrests by Race and Ethnicity, 2015." 2015 Crime in the United States. Federal Bureau of Investigation. http://ucr.fbi.gov/crime-in-the-u.s/2015/crime-in-the-u.s.-2015/tables/table-43.

Tesler, Michael. "Jemele Hill's The Mainstream: Most Americans Think Donald Trump's a Racist." *Huffington Post*, September 15, 2017. https://www.huffingtonpost.com/entry/jemele-hills-the-mainstream-most-americans-think_us_59bad6ace4b0390a1564dbf6.

Wang, Amy B. "One Group Loved Trump's Remarks About Charlottesville: White Supremacists; 'No Condemnation at All' from the President, a Neo-Nazi Website Wrote." *Washington Post*, August 13, 2017.

Williams, Katie Bo. "FBI Has 1,000 Open Domestic Terror Investigations: Director." *Hill*, September 27, 2017. http://thehill.com/policy/national-security/352670-fbi-has-1000-open-domestic-terror-investigations-director.

Chapter 1

"August 4, 1964: Bodies of Chaney, Goodman, and Schwerner Discovered." SNCC Digital Gateway. https://snccdigital.org/events/bodies-chaney-goodman-schwerner-discovered.

Bagdikian, Ben. "Negro Youth's New March on Dixie." *Saturday Evening Post*, September 8, 1962.

Berman, Ari. "Did Republicans Rig the Election?" *Nation*, November 15, 2016. https://www.thenation.com/article/did-republicans-rig-the-election.

———. *Give Us the Ballot: The Modern Struggle for Voting Rights in America*. New York: Farrar, Strauss, and Giroux, 2015.

Beschloss, Michael. *Taking Charge: The Johnson White House Tapes, 1963–1964*. New York: Touchstone, 1998.

Brown, W. David. "Inexcusable Action." *Pascagoula Chronicle*, June 24, 1964.

Bullock, Charles S., Ronald Keith Gaddie, and Justin J. Wert. *The Rise and Fall of the Voting Rights Act.* Norman: University of Oklahoma Press, 2016.

Burner, Eric. *And Gently He Shall Lead Them: Robert Parris Moses and Civil Rights in Mississippi.* New York and London: New York University Press, 1994.

Colby, David C. "The Voting Rights Act and Black Registration in Mississippi." *Publius* 16, no. 4 (1986): 123–137.

Crespino, Joseph. *In Search of Another Country: Mississippi and the Conservative Counterrevolution.* Princeton, New Jersey: Princeton University Press, 2007.

Daly, Charles, editor. *The Media and the Cities.* Chicago: University of Chicago Press, 1968.

Dittmer, John L. *Local People: The Struggle for Civil Rights in Mississippi.* Urbana: University of Illinois Press, 1994.

Eastland, James. Telephone conversation with President Lyndon Johnson, June 23, 1964. Miller Center of Public Affairs at the University of Virginia. https://millercenter.org/the-presidency/secret-white-house-tapes/conversation-james-eastland-june-23-1964.

Emmerich, J. O. "Highlights in the Headlines." [McComb, GA] *Enterprise-Journal,* July 28, 1948.

Federal Bureau of Investigation. "Mississippi Burning (MIBURN)." FBI Records: The Vault. https://vault.fbi.gov/Mississippi%20Burning%20%28MIBURN%29%20Case.

Forman, James. *The Making of Black Revolutionaries.* Illustrated Edition. Seattle: University of Washington Press, 1997.

Freedom Summer. Directed by Stanley Nelson. New York: Firelight Films, 2014.

George, Carol V. R. *One Mississippi, Two Mississippi: Methodists, Murder, & the Struggle for Racial Justice in Neshoba County.* New York: Oxford University Press, 2015.

Hamer, Fannie Lou. "Testimony Before the Credentials Committee." Democratic National Convention, Atlantic City, New Jersey, August 22, 1964.

Hampton, Henry, and Steve Fayer. *Voices of Freedom: An Oral History of the Civil Rights Movement from 1950s through the 1980s.* New York: Bantam Books, 1990.

"Information Sheet: Project Mississippi." Civil Rights Movement Veterans, Hosted by Tougaloo College. http://www.crmvet.org/docs/fs64fact.pdf.

Kennedy, John F. "The President's News Conference." September 13, 1962. The American Presidency Project. http://www.presidency.ucsb.edu.

Keyssar, Alexander. *The Right to Vote: The Contested History of Democracy in the United States*. Revised edition. New York: Basic Books, 2009.

Kraske, Steve. "The Chat: Kansas Senate Minority Leader Calls Kris Kobach the Most Racist Politician in America." *Kansas City Star*, March 8, 2015. http://www.kansascity.com/news/local/news-columns-blogs/the-buzz/article12949031.html.

Krebs, Albin. "Find Boys, Parents Beg." *Boston Globe*, June 23, 1964.

The Leadership Conference Education Fund. "The Great Poll Closure." November 2016. http://civilrightsdocs.info/pdf/reports/2016/poll-closure-report-web.pdf.

Levitt, Justin. "The Truth About Voter Fraud." Brennan Center for Justice. 2007. https://www.brennancenter.org/sites/default/files/legacy/The%20Truth%20About%20Voter%20Fraud.pdf.

Litwack, Leon F. *Trouble in Mind: Black Southerners in the Age of Jim Crow*. New York: Vintage Books, 1999.

Lopez, German. "How the Voting Rights Act Transformed Black Voting Rights in the South, in One Chart." *Vox*, August 6, 2015. https://www.vox.com/2015/3/6/8163229/voting-rights-act-1965.

"Low Turnout Eases Path for Donald Trump, Sen. Ron Johnson Wisconsin." *Chicago Tribune*, November 9, 2016. http://www.chicagotribune.com/news/nationworld/midwest/ct-how-did-trump-win-wisconsin-low-turnout-20161109-story.html.

Martin, Louis. "Blacks Won Some Key Races." *Chicago Daily Defender*, November 11, 1972.

Martin Luther King Jr. Papers Project. *The Student Voice 1960-1965, Periodical of the Student Nonviolent Coordinating Committee*. Westport, CT: Meckler, 1990.

Mays, Benjamin E. "How Andy Young Became Congressman." *Chicago Daily Defender*, November 25, 1972.

McAdam, Doug. *Freedom Summer*. New York: Oxford University Press, 1988.

"The Mississippi Freedom Summer: Bob Moses on Reality Asserts Itself." Interview with Paul Jay. June 20, 2014. http://therealnews.com/t2/story:12021:The-Mississippi-Freedom-Summer—Bob-Moses-on-Reality-Asserts-Itself-%2819%29.

Moses, Robert. Letter from Robert Moses, Program Director, COFO, Jackson, Mississippi. Civil Rights Movement Veterans. http://www.crmvet.org/docs /fs64_accept.pdf.

Moses, Robert, and Charles E. Cobb Jr. *Radical Equations: Civil Rights from Mississippi to the Algebra Project*. Boston: Beacon, 2001.

Romaine, Anne. "The Mississippi Freedom Democratic Party Through August, 1964." Master's thesis, University of Virginia, 1970.

Schultz, Debra L. *Going South: Jewish Women in the Civil Rights Movement*. New York: New York University Press, 2001.

Sitton, Claude. "Mississippi Drags River in Search for Rights Aides." *New York Times*, June 28, 1964.

Skewes, James B. "We Make Poor Slaves." *Meridian Star*, June 12, 1964.

The Streets of Greenwood. Directed by Jack Willis, John Reavis, and Fred Wardenburg. New Time Films, 1964.

Sugarman, Tracy. *Stranger at the Gates: A Summer in Mississippi*. New York: Hill and Wang, 1966.

Sullens, Fred. "It's Time for Thinking." [Jackson, MS] *Daily News*, August 1, 1954.

"Three Rights Workers Missing." *Washington Post*, June 23, 1964.

Trimble, Elliot. "We Should Be Unified on This Important Issue." *Natchez Democrat*, August 15, 1954.

Trump, Donald J. "In addition to winning the Electoral College..." Post on Twitter, November 27, 2016, 12:30 p.m. https://twitter.com/realdonaldtrump /status/802972944532209664?lang=en.

———. "I will be asking for a major investigation..." Post on Twitter, January 25, 2017, 4:10 a.m. https://twitter.com/realdonaldtrump/status/8242278249 03090176?lang=en.

———. "Serious voter fraud..." Post on Twitter, November 27, 2016, 4:31 p.m. https://twitter.com/realdonaldtrump/status/803033642545115140?lang=en.

Visser-Maessen, Laura. *Robert Parris Moses: A Life in Civil Rights and Leadership at the Grassroots*. Chapel Hill: University of North Carolina Press, 2016.

Walt, Thatcher. "A Challenge for Leflore County." [Greenwood, MS] *Commonwealth*. June 22, 1964.

Ward, James. "Plate Passing Philosophy." [Jackson, MS] *Daily News*, July 22, 1964.

Watson, Bruce. *Freedom Summer: The Savage Season of 1964 That Made Mississippi Burn and Made America a Democracy*. New York: Penguin Books, 2010.

Weill, Susan. *In a Madhouse's Din: Civil Rights Coverage by Mississippi's Daily Press, 1948–1968*. Westport, CT: Praeger, 2002.

William Crawford v. Marion County Election Board. 553 U.S. 181 (2008) (Docket No. 07-21).

Zinn, Howard. *SNCC: The New Abolitionists*. Cambridge, MA: South End, 1964.

Chapter 2

Anderson, Carol. *White Rage: The Unspoken Truth of Our Racial Divide*. New York: Bloomsbury, 2016.

Bader, Hans. "How Eric Holder's Disparate Impact Crusade Leads to Quotas." *Daily Caller*, June 5, 2014. http://dailycaller.com/2014/06/05/how-eric-holders-disparate-impact-crusade-leads-to-quotas.

"Be Calm, Faubus Urges Arkansas." *Los Angeles Times*, September 27, 1957.

Beer, William. "Real-Life Costs of Affirmative Action." *Wall Street Journal*, August 7, 1986.

Bolton, Charles C. *The Hardest Deal of All: The Battle over School Integration in Mississippi, 1870–1980*. Jackson: University Press of Mississippi, 2005.

Brown, Emma. "Trump's Education Department Nixes Obama-Era Grant Program for School Diversity." *Washington Post*, March 29, 2017. https://www.washingtonpost.com/?utm_term=.303247310ce1.

Coleman McGee, Meredith. *James Meredith: Warrior and the America that Created Him*. Santa Barbara: Praeger, 2013.

Democratic Party Platforms: "1960 Democratic Party Platform." July 11, 1960. The American Presidency Project. http://www.presidency.ucsb.edu/ws/index.php?pid=29602.

DeVos, Betsy. "Statement from Secretary of Education Betsy DeVos Following Listening Session with Historically Black Colleges and University Leaders." US Department of Education, February 28, 2017. https://www.ed.gov/news/press-releases/statement-secretary-education-betsy-devos-following-listening-session-historically-black-college-and-university-leaders.

Diggs, Mitchell. "UM Enrollment Soars Past 23,800 Students." University of Mississippi, September 10, 2015. https://news.olemiss.edu/um-enrollment-soars-past-23800-students/.

Douglas-Gabriel, Danielle. "After White House Courts HBCUs, Budget Disappoints School Leaders." *Washington Post*, March 16, 2017. https://www.washingtonpost.com/?utm_term=.a7fa5c13122b.

Douglass, Frederick. *Narrative of the Life of Frederick Douglass an American Slave, Written by Himself.* 1845. Reprinted. Cambridge, MA: The Belknap Press of Harvard University Press, 2009.

Doyle, William. *An American Insurrection: James Meredith and the Battle of Oxford, Mississippi, 1962.* New York: Doubleday, 2001.

Eagles, Charles W. *The Price of Defiance: James Meredith and the Integration of Ole Miss.* Charlotte: University of North Carolina Press, 2009.

Federal Writers Project. *North Carolina Slave Narratives: A Folk History of Slavery in North Carolina from Interviews with Former Slaves.* Washington, DC: Public Works Administration.

————. *Slave Narratives: A Folk History of Slavery in the United States from Interviews with Former Slaves Texas Narratives (Complete).* Washington, DC: Public Works Administration.

Finney, John W. "Congress Is Split on Use of Troops; Johnston Calls for Faubus to Resist President but Others Hail His Move." *New York Times*, September 2, 1957.

Freedman, Max. "South Invokes Obsolete Law: Civil War Issue." (London) *Guardian*, September 25, 1962.

Gonyea, Don. "Majority of White Americans Say They Believe Whites Face Discrimination." National Public Radio, October 24, 2017. https://www.npr.org/2017/10/24/559604836/majority-of-white-americans-think-theyre-discriminated-against.

Haldeman, H. R. *The Haldeman Diaries: Inside the Nixon White House.* New York: G. P. Putnam's Sons, 1994.

Harriot, Michael. "Morehouse College President: We Got Played." *Root*, March 2, 2017. https://www.theroot.com/morehouse-college-president-we-got-played-1792916254.

Hochschild, Arlie Russell. *Strangers in Their Own Land: Anger and Mourning on the American Right.* New York: New Press, 2016.

Kumar, Anita, and William Douglas. "Trump Seeks to Outdo Obama in Backing Black Colleges." McClatchy, February 27, 2017. https://www.whitehouse.gov/briefings-statements/president-trump-seeks-outdo-obama-backing-black-colleges.

Livingston, Gretchen. "It's No Longer a 'Leave It to Beaver' World for American Families—But It Wasn't Back Then, Either." Pew Research Center, December 30, 2015. http://www.pewresearch.org/fact-tank/2015/12/30 /its-no-longer-a-leave-it-to-beaver-world-for-american-families-but-it-wasnt -back-then-either/.

Lynch, Frederick. "Tales from an Oppressed Class." *Wall Street Journal*, November 11, 1991.

Margo, Robert A. *Race and Schooling in the South, 1880–1950: An Economic History*. Chicago: University of Chicago Press, 1990.

Meredith, James. *Three Years in Mississippi*. Bloomington: Indiana University Press, 1966.

Meredith, James, and William Doyle. *A Mission from God: A Memoir and Challenge for America*. New York: Atria Books, 2012.

Meridian Star. August 5, 1962.

Meyerson, Collier. "What Is the Future of Affirmative Action Under Jeff Session's Department of Justice?" *Nation*, August 3, 2017. https://www.thenation .com/article/what-is-the-future-of-affirmative-action-under-jeff-sessionss -department-of-justice.

Minnery, Gerald M. "Air Force Enlistee Recalls Meredith as 'Tough Sergeant.'" [Baltimore] *Afro-American*, February 23, 1963.

"Negro Student Victory in Mississippi." *Austin Statesman*, June 26, 1962.

Newton, Michael. *The Ku Klux Klan in Mississippi: A History*. Jefferson, NC: McFarland, 2010.

Nixon, Richard. *RN: The Memoirs of Richard Nixon*. New York: Grosset and Dunlap, 1978.

Orfield, Gary, and Erica Frankenberg. *Brown at 60: Great Progress, a Long Retreat and an Uncertain Future*. The Civil Rights Project, May 15, 2014. https:// www.civilrightsproject.ucla.edu/research/k-12-education/integration-and -diversity/brown-at-60-great-progress-a-long-retreat-and-an-uncertain-future /Brown-at-60-051814.pdf.

Patterson, Brandon E. "Trump Vowed to 'Absolutely Prioritize' Black Colleges. Then Came His Budget." *Mother Jones*, June 1, 2017. https://www.motherjones .com/politics/2017/06/historically-black-colleges-universities-hbcu-trump/.

Patterson, Joe. "Mississippi Fighting 'Lost Cause.'" [Baltimore] *Afro-American*, July 7, 1962.

Pew Research Center. "On Views of Race and Inequality, Blacks and Whites Are Worlds Apart." June 27, 2016. http://www.pewsocialtrends.org/files/2016/06 /ST_2016.06.27_Race-Inequality-Final.pdf.

Public Religion Research Institute and Brookings Institute. "How Immigration and Concerns About Cultural Changes Are Shaping the 2016 Election." June 23, 2016. https://www.brookings.edu/wp-content/uploads/2016/06/20160623 _prri_jones_presentation.pdf.

Sansing, David G. *The University of Mississippi: A Sesquicentennial History.* Jackson: University Press of Mississippi, 1999.

Savage, Charlie. "Justice Dept. to Take on Affirmative Action in College Admissions." *New York Times*, August 1, 2017. https://www.nytimes .com/2017/08/01/us/politics/trump-affirmative-action-universities.html.

Scott, Bobby. "Scott Condemns Trump Administration's Decision to Pull Funding for School Diversity." Education & The Workforce Committee Democrats, March 30, 2017. http://democrats-edworkforce.house.gov/media /press-releases/scott-condemns-trump-administrations-decision-to-pull -funding-for-school-diversity.

Skates, Ray. *Mississippi: A Bicentennial History.* New York: W. W. Norton, 1979.

Sullens, Fred. "Bloodstains on the White Marble Steps." [Jackson, MS] *Daily News*, May 18, 1954.

"Table 219.70: Percentage of High School Dropouts Among Persons 16 to 24 Years Old (Status Dropout Rate), by Sex and Race/Ethnicity: Selected Years, 1960 Through 2015." National Center for Education Statistics.

"Test at Ole Miss." *Christian Science Monitor*, September 26, 1962.

Thomas, William. "Meredith: I Came with a Plan to Destroy the System." *Memphis Commercial Appeal*, September 1, 1982.

"The University of Alabama Students by Race/Ethnicity: Fall 2016." University of Alabama Office of Institutional Research and Assessment. http://oira .ua.edu/factbook/reports/student-enrollment/fall-term/students-by-race-and -ethnicity.

"U.S. Departments of Education and Justice Release School Discipline Guidance Package to Enhance School Climate and Improve School Discipline Policies/Practices." US Department of Education. January 8, 2014. https://www .ed.gov/news/press-releases/us-departments-education-and-justice-release -school-discipline-guidance-package-.

Waldman, Annie. "DeVos Pick to Head Civil Rights Office Once Said She Faced Discrimination for Being White." ProPublica, April 14, 2017. https://www.propublica.org/article/devos-candice-jackson-civil-rights -office-education-department.

The White House. "My Brother's Keeper 2016 Progress Report: Two Years of Expanding Opportunity and Creating Pathways to Success." 2016. https:// www.whitehouse.gov/sites/whitehouse.gov/files/images/MBK-2016-Progress -Report.pdf.

Wilkie, Curtis. *Dixie: A Personal Odyssey Through Events That Shaped the Modern South.* New York: Lisa Drew Book/Scribner, 2001.

Wilkins, Roy. "A New 'Mr.' for 'Ole Miss.'" *New York Amsterdam News*, July 14, 1962.

Will, George F. "You'd Think It Was the Warren Court." *Washington Post*, April 2, 1987.

Williams, Juan. "The Scandal of K-12 Education." *Wall Street Journal*, July 4, 2016. https://www.wsj.com/articles/the-scandal-of-k-12-education-146767 3395.

Wilson Jr., John Silvanus. "Office of the President: Statement on HBCU Presidents Visit to White House." Morehouse College, March 1, 2017. http://www .morehouse.edu/collegestatements/officeofthepresidentstatementonhbcupresi dentsvisittowhitehouse.html.

Chapter 3

Blight, David. "Lecture 25: The 'End' of Reconstruction: Disputed Election of 1876, and the 'Compromise of 1877.'" Lecture, Yale University, Open Yale Courses. https://oyc.yale.edu/history/hist-119/lecture-25.

———. "Lecture 26: Race and Reunion: The Civil War in American Memory." Lecture, Yale University, Open Yale Courses. https://oyc.yale.edu /history/hist-119/lecture-26.

Bump, Philip. "Trump's Speech Encouraging Police to Be 'Rough,' Annotated." *Washington Post*, July 28, 2017. https://www.washingtonpost.com/news/politics /wp/2017/07/28/trumps-speech-encouraging-police-to-be-rough-annotated.

Campbell, James. *Crime and Punishment in African American History.* New York: Palgrave Macmillan, 2013.

"Criminal Justice Fact Sheet." NAACP. http://www.naacp.org/criminal-justice -fact-sheet.

Dallek, Robert. *An Unfinished Life: John F. Kennedy, 1917–1963.* Boston: Little, Brown, 2003.

De Blasio, Bill, and James P. O'Neill. "Transcript: Mayor de Blasio, Police Commissioner O'Neill Delivers Remarks in Response to Attorney General Sessions' Comments on NYC Crime." New York City, April 21, 2017. http:// www1.nyc.gov/office-of-the-mayor/news/253-17/transcript-mayor-de-blasio -police-commissioner-o-neill-deliver-remarks-response-attorney.

"Department of Justice Sends Letter to Nine Jurisdictions Requiring Proof of Compliance with 8 U.S.C. 1373." Office of Public Affairs, US Department of Justice, April 21, 2017. https://www.justice.gov/opa/pr/department-justice -sends-letter-nine-jurisdictions-requiring-proof-compliance-8-usc-1373.

Dirksen, Everett. "The Congressional Front." February 9, 1935. Dirksen Congressional Center. http://www.dirksencenter.org/lincoln/Dirksen/documents _index.htm.

———. "Lincoln Day Address, 1941." Dirksen Congressional Center. http:// www.dirksencenter.org/lincoln/Dirksen/documents_index.htm.

———. Senate Floor Speech on June 10, 1964. In *Landmark Debates in Congress: From the Declaration of Independence to the War in Iraq*, edited by Stephen W. Stathis. Washington, DC: CQ, 2009.

Douglass, Frederick. *The Life and Times of Frederick Douglass, Written by Himself*. Hartford, CT: Park Publishing, 1882.

Foner, Eric. *Reconstruction: America's Unfinished Revolution, 1863–1877*. New York: Perennial Classics, 2002.

Garrettson, Charles L. *Hubert H. Humphrey: The Politics of Joy*. New Brunswick: Transaction Publishers, 1993.

Graham, Hugh Davis. *Collision Course: The Strange Convergence of Affirmative Action and Immigration Policy in America*. New York: Oxford University Press, 2002.

Gurman, Sadie. "Zealous Prosecutor Leading Review of Violent Crime in Cities." *U.S. News & World Report*, May 29, 2017.

Horwitz, Jeff, and Jake Pearson. "Few If Any Minority Senior Execs in Trump's Empire." Associated Press, June 16, 2016. https://apnews .com/426e763d7a38472d9c1df8b799725084.

Horwitz, Sari. "How Jeff Sessions Wants to Bring Back the War on Drugs." *Washington Post*, April 8, 2017.

Jenkins, Aric. "Read President Trump's NFL Speech on National Anthem Protests." *Time*, September 23, 2017. http://time.com/4954684/donald-trump-nfl -speech-anthem-protests.

Johnson, Lyndon B. "Address Before a Joint Session of the Congress." November 27, 1963. PBS, http://www.pbs.org/ladybird/epicenter/epicenter_doc_speech.html.

Kennedy, John F. "Meeting with Americans for Democratic Action Leaders, May 4, 1963." In *Listening In: The Secret White House Recordings of John F. Kennedy*, selected and introduced by Ted Widmer. New York: Hyperion, 2012.

———. "Radio and Television Report to the American People on Civil Rights," June 11, 1963. The American Presidency Project. http://www.presidency.ucsb.edu/ws/?pid=9271.

———. "Special Message to the Congress on Civil Rights." February 28, 1963. The American Presidency Project. http://www.presidency.ucsb.edu/ws/?pid=9581.

Kennedy, Robert F. "Statement of the Honorable Robert F. Kennedy, Attorney General of the United States, Issued at 11 A.M., May 24, 1961." May 24, 1961. Department of Justice. https://www.justice.gov/sites/default/files/ag/legacy/2011/01/20/05-24-1961c.pdf.

King Jr., Martin Luther. "A Bold Design for a New South." *Nation*, March 30, 1963. https://www.thenation.com/article/archive-bold-design-new-south.

Levingston, Steven. *Kennedy and King: The President, the Pastor, and the Battle over Civil Rights*. New York: Hachette Books, 2017.

Lewis, John. "Rep. John Lewis Senate Testimony in Sen. Sessions Confirmation Hearing: Full Written Testimony Submitted for the Record Video of Congressman Lewis' Testimony." January 11, 2017. https://johnlewis.house.gov/media-center/press-releases/rep-john-lewis-senate-testimony-sen-sessions-confirmation-hearing.

Loewen, James W. "Showing *Pekin* in IL..." Something Has Gone Very Wrong...: The Homepage of James W. Loewen. http://sundown.tougaloo.edu/sundowntownsshow.php?id=1817.

———. *Sundown Towns: A Hidden Dimension of American Racism*. New York: New Press, 2005.

Martin, Jill. "Michael Bennett: 'I Can't Stand for the National Anthem.'" CNN, August 17, 2017. https://www.cnn.com/2017/08/16/sport/seahawks-michael-bennett-not-standing-for-national-anthem/index.html.

Murdock, Sebastian. "Philly Police Union President Calls Black Lives Matter Activists 'A Pack of Rabid Animals.'" *Huffington Post*, September 5, 2017.

https://www.huffingtonpost.com/entry/philly-police-union-president-calls
-black-lives-matter-activists-a-pack-of-rabid-animals_us_59aacc02e4b0dfaaf
cf0bc55.

Nelson, Steven. "Jeff Sessions Veers Off-Script, Bashes Pot Use but Steers Clear of Claim It's 'Slightly Less Awful' Than Using Heroin." *U.S. News & World Report*, March 15, 2017. https://www.usnews.com/news/articles/2017-03-15 /jeff-sessions-veers-off-script-bashes-pot-use-but-steers-clear-of-claim-its -slightly-less-awful-than-heroin-abuse.

"1960 Democratic Party Platform. July 11, 1960." The American Presidency Project. http://www.presidency.ucsb.edu/ws/index.php?pid=29602.

Obama, Barack. "Remarks by the President at LBJ Presidential Library Civil Rights Summit." Speech, Austin, TX, April 10, 2014. https://obamawhite house.archives.gov/the-press-office/2014/04/10/remarks-president-lbj -presidential-library-civil-rights-summit.

Pew Research Center. "On Views of Race and Inequality, Blacks and Whites Are Worlds Apart." June 27, 2016. http://www.pewsocialtrends.org/files/2016/06 /ST_2016.06.27_Race-Inequality-Final.pdf.

Purdum, Todd S. *An Idea Whose Time Has Come: Two Presidents, Two Parties, and the Battle for the Civil Rights Act of 1964*. New York: Henry Holt, 2014.

Risen, Clay. *The Bill of the Century: The Epic Battle for the Civil Rights Act*. New York: Bloomsbury Press, 2014.

Rosen, Elliot A. *The Republican Party in the Age of Roosevelt: Sources of Anti-Government Conservatism in the United States*. Charlottesville: University of Virginia Press, 2014.

"Russell Rips Halleck for Aid to Rights Bill." *Chicago Tribune*, November 12, 1963.

Sessions, Jeff. "Attorney General Sessions Delivers Remarks at the Heritage Foundation's Legal Strategy Forum." Speech, Washington, DC, October 26, 2017. https://www.justice.gov/opa/speech/attorney-general-sessions-delivers -remarks-heritage-foundation-s-legal-strategy-forum.

———. "Jeff Sessions: 'Avoid Harmful Federal Intrusion.'" *USA Today*, April 17, 2017. https://www.usatoday.com/story/opinion/2017/04/17/jeff-sessions -avoid-harmful-federal-intrusion-editorials-debates/100579848/.

———. Memorandum for the Acting Director Federal Bureau of Prisons, February 21, 2017. Office of the Attorney General.

———. Memorandum from the Attorney General Jeff Sessions for Heads of Department Components and United States Attorneys. March 31, 2017. Office of the Attorney General.

———. Memorandum to United States Attorneys Heads of Department Components on Revised Treatment of Transgender Employment Discrimination Claims Under Title VII of the Civil Rights Act of 1964. October 4, 2017. Office of the Attorney General.

Skewes, James B. "Gap Is Widening." *Meridian Star*, July 5, 1964.

Slack, Donavan. "Biden Says 'Transgender Discrimination Civil Rights Issue of Our Time." *Politico*, October 30, 2012. https://www.politico.com /blogs/politico44/2012/10/biden-says-transgender-discrimination-civil-rights -issue-of-our-time-147761.

"The Southern Manifesto." Eighty-Fourth Congress, Second Session. *Congressional Record*, vol. 102, part 4 (March 12, 1956). Washington, DC: Governmental Printing Office, 1956.

Tatum, Sophie. "Athletes, Activists Spar on Kneeling National Anthem Protests." CNN, September 28, 2017. https://www.cnn.com/2017/09/27/politics /cnn-nfl-kneeling-protests-town-hall-ac360/index.html.

Truman, Harry S. "Address Before the National Association for the Advancement of Colored People." Speech, June 29, 1947. The American Presidency Project. http://www.presidency.ucsb.edu/ws/index.php?pid=12686.

Trump, Donald J. "Remarks by President Trump in Listening Session with the Fraternal Order of Police." Listening Session, Washington, DC, March 28, 2017. https://www.whitehouse.gov/briefings-statements/remarks-president -trump-listening-session-fraternal-order-police.

United Press International. "Rights Plan Hit by Southern Bloc: Thurmond Says Proposals Recall Reconstruction." *New York Times*, June 20, 1963.

Woods, Baynard. "Democracy in Crisis: The Death of Freddie Gray and the Future of Police Reform." *City Paper*, April 25, 2017. http://www.citypaper .com/news/dic/bcp-042617-democracy-in-crisis-police-reform-20170425 -story.html.

Yates, Sally Q., Deputy Attorney General. Memorandum for the Acting Director Federal Bureau of Prisons, August 18, 2016. U.S. Department of Justice Office of the Deputy Attorney General.

Ye Hee Lee, Michelle. "Jeff Sessions's Comments on Race: For the Record." *Washington Post*, December 2, 2016. https://www.washingtonpost.com/news /fact-checker/wp/2016/12/02/jeff-sessionss-comments-on-race-for-the-record.

Chapter 4

Alcindor, Yamiche. "Uproar over Omarosa Manigault-Newman at Black Journalists Convention." *New York Times*, August 11, 2017. https://www.nytimes.com/2017/08/11/us/politics/omarosa-manigault-newman-nabj.html.

"At This Hour: Manhunt Underway for London Subway Bomber; North Korea Launches Missile over Japan; U.N. Security Council Meets Soon About North Korea; Trump Demands Apology from ESPN for 'Untruth'; Trump Blames 'Both Sides' for Charlottesville Again." CNN, September 15, 2017. http://transcripts.cnn.com/TRANSCRIPTS/1709/15/ath.01.html.

Baldwin, James. "The Dangerous Road Before Martin Luther King." *Harper's* 222, February 1961.

———. "Dark Days." *Esquire*, October 1980.

———. "Faulkner and Desegregation." *Partisan Review* 23, Fall 1956.

———. "Fifth Avenue, Uptown." *Esquire* 54, July 1960.

———. *The Fire Next Time*. New York: Dial, 1963.

———. "Freaks and the American Ideal of Manhood." *Playboy*, January 1985.

———. Interview with Kenneth Clark. WGBH-TV, New York City, May 24, 1963. Reprinted in *Conversations with James Baldwin*, edited by Fred L. Standley and Louis H. Pratt. Jackson: University Press of Mississippi, 1989.

———. "Letter from a Region in My Mind." *New Yorker* 38, November 17, 1960.

———. "Notes of a Native Son." *Harper's*, 1955.

———. *Notes of a Native Son*. Boston: Beacon, November 1955.

———. "They Can't Turn Back." *Mademoiselle* 51, August, 1960.

Blay, Zeba. "Martin Luther King III Says Meeting with Trump Was 'Very Constructive.'" *Huffington Post*, January 17, 2017. https://www.huffingtonpost.com/entry/martin-luther-king-iii-says-meeting-with-trump-was-very-constructive_us_587e3974e4b0d4cc0884a848.

Booker, Brakkton. "Trump's African American: 'I Am Not a Trump Supporter.'" National Public Radio, June 5, 2016. https://www.npr.org/sections/thetwo-way/2016/06/05/480864303/trumps-african-american-i-am-not-a-trump-supporter.

Bush, George W. Address at the Annual Convention of the NAACP. Speech, Baltimore, Maryland, July 11, 2000.

———. Address at the Annual Convention of the NAACP. Speech, Washington, DC, July 20, 2006.

Deb, Sopan. "What's Behind Trump's Cancellation of Endorsement Event with Black Pastors." CBS News, November 30, 2015. https://www.cbsnews.com/news/black-pastor-who-organized-trump-meeting-calls-endorsement-talk-mix-up.

Eckman, Fern Marja. *The Furious Passage of James Baldwin*. Lanham, MD: M. Evans, 1966.

"English Ovation for James Baldwin." *New York Times*, February 19, 1965.

Ernst, Douglas. "NFL Legend Jim Brown Praises Donald Trump: 'I Fell in Love with Him.'" *Washington Times*, December 14, 2016. https://www.washingtontimes.com/news/2016/dec/14/jim-brown-nfl-legend-praises-trump-after-supportin/.

"Ex-Rep. JC Watts: Trump Doesn't 'Speak with Clarity' on Charlottesville." *Newsmax*, August 17, 2017. https://www.newsmax.com/politics/jc-watts-trump-charlottesville-comments/2017/08/17/id/808288/.

Godsell, Geoffrey. "Baldwin: 'I'm Not Mad...I Am Worried.'" Review of *The Fire Next Time. Christian Science Monitor*, February 21, 1963.

Heil, Emily. "White House Reporter April Ryan and Trump Aide Omarosa Manigault Used to Be Friends. Now Their Feud Is at Epic Levels." *Washington Post*, August 11, 2017.

Leary, Alex, Tampa Bay Times. "At Tampa Rally, Donald Trump Promises He'll Win Florida." *Miami Herald*, November 5, 2016. http://www.miamiherald.com/news/politics-government/election/article112774528.html.

Leeming, David. *James Baldwin: A Biography*. New York: Alfred A. Knopf, 1994.

Lusane, Clarence. *The Black History of the White House*. San Francisco: City Lights Books, 2010.

Manigault, Omarosa. Interview with Michael Strahan on *Good Morning America*. Quoted in Veronica Stracqualursi, "Omarosa Manigault Speaks Out About WH Exit: 'I Have Seen Things That Have Made Me Uncomfortable." ABC News, December 14, 2017. http://abcnews.go.com/Politics/omarosa-manigault-speaks-wh-exit-things-made-uncomfortable/story?id=51786749.

Mettler, Katie, and Lindsey Bever. "The Strange Story of That 'Blacks for Trump' Guy Standing Behind POTUS at His Phoenix Rally." *Washington Post*, April 23, 2017.

Nakamura, David. "Trump Says Recent Antifa Violence Justifies His Condemnation of Both Sides in Charlottesville." *Washington Post*, September 14, 2017.

Pasley, Virginia. "A Mind-Jolting Book." Review of *The Fire Next Time*. *Newsday*, February 2, 1963.

Plott, Elaina. "No One Knows What Omarosa Is Doing in the White House—Even Omarosa." *Daily Beast*, November 13, 2017. https://www.thedailybeast.com/no-one-knows-what-omarosa-is-doing-in-the-white-houseeven-omarosa.

———. "Why Pastor Darrell Scott Is Hoping Black Voters Give Trump a Chance." *National Review*, December 7, 2015. https://www.nationalreview.com/2015/12/donald-trump-black-pastor-darrell-scott-voter-outreach/.

Reagan, Ronald. Address at the Annual Convention of the NAACP. Denver, June 29, 1981. http://www.americanrhetoric.com/speeches/ronaldreagannaacp1981.htm.

Rose, Lacey. "Steve Harvey Unleashed: A New Show, His Private Trump Sit-Down and That Infamous Leaked Memo." *Hollywood Reporter*, September 5, 2017. https://www.hollywoodreporter.com/features/steve-harvey-unleashed-a-new-show-his-private-trump-sitdown-infamous-leaked-memo-1034591.

Rye, Angela. Interview with Charlemagne the God. *The Breakfast Club*, Power 105.1, New York City, December 18, 2017. https://www.youtube.com/watch?v=_ybtKENDZ4g&t=1s.

Schlesinger, Arthur. *Robert Kennedy and His Times*. Boston: Mariner Books, 2002.

Schultheis, Emily. "Kanye West Meets with Donald Trump at Trump Tower." CBS News, December 13, 2016. https://www.cbsnews.com/news/kanye-west-donald-trump-trump-tower-meeting.

Schwartz, Ian. "Marc Lamont Hill: 'Mediocre Negroes Being Dragged in Front of TV As Photo-Op for Trump." RealClearPolitics, January 16, 2017. https://www.realclearpolitics.com/video/2017/01/16/marc_lamont_hill_mediocre_negroes_being_dragged_in_front_of_tv_as_photo-op_for_trump.html.

Scott, Tim. Interview with Nancy Cordes. CBS Evening News, September 13, 2017. https://www.cbsnews.com/news/sen-tim-scott-trump-very-receptive-to-listening.

———. "Statement from Our Office on the President's Comments This Afternoon." Twitter Post. September 14, 2017, 1:33 P.M. https://twitter.com/senatortimscott/status/908428535353810944.

Sowell, Thomas. Interview with Ben Shapiro. *The Ben Shapiro Show* (podcast), episode 188. September 28, 2016. https://www.youtube.com/watch?v=LGDobadAHvI&t=421s.

———. "Ronald Reagan (1911–2004). Town Hall, June 8, 2004. https://townhall.com/columnists/thomassowell/2004/06/08/ronald-reagan-1911-2004-n1417169.

———. "Trump v. Clinton: An Unmitigated Disaster." *National Review*, May 6, 2016. https://www.nationalreview.com/2016/05/donald-trump-hillary-clinton-american-disaster/.

Thomas, Shawna. "Sen. Scott Says Trump's Moral Authority Was Compromised by His Tues. Comments on Charlottesville." *Vice News*, August 17, 2017. https://news.vice.com/en_us/article/j5dab3/tim-scott-trump-charlottesville-race.

Wakefield, Dan. "Disturbing Letters." Review of *The Fire Next Time*. *New York Times*, April 7, 1963.

"Watch: Ray Lewis Claims Donald Trump Is Aware of His Divisiveness." *BET*, December 15, 2016. https://www.bet.com/news/sports/2016/120/15/ray-lewis-claims-donald-trump-is-aware-of-his-divisiveness.html.

WGN Web Desk, and Tahman Bradley. "Trump's Discussion with Ohio Pastor About Chicago Violence Baffles Leaders Here." *WGNTV*, February 1, 2017. http://wgntv.com/2017/02/01/trumps-discussion-with-ohio-pastor-about-chicago-violence-baffles-religious-leader-here.

Williams, Vanessa. "African American Businessman: 'Donald Trump Is Not Racist, Guys.'" *Washington Post*, April 16, 2016.

Chapter 5

Abramson, Alana. "Read Ivanka Trump's Remarks About Her Father and Her White House Role." *Time*, April 25, 2017. http://time.com/4753986/ivanka-trump-womens-20-summit-berlin-germany-read-transcript.

"African American Income." Black Demographics, 2015. http://blackdemographics.com/households/african-american-income.

Anderson, Jervis. *A. Philip Randolph: A Biographical Portrait*. New York: Harcourt Brace Jovanovich, 1972.

Barber, Lucy G. *Marching on Washington: The Forging of an American Political Tradition*. Berkeley: University of California Press, 2002.

Bates, Beth Tompkins. *Pullman Porters and the Rise of Protest Politics in Black America, 1925–1945*. Chapel Hill: University of North Carolina Press, 2001.

Bynum, Cornelius. *A. Philip Randolph and the Struggle for Civil Rights*. Urbana: University of Illinois Press, 2010.

Campbell, Colin. "Donald Trump Changes Tune on Wages After Bernie Sanders Broadside." *Business Insider*, December 28, 2015. http://www.businessinsider.com/donald-trump-bernie-sanders-wages-high-low-2015-12.

Chicago Defender. September 26, 1942.

Cohen, Patricia. "Public-Sector Jobs Vanish, Hitting Blacks Hard." *New York Times*, May 24, 2015. https://www.nytimes.com/2015/05/25/business/public-sector-jobs-vanish-and-blacks-take-blow.html.

Crisis. July 1940.

Davidson, Joe. "Trump Links Federal Hiring Freeze to Fighting Corruption." *Washington Post*, October 24, 2016.

Ellison, Charles D. "Trump's Federal-Workforce Plan Will Blow Up the Black Middle Class…and a Lot More." *Root*, November 23, 2016. https://www.theroot.com/trump-s-federal-workforce-plans-will-blow-up-the-black-1790857869.

Farley, Robert. "DNC Chair on Trump and Overtime Pay." FactCheck, February 28, 2017. https://www.factcheck.org/2017/02/dnc-chair-on-trump-and-overtime-pay.

"Federal Equal Opportunity Recruitment Program (FEORP) Report to Congress." United States Office of Personnel Management, 2014. https://www.opm.gov/policy-data-oversight/diversity-and-inclusion/reports/feorp-2014.pdf.

"500 Enthusiastic Porters Loudly Cheer Proposed Porters' Union." *New York Age*, September 2, 1925.

Fleming, James. "Pullman Porters Win Pot of Gold." *Crisis* 44 (November 1937): 332–333.

Fletcher, Michael A. "Blacks Lose Ground in U.S. Military." *Root*, May 31, 2010. https://www.theroot.com/blacks-lose-ground-in-the-u-s-military-1790879720.

"Full Transcript: President Obama's Speech on the 50th Anniversary of the March on Washington." *Washington Post*, August 28, 2013.

Gersen, Michael. "Trump Has Revealed Who He Is; Now It's Our Turn." *Washington Post*, January 15, 2018.

Goodwin, Doris Kearns. *No Ordinary Time: Franklin and Eleanor Roosevelt: The Home Front in World War II.* New York: Simon & Schuster, 1994.

Harris, William H. *Keeping the Faith: A. Philip Randolph, Milton P. Webster, and the Brotherhood of Sleeping Car Porters, 1925–37.* Urbana: University of Illinois Press, 1978.

Hillman, Sidney. "Letter to All Holders of Defense Contracts." *Crisis* (May 1941): 151.

Horwitz, Jeff, and Jake Pearson. "Few If Any Minority Senior Execs in Trump's Empire." Associated Press, June 16, 2016. https://apnews.com/426e763d7a38472d9c1df8b799725084.

Jan, Tracy. "These Americans May Suffer the Most from a Trump Hiring Freeze." *Washington Post*, January 27, 2017.

Jones, Rhonda. "A. Philip Randolph, Early Pioneer: The Brotherhood of Sleeping Car Porters, National Negro Congress, and the March on Washington Movement." In *The Economic Civil Rights Movement: African Americans and the Struggle for Economic Power*, edited by Michael Ezra. New York: Routledge, 2013.

Jones, William P. *The March on Washington: Jobs, Freedom, and the Forgotten History of Civil Rights*. New York: W.W. Norton, 2013.

Kersten, Andrew E. *A. Philip Randolph: A Life in the Vanguard*. Lanham, MD: Rowman & Littlefield, 2007.

Kersten, Andrew E., and Clarence Lang. *Reframing Randolph: Labor, Black Freedom, and the Legacies of A. Philip Randolph*. New York: New York University Press, 2015.

Krieg, Gregory. "What the 'Deconstruction of the Administrative State' Really Looks Like." CNN, March 30, 2017. https://www.cnn.com/2017/03/30/politics/trump-bannon-administrative-state/index.html.

Lucander, David. *Winning the War for Democracy: The March on Washington Movement*. Urbana: University of Illinois Press, 2014.

Mann, Ted. "White House Won't Require Firms to Report Pay by Gender, Race." *Wall Street Journal*, August 29, 2017. https://www.wsj.com/articles/white-house-wont-require-firms-to-report-pay-by-gender-race-1504047656.

McKinney, Jeffrey. "MBDA Would Be Abolished If Trump Budget Cuts Supported." *Black Enterprise*, March 23, 2017. http://www.blackenterprise.com/mbda-abolished-trump-budget-cuts/.

Morsell, John A. "Black Progress or Illiberal Rhetoric?" *Crisis*, June/July 1973.

Murray, Pauli, and Caroline Ware. *Forty Years of Letters in Black & White*, edited by Anne Firor Scott. Chapel Hill: University of North Carolina Press, 2006.

National Urban League. *African Americans and the Minimum Wage*. April 2014. http://civilrightsdocs.info/pdf/minimumwage/african-americans-minimum-wage.pdf.

Naylor, Bryan. "Trump Lifting Federal Hiring Freeze." NPR, April 12, 2017. https://www.npr.org/2017/04/12/523473051/trump-lifting-federal-hiring-freeze.

Newsome, Yvonne D., and F. Nii-Amoo DoDoo. "Explaining the Decline in Black Women's Earnings." In *Race, Work, and Family in the Lives of African Americans*, edited by Marlese Durr and Shirley A. Hill. Lanham, MD: Rowman & Littlefield, 2006.

New York Age. October 19, 1940.

Norrell, Robert J. *The House I Live In: Race in the American Century*. New York: Oxford University Press, 2005.

Obama, Barack. "Memorandum for the Secretary of Labor: Updating and Modernizing Overtime Regulations." The White House Office of the Press Secretary, March 13, 2014. https://obamawhitehouse.archives.gov/the-press-office/2014/03/13/presidential-memorandum-updating-and-modernizing-overtime-regulations.

O'Donnell, John R., and James Rutherford. *Trumped! The Inside Story of the Real Donald Trump—His Cunning Rise and Spectacular Fall*. New York: Simon & Schuster, 1991.

Patten, Eileen. "Racial, Gender Wage Gaps Persist in U.S. Despite Some Progress." Pew Research Center, July 1, 2016. http://www.pewresearch.org/fact-tank/2016/07/01/racial-gender-wage-gaps-persist-in-u-s-despite-some-progress.

Paumgarten, Nick. "The Death and Life of Atlantic City." *New Yorker*, September 7, 2015. https://www.newyorker.com/magazine/2015/09/07/the-death-and-life-of-atlantic-city.

Pitts, Steven. "Research Brief: Black Workers and the Public Sector." University of California Berkeley Center for Labor Research and Education, April 4, 2011. http://laborcenter.berkeley.edu/pdf/2011/blacks_public_sector11.pdf.

Politico Staff. "Full Transcript: Second 2016 Presidential Debate." *Politico*, October 10, 2016. https://www.politico.com/story/2016/10/2016-presidential-debate-transcript-229519.

Proctor, Bernadette D., Jessica L. Semega, and Melissa A. Kollar. *Income and Poverty in the United States, 2015*. US Census Bureau, Current Population

Reports, P60-256(RV). Washington, DC: US Government Printing Office, 2016.

Randolph, A. Philip. "A. Philip Randolph's 1963 March on Washington Speech." *Florida Times-Union*, August 20, 2013. http://www.jacksonville.com /article/20130820/NEWS/801247969.

———. " 'Defense Rotten'—Randolph." *Pittsburg Courier*, January 25, 1941.

Rao, Neomi. Memorandum to Acting Chair Victoria Lipnic, Equal Employment Opportunity Commission, August 29, 2017. Executive Office of the President, Office of Management and Budget.

"Report on The Messenger, New York: Editors, A. Philip Randolph, Chandler Owen, Victory R. Daily, W. A. Domingo, William N. Colson." In *A Report on the Activities of the Bureau of Investigation of the Department of Justice Against Persons Advising Anarchy, Sedition, and the Forcible Overthrow of Government*. Washington, DC: Government Printing Office, 1919.

"Roosevelt's Executive Order." *Chicago Defender*, July 12, 1941.

Stanhope, Kate. "THR Spoke with Several Former Contestants on 'The Apprentice,' As Well As Individuals Who Worked with Trump on the Miss USA and Miss Universe Pageants." *Hollywood Reporter*, October 11, 2016. https:// www.hollywoodreporter.com/news/tapes-no-tapes-apprentice-alums-936981.

Sullivan, Laura, Tatjana Meschede, Lars Dietrich, Thomas Shapiro, Amy Traub, Catherine Ruetschlin, and Tamara Draut. "The Racial Wealth Gap: Why Policy Matters." *Demos* and Institute for Assets & Social Policy, Brandeis University, 2015.

Taylor, Jessica. "Another Reversal: Trump Now Says Counterprotesters Also to Blame for Charlottesville." NPR, August 15, 2017. https:// www.npr.org/2017/08/15/543743845/another-reversal-trump-now-says -counterprotesters-also-to-blame-for-charlottesvi.

Theodos, Brett, Christina Plerhoples Stacy, and Helen Ho. "Taking Stock of the Community Development Block Grant." Urban Institute, April 2017.

Trump, Donald J. "Remarks at the Summit Sports and Ice Complex in Dimondale, Michigan." August 19, 2016. The American Presidency Project. http://www.presidency.ucsb.edu/ws/index.php?pid=123197.

"Trump Would Slash Department of Education, Reverse Worker Overtime Rules." *Circa*, August 11, 2016. https://www.circa.com/story/2016/08/11 /politics/trump-would-slash-department-of-education-reverse-worker -overtime-rules.

Tye, Larry. *Rising from the Rails: Pullman Porters and the Making of the Black Middle Class*. New York: Henry Holt, 2005.

United States Department of Labor. "Labor Force Statistics from the Current Population Survey." Bureau of Labor Statistics, 2016.

———. "Overtime for White Collar Workers: Overview and Summary of Final Rule." https://www.dol.gov/sites/default/files/overtime-overview.pdf.

United States Postal Service. "2010 Comprehensive Statement on Postal Operations: Workforce Diversity and Inclusiveness." https://about.usps.com /strategic-planning/cs09/CSPO_09_087.htm.

Urrutia, Luz. "Small Businesses and Low-Income Americans Will Lose Under New Budget Cuts to CDFI and NMTC Programs." *Forbes*, November 10, 2017.

Vicens, A. J., and Natalie Schreyer. "The Trump Files: Watch Donald Say He Would Have Done Better as a Black Man." *Mother Jones*, June 20, 2016. https://www.motherjones.com/politics/2016/06/donald-trump-black-man -advantage/.

"White House Blesses Jim Crow." *Crisis* (November 1940): 350–351.

White, Walter. *A Man Called White: The Autobiography of Walter White*. 1948. Reprint: Athens: University of Georgia Press, 1995.

———. "'It's Our Country, Too': The Negro Demands the Right to Be Allowed to Fight for It." *Saturday Evening Post*, December 14, 1940.

Wynn, Neil A. *The African American Experience During World War II*. Lanham, MD: Rowman & Littlefield, 2010.

Yang, Jenny R. "Remarks of Chair Jenny R. Yang at the White House Equal Pay Event." Speech, Washington, DC, January 29, 2016. U.S. Equal Employment Opportunity Commission.

Ye Hee Lee, Michelle. "Trump's Misleading Claim That 48 Percent of Black Youths Are Unemployed." *Washington Post*, August 24, 2016.

Chapter 6

Andrews, Jeff. "HUD, Affordable Housing Programs Get a Boost in Latest Congressional Spending Bill." *Curbed*, March 22, 2018. https://www .curbed.com/2018/3/22/17151758/congressional-spending-bill-hud -affordable-housing.

Asch, Chris Meyers, and George Derek Musgrove. *Chocolate City: A History of Race and Democracy in the Nation's Capital*. Durham: University of North Carolina Press, 2017.

Atta-Mensah, Afua, Lavon Chambers, and Patrick Purcell. "Trump's Planned HUD Cut Would Devastate Working Families." *New York Amsterdam News*, April 27, 2017. http://amsterdamnews.com/news/2017/apr/27/trumps-planned-hud-cuts-would-devastate-working-fa/?fb_comment_id=1441862975873371_1472874192772249#f3a58bdb5ac4144.

Badger, Emily. "How Donald Trump Abandoned His Father's Middle-Class Housing Empire for Luxury Building." *Washington Post*, August 10, 2015.

———. "How Section 8 Became a 'Racial Slur.'" *Washington Post*, June 15, 2015.

Baker, Russell. "Kennedy Accused on Urban Moves: G.O.P. Sees Racism in Plan to Create Cabinet Post." *New York Times*, January 26, 1962.

Blake, Aaron. "The First Trump-Clinton Presidential Debate Transcript, Annotated." *Washington Post*, September 26, 2016. https://www.washingtonpost.com/?utm_term=.3c47c41da8af.

Carson, Ben. *One Nation: What We Can All Do to Save America's Future*. New York: Sentinel, 2014.

Carson, Ben, and Candy Carson. *A More Perfect Union: What We the People Can Do to Reclaim Our Constitutional Liberties*. New York: Sentinel, 2015.

Choi, David. "The FBI Released Hundreds of Pages Related to a 1970s Housing Discrimination Lawsuit Against Trump." *Business Insider*, February 15, 2017. http://www.businessinsider.com/fbi-report-trump-housing-discrimination-2017-2.

"City of Philadelphia and the Philadelphia Housing Authority Assessment of Fair Housing." October 27, 2016. http://www.pha.phila.gov/media/170834/assessment_of_fair_housing_2016-web.pdf.

Clark, Joseph. "To Come to the Aid of Their Cities." *New York Times*, April 30, 1961.

Cohen, Rachel M. "School Closures: A Blunt Instrument." *American Prospect*, April 11, 2016. http://prospect.org/article/school-closures-blunt-instrument-0.

"The Community Development Block Grant (CDBG) Program: Frequently Asked Questions." 40 Years CDBG Building Better Neighborhoods, Department of Housing and Urban Development. https://www.hudexchange.info/onecpd/assets/File/The-Community-Development-Block-Grant-FAQ.pdf.

"Country Public Housing Chief Sees Trump Budget as 'Doomsday Scenario.'" CBS, April 12, 2017. http://chicago.cbslocal.com/2017/04/12/housing-authority-cook-county-president-donald-trump-doomsday-scenario-budget.

Dean, John P. "Only Caucasian: A Study of Race Covenants." *Journal of Land & Public Utility Economics* 23, no. 4 (Nov. 1947): 428–432.

Diamond, Jeremy. "Ben Carson Sits for Hearing Amid Questions About Qualifications." CNN, January 12, 2017. https://www.cnn.com/2017/01/12/politics/ben-carson-hud-confirmation-hearing/index.html.

Dovey, Rachel. "HUD May Be Trying to Quietly Kill Obama-Era Fair Housing Rule." *Next City*, January 8, 2018. https://nextcity.org/daily/entry/hud-may-be-trying-to-quietly-kill-obama-era-fair-housing-rule.

Du Bois, W. E. B. *Dusk of Dawn*. New York: Harcourt, Brace, 1940.

Giambrone, Andrew. "DC Public Housing May Get Major Funding Cuts Under Trump." *Washington City Paper*, March 14, 2017. https://www.washingtoncitypaper.com/news/housing-complex/blog/20854791/dc-public-housing-may-get-major-funding-cuts-under-trump.

Glaeser, Edward, and Jacob Vigdor. "The End of the Segregated Century: Racial Separation in America's Neighborhoods." Center for State and Local Leadership at the Manhattan Institute, January 2012.

Goetz, Edward G., Tony Damiano, and Jason Hicks. "Racially Concentrated Areas of Affluence: A Preliminary Investigation (Draft)." Humphrey School of Public Affairs, University of Minnesota. http://www.cura.umn.edu/sites/cura.advantagelabs.com/files/publications/DRAFT-Racially-Concentrated-Areas-of-Affluence-A-Preliminary-Investigation.pdf.

Grabar, Henry. "Watch Rep. Al Green Roast Ben Carson Like a Marshmallow." *Slate*, October 25, 2017. http://www.slate.com/blogs/the_slatest/2017/10/25/ben_carson_does_not_want_to_talk_about_the_housing_budget.html.

Horowitz, Jason. "Donald Trump's Old Queens Neighborhood Contrasts with the Diverse Area Around it." *New York Times*, September 22, 2015. https://www.nytimes.com/2015/09/23/us/politics/donald-trumps-old-queens-neighborhood-now-a-melting-pot-was-seen-as-a-cloister.html.

———. "Fred Trump Taught His Son the Essentials of Showboating Self-Promotion." *New York Times*, August 12, 2016. https://www.nytimes.com/2016/08/13/us/politics/fred-donald-trump-father.html.

Ihejirika, Maudlyne. "Chicago Remains Among Most Segregated U.S. Cities." *Chicago Sun Times*, March 2, 2016. https://chicago.suntimes.com/chicago-politics/chicago-racial-segregation-studies.

"Impact of the Trump/Carson HUD Budget Cuts in Chicago, Illinois." Affordable Housing Online, May 23, 2017. https://affordablehousingonline.com/FY18-HUD-Budget-Cuts/Illinois/Chicago.

Johnson, Lyndon. "Special Message to the Congress Proposing Further Legislation to Strengthen Civil Rights," April 28, 1966. The American Presidency Project. http://www.presidency.ucsb.edu/ws/index.php?pid=27566.

Kaufman, Will. "In Another Newly Discovered Song, Woody Guthrie Continues His Assault on 'Old Man Trump.'" The Conversation, September 5, 2016. https://theconversation.com/in-another-newly-discovered-song-woody-guthrie-continues-his-assault-on-old-man-trump-64221.

———. "Woody Guthrie, 'Old Man Trump' and a Real Estate Empire's Racist Foundations." The Conversation, January 21, 2016. https://theconversation.com/woody-guthrie-old-man-trump-and-a-real-estate-empires-racist-foundations-53026.

Kennedy, John F. "Special Message to the Congress on Housing and Community Development," March 9, 1961. The American Presidency Project.

———. "Statement by Senator John F. Kennedy, on Use of Civil Rights Legislation," August 9, 1960. The American Presidency Project. http://www.presidency.ucsb.edu/ws/index.php?pid=25717.

The Kerner Report: The National Advisory Commission on Civil Disorders. 1968. Reprint. Princeton: Princeton University Press, 2016.

Lane, Ben. "Civil Rights, Housing, Community Development Groups Slam HUD's Fair Housing Rule Decay." *Housing Wire*, January 8, 2018. https://www.housingwire.com/articles/42230-civil-rights-housing-community-development-groups-slam-huds-fair-housing-rule-delay.

"Let Democracy Flourish." *Chicago Defender*, May 8, 1948.

Litwack, Leon F. *North of Slavery: The Negro in the Free States, 1790–1860*. Chicago: University of Chicago Press, 1961.

"Low-Income Housing Tax Credits." Office of Policy Development and Research, Department of Housing and Urban Development, July 10, 2017. https://www.huduser.gov/portal/datasets/lihtc.html.

Mahler, Jonathan, and Steve Eder. "'No Vacancies' for Blacks: How Donald Trump Got His Start, and Was First Accused of Bias." *New York Times*, August 27, 2016. https://www.nytimes.com/2016/08/28/us/politics/donald-trump-housing-race.html.

Massey, Douglas S., and Nancy A. Denton. *American Apartheid: Segregation and the Making of the Underclass*. Cambridge, MA: Harvard University Press, 1993.

Meyer, Stephen Grant. *As Long as They Don't Move in Next Door: Segregation and Racial Conflict in American Neighborhoods*. Lanham, MD: Rowman & Littlefield, 2000.

Miller, Nathan. "Weaver Cites Riots in Plea: Wants Increased Funds for City Housing." [Baltimore] *Sun*, July 18, 1967.

New York City Housing Authority. "NYCHA 2017 Fact Sheet." April 13, 2017. https://www1.nyc.gov/assets/nycha/downloads/pdf/factsheet.pdf.

———. "Special Tabulation of Resident Characteristics." January 2015. https://www1.nyc.gov/assets/nycha/downloads/pdf/res_data.pdf.

Novogradac, Michael. "Final Tax Reform Bill Would Reduce Affordable Rental Housing Production by Nearly 235,000 Homes." Novogradac & Company, December 19, 2017. https://www.novoco.com/notes-from-novogradac/final-tax-reform-bill-would-reduce-affordable-rental-housing-production-nearly-235000-homes.

Office of Management and Budget. "America First: A Budget Blueprint to Make America Great Again." https://www.whitehouse.gov/wp-content/uploads/2017/11/2018_blueprint.pdf.

———. "An American Budget: Efficient, Effective, Accountable, Fiscal Year 2019." https://www.whitehouse.gov/wp-content/uploads/2018/02/budget-fy2019.pdf.

Pendall, Rolf, and Leah Hendey. "A Brief Look at the Early Implementation of Choice Neighborhoods." Washington, DC: Urban Institute, 2013. https://www.urban.org/sites/default/files/publication/24126/412940-A-Brief-Look-at-the-Early-Implementation-of-Choice-Neighborhoods.PDF.

Povich, Elaine S. "Talk of Federal Tax Cuts Chills Affordable Housing Market." The Pew Charitable Trusts, April 25, 2017. http://www.pewtrusts.org/en/research-and-analysis/blogs/stateline/2017/04/25/talk-of-federal-tax-cuts-chills-affordable-housing-market.

Pritchett, Wendell E. *Robert Clifton Weaver and the American City: The Life and Times of an Urban Reformer*. Chicago: University of Chicago Press, 2008.

Raskin, A. H. "Washington Gets 'the Weaver Treatment.'" *New York Times*, May 14, 1961.

Rich, Motoko. "Restrictive Covenants Stubbornly Stay on the Books." *New York Times*, April 21, 2005. http://www.nytimes.com/2005/04/21/garden /restrictive-covenants-stubbornly-stay-on-the-books.html.

Roberts, Sam. "Nation's Cities Almost Free of Segregation, Study Finds." *New York Times*, January 30, 2012. http://www.nytimes.com/2012/01/31/us /Segregation-Curtailed-in-US-Cities-Study-Finds.html.

Rothstein, Richard. *The Color of Law: A Forgotten History of How Our Government Segregated America*. New York: Liveright, 2017.

Smith, Greg B. "Trump's Budget Proposal Would Cost NYCHA Tenants Dearly." *New York Daily News*, May 23, 2017. http://www.nydailynews.com/news /politics/trump-budget-proposal-cost-nycha-tenants-dearly-article-1.3190240.

Squires, Gregory D., editor. *The Fight for Fair Housing: Causes, Consequences, and Future Implications of the 1968 Federal Fair Housing Act*. New York: Routledge, 2018.

"Strictly Political." *Washington Star*, February 20, 1962.

Sullivan, Sean. "Trump Talks of 'Ghettos' in Describing Urban African American Areas." *Washington Post*, October 27, 2016, https://www.washingtonpost .com/?utm_term=.8cf8d641ceae.

Trump, Donald J. "The Inaugural Address." Speech, Washington, DC, January 20, 2017. https://www.whitehouse.gov/briefings-statements/the-inaugural-address.

United States Congress. *Fair Housing Act: Hearings Before the Subcommittee on Civil and Constitutional Rights of the House Committee on the Judiciary, 95th Congress, 2nd Session*. Washington, DC: U.S. Government Printing Office, 1978.

United States v. Trump Management, Inc. Civil Action No. 73 C 1529 (United States District Court Eastern District New York, June 10, 1975). https://www .clearinghouse.net/chDocs/public/FH-NY-0024-0034.pdf.

"Warren Criticizes 'Class' Parades, Police Head Declares Neither Fascisti Nor Klan Had Any Place in Memorial March; Klan Assails Policemen; No Progress Made in Tracing the Slayers of Two Italians—Seven Arraigned in Queens Battle." *New York Times*, June 1, 1927.

"Weaver in Plea for New Agency: He Tells Mayors Housing Set-Up Is 'Monstrosity.'" *New York Times*, June 15, 1961.

Weaver, Robert Clifton. "Race Restrictive Housing Covenants." *Journal of Land and Public Utility Economics* 20 (August 1944): 183–193.

BIBLIOGRAPHY

Weiss, Nancy J. *Farewell to the Party of Lincoln: Black Politics in the Age of FDR.* Princeton, NJ: Princeton University Press, 1983.

Whitford, Emma. "NYCHA Embraces Private Development to Fight 'Financial Death Spiral.'" *Gothamist*, March 14, 2017. http://gothamist.com/2017/03/14/nycha_budget_fight.php.

Wilson, Megan R. "FBI Releases Documents Related to Trump Apartment Discrimination Case." *Hill*, February 15, 2017. http://thehill.com/home news/news/319788-fbi-releases-documents-related-to-trump-apartment -discrimination-case.

Index

Fox News

JUAN WILLIAMS has covered and written about American politics for four decades. He is currently a columnist for the *Hill* and was a longtime writer and correspondent for the *Washington Post* and NPR. Most notably, Juan is currently a cohost of Fox News Channel's roundtable debate show *The Five* and makes regular appearances across the network on shows like *FoxNews Sunday with Chris Wallace* and *Special Report with Brett Baier*, where he regularly challenges the orthodoxy of the network's conservative stalwarts. He is also the author of numerous books, including *Eyes on the Prize*, *Thurgood Marshall*, *Enough*, *Muzzled*, and *We the People*.